DATE DUE

MAY 0 5 2010	
NOV 2 9 2012	

DEMCO, INC. 38-2931

BIOLOGICAL CONTROL OF WEEDS: A WORLD CATALOGUE OF AGENTS AND THEIR TARGET WEEDS

THIRD EDITION

Editor: **M.H. JULIEN**

CSIRO Division of Entomology,
Long Pocket Laboratories,
Private Bag No. 3,
Indooroopilly,
Brisbane,
Queensland 4068,
Australia

C·A·B *International*

In association with

ACIAR
(Australian Centre for International Agricultural Research)

C·A·B International   Tel: Wallingford (0491) 32111
Wallingford   Telex: 847964 (COMAGG G).
Oxon OX10 8DE   Telecom Gold/Dialcom: 84: CAU001
UK   Fax: (0491) 33508

Published in Association with
ACIAR
(Australian Centre for International Agricultural Research)
GPO Box 1571
Canberra
ACT 2601
Australia

Tel: (062) 48 8588
Fax: (062) 57 3051
Telex: AA 62419
E−Mail: Dialcom: 6007:IAR001

A catalogue entry for this book is available from the British Library

ISBN 0−85198−766−4

Printed and bound in the UK

Cover photos: The flea-beetle *Agasicles hygrophila* and its target weed *Alternanthera philoxeroides* in Australia.

CONTENTS

FOREWORD

The field of biological control of weeds continues to expand and the original idea of producing a catalogue that would be updated on a regular basis without major difficulty seems to have more and more value as a means of keeping track of the world scene. This is the third edition, five years after the second, and again, a considerable increase in activity can be noticed in many areas around the world.

There has been an increase in the use of biological control in developing countries and in the use of biological control to combat weeds invasive in natural environments in addition to tackling agricultural problems. Both can be related to the increasing worldwide concern over the environment. The need to conserve natural resources and ensure the continued existence of an environment that can maintain life on earth as we know it has resulted in a major effort to produce ecologically sustainable systems of production, particularly in agriculture, and biological control of weeds plays a key role in this endeavour. Worldwide, weeds are acknowledged as a major impediment to agricultural production and a system of control that does not require continuous expense or high technology, is non-disruptive ecologically and maintains biodiversity, is of increasing appeal to developing countries as well as to the more developed nations. This catalogue is invaluable in establishing the credentials of the science to new audiences possibly unfamiliar with the methodology. The acceptability of biological control as a means of combating a diverse array of weed problems in many countries is readily apparent from this catalogue, both as evidence of credibility in its effectiveness and as a demonstration that fears over perceived risks are unfounded and with appropriate precautions, they should not be an impediment to its use.

Concern over risks is often based on ignorance and as mentioned by David Greathead in the Preface to the second edition, scientists must explain more and more what they are doing. This is particularly so for biological control scientists and this catalogue is a valuable resource base for doing that.

The possible risk to native flora from the introduction of exotic biological control agents is the other side of the coin to the need to use a non-disruptive, environmentally safe system to protect native habitats, including their flora, threatened by the invasion of exotic species. Biological control scientists are being asked to help combat exotic species invading National Parks and other areas of native vegetation, but at the same time, being impressed upon to be doubly sure of any risks from any agents they might introduce.

Biological control is increasingly needed to maintain and increase agricultural production without unwanted side effects; it is needed to protect natural habitats and the diversity of species, and in the face of such an increased demand, needs to be increasingly knowledgeable of any side effects. As a scientific methodology it must become increasingly efficient and should be exploited to the maximum. Despite the need and the clear benefits, many countries are having difficulties in maintaining funds to science. Biological control therefore must justify its support not only by its track record, but by the ability to predict its probable benefits as well as the level of any risk. Our capacity to do this is only increasing slowly and many of the questions posed by Peter Harris in the Preface to the first edition of this catalogue ten years ago remain unanswered. We need to know much more about how the system works. How do, and how will, different agents affect weed populations and perhaps non-target populations, under different conditions? While we continue to have difficulty in grappling with these vital questions, there is no doubt that this catalogue remains the best resource base and starting point for much of the research required.

J.M. Cullen
Assistant Chief and Head
Biological Control of Weeds Section
CSIRO Division of Entomology
Canberra, Australia.

INTRODUCTION

This third edition of the catalogue includes information on releases made since the previous edition was collated, that is, releases made between early 1986 and the end of 1990. It also includes all previously catalogued releases with updated information and updated references where applicable.

The original catalogue, published in 1982, recorded 499 releases of exotic agents between the late 19th Century and 1980. The second edition (published in 1987) recorded 100 new releases during the intervening five years. This new edition records 130 new releases of exotic invertebrates during the five years since the second edition. The increasing frequency of releases shows that biological control of weeds is alive and well. In fact biological control is a viable alternative to other control methods for some weeds, and provides the only practical, economical or environmentally acceptable method of control for others.

In this catalogue:

> **LIST A** deals with exotic invertebrates and fungi that have been released for biological control and their target weeds. There are numerous organisms that have been studied and many that have been introduced into quarantine facilities in exotic countries but were not released. These are not listed here.

> **LIST B** deals with exotic vertebrates utilised to control weeds. The list consists entirely of fish species but it must be remembered that other species have been and are being utilised on a wide scale to control weeds, e.g., sheep, cattle, goats. Others have been considered or used on a lesser scale, e.g., manatees, geese.

> **LIST C** deals with organisms utilised within their native ranges to control weeds. There has been a rapid increase in the number of fungi that have been or are being assessed as potential control agents. Most of these were collected from their target weed within the weedy range. A small number has proved suitable for wide practical use. I have chosen to list only those that have been used widely or have undergone large scale field trials and are being developed further. Charudattan (1991), reference number 73, presents a comprehensive list of fungi that have been or are being assessed and their current status.

> **LIST D** deals with organisms that have been released as biological control agents and now occur in countries other than those into which they were released. It also includes organisms found in exotic ranges where they were not deliberately released but are useful control agents.

The lists' headings are as follows, with some explanations.

Weed and its origin

The target weeds are listed alphabetically under plant family names which are listed alphabetically.

If more than one name for the same plant has been used recently in the literature cited, each name is included in the index with appropriate referencing to the name used in the lists. Articles which were consulted for plant taxonomy, synonymy and origins are included in the references.

The country or region of origin of the weed and the widely used common name(s) are also listed; the latter being indexed.

Agent and taxonomic references

The names of the agents are listed alphabetically after their target weed. Synonyms and old names used in the literature cited are included in the index and referenced to the name used in the lists.

Released

This is the year when the first release was carried out. If there was a second or third, etc. importation and release of material in later years, this has also been included if the initial release failed or if the subsequent release material was from a different source.

Status and degree of control

The comments in this column are a brief précis of the literature cited and information obtained through personal communication. Where possible the origin of each organism is given and if it was not obtained directly from its original source, the countries or regions from where it was obtained are given.

Research organisation

A list of research units and their corresponding abbreviations is provided.

General references

The references, including personal communications, are listed alphabetically and given a number which is shown in the lists.

ACKNOWLEDGEMENTS

I thank those people, listed below, who contributed information for this edition. I also thank contributors to the 1982 and 1987 catalogues, listed in those editions, since much of the information has again been presented here.

Special thanks to Lloyd Andres and Charles Turner, USDA, who compiled the entries for the whole of USA, a formidable catalogue in its own right.

Thanks to Jim Cullen, CSIRO, for providing encouragement and resources; Rose Broe, CSIRO, who very capably assisted in the collation and preparation of this edition; Del Dunn, CSIRO, for assistance with word processing; Patrick Ledwith and June Farkas, CSIRO, for obtaining references; Peter Cranson, Ted Edwards, Ian Naumann and Tom Weir, ANIC, Division of Entomology, CSIRO, for advice on insect names, and numerous other people who checked information and advised me of errors, omissions and additions.

I am particularly grateful to the Australian Centre for International Agricultural Research, its Director, George Rothschild, and Research Services Officer, Paul Ferrar, for a grant which supported the preparation of this catalogue.

CONTRIBUTORS AND THEIR ADDRESSES

L.A. Andres, USDA-ARS, Biological Control of Weeds Unit, 800 Buchanan Street, Albany, California 94710, U.S.A.

E. Bruzzese, Keith Turnbull Research Institute, Ballarto Road, Frankston, Victoria 3199, Australia.

R. Charudattan, Plant Pathology Department, University of Florida, Gainesville, Florida 32611, U.S.A.

G.P. Donnelly, The Alan Fletcher Research Station, 27 Magazine Street, Sherwood 4075, Australia.

P. Harris, Agriculture Canada, Research Station, Box 440, Regina, Saskatchewan S4P 3A2, Canada.

J.H. Hoffmann, University of Cape Town, Zoology Department, Rondebosch 7700, Republic of South Africa.

J. Igrc, University of Zagreb, Institute for Plant Protection, Simunska 25, POB 281, 41000 Zagreb, Yugoslavia.

M.O. Isherwood, jr. Department of Agriculture, 1428 So. King Street, Hawaii 96814-2512, U.S.A.

K.P. Jayanth, Indian Institute of Horticultural Research, Hessaraghatta Lake Post, Bangalore 560 089, India.

T. Jessep, DSIR, Plant Protection, Canterbury Agriculture and Science Centre, Ellesmere Road, Lincoln, Christchurch, New Zealand.

P.J. Joy, Kerala Agricultural University, College of Horticulture, Vellanikkara, Trichur 680 654, S. India.

O.V. Kovalev, Zoological Institute, Academy of Sciences, Leningrad 199034, U.S.S.R.

A. Naito, National Agriculture Research Center, Yatabe, Tsukuba 305, Japan.

B. Napompeth, National Biological Control Research Center, P.O. Box 52, Bangkok, 10900, Thailand.

S. Neser, Department of Agriculture and Water Supply, Plant Protection Research Institute, Private Bag X134, Pretoria 0001, Republic of South Africa.

C. Turner, USDA-ARS, Biological Control of Weeds Unit, 800 Buchanan Street, Albany, California 94710, U.S.A.

P. Syrett, DSIR, Plant Protection, Canterbury Agriculture and Science Centre, Ellesmere Road, Lincoln, Christchurch, New Zealand.

R. Wang, Biological Control Laboratory, Chinese Academy of Sciences, 30 Bai Shi Qiao Road, Beijing, People's Republic of China.

List A: Exotic invertebrates and fungi released and their target weeds

Weed and its origin*	Agent and taxonomic references*	Released*	Status and degree of control*	Research organisation*	General references*
AMARANTHACEAE					
Alternanthera philoxeroides (Martius) Grisebach South America (alligator weed)	*Agasicles hygrophila* Selman & Vogt (Coleoptera: Chrysomelidae)	1977	**AUSTRALIA.** Ex Argentina via Florida, U.S.A. Successful control of floating mats within two years of release. No effect in terrestrial habitat.	CSIRO	337
		1981	**NEW ZEALAND.** Ex Argentina via U.S.A. via Australia. Widely established and destroys most foliage annually. Weed mat regrows in spring.	DSIR	525,557
		1986	**PEOPLE'S REPUBLIC OF CHINA.** Ex Argentina via Florida, U.S.A. Released into field cages in Sichuan and Zhejiang Provinces. Status unknown.	CAAS	683
		1982	**THAILAND.** Ex Argentina via U.S.A. via Australia. Established and spread around Bangkok and the lower Central Plain area. Excellent control.	NBCRC	468,469
		1964	**UNITED STATES OF AMERICA.** Ex Argentina. Impact good in many situations; variable in others. Initial effects spectacular in coastal regions. Populations are sensitive to hot dry summers and cold winters. Effectiveness limited to coastal, warmer regions except when supplementary releases are made in early summer. Other control measures generally unnecessary in FL, LA and TX. Well established in SC, GA, AL and MS. Not established in AR, CA, NC and TN. Not effective against the terrestrial form of the weed.	USDA (3,5, 7,13)	57,58, 116

* See 'Introduction' for explanation of headings.

List A continued

(AMARANTHACEAE continued)

Weed and its origin*	Agent and taxonomic references*	Released*	Status and degree of control*	Research organisation*	General references*
	Amynothrips andersoni O'Neill (Thysanoptera: Phlaeothripidae)	1967	**UNITED STATES OF AMERICA.** Ex Argentina. Established in FL, GA and SC. Establishment not confirmed in AL, CA, MS and TX. Impact uncertain; reduces rates of growth in some cases. Overwinters successfully and significant populations are active early in the season. May be unfavourable interaction with *Agasicles hygrophila* and *Vogtia malloi*. Not effective against the terrestrial form of the weed	USDA (3,5, 7,13)	57,116
	Disonycha argentinensis Jacoby (Coleoptera: Chrysomelidae)	1980	**AUSTRALIA.** Ex southern Brazil. Not established.	CSIRO	341
		1982	**NEW ZEALAND.** Ex Brazil via Australia. Not established.	DSIR	556,557
	Vogtia malloi Pastrana (Lepidoptera: Pyralidae)	1977	**AUSTRALIA.** Ex Argentina via Florida, U.S.A. Established and spread throughout the aquatic habitat. Effects masked by devastation caused by *Agasicles hygrophila*. Effective in small semi-aquatic habitats not destroyed by *Agasicles hygrophila*. Present but not effective in terrestrial situations.	CSIRO	337,339
		1984	**NEW ZEALAND.** Ex Argentina via U.S.A. via Australia. Not established.	DSIR	556,557, 710
		1987	Ex Argentina via U.S.A. via Australia. Well established and reducing spread of weed at three sites.		

* See 'Introduction' for explanation of headings.

List A continued

Weed and its origin*	Agent and taxonomic references*	Released*	Status and degree of control*	Research organisation*	General references*
(AMARANTHACEAE continued)					
		1971	**UNITED STATES OF AMERICA.** Ex Argentina. Reduces growth of floating mats in lower MS by 50 to 90%, but alligator weed has strong regenerative capacity, and *Vogtia malloi* reinfestations are uneven, and in coastal areas may be cyclical over a period of several years. Also established in AR, FL, LA, SC and TX. Not effective against the terrestrial form of the weed.	USDA (3,5, 7,13)	57,116
ANACARDIACEAE					
Schinus terebinthifolius Raddi South America (Christmas berry, Brazilian pepper tree, Brazilian holly, wilelaika)	*Crasimorpha infuscata* Hodges Lepidoptera: Gelechiidae)	1961	**HAWAII, U.S.A.** Ex Brazil. Released on Hawaii. Not established.	HDOA	141,212, 220,376
	Episimus utilis Zimmerman (Lepidoptera: Tortricidae)	1954	**HAWAII, U.S.A.** Ex Brazil. Released on Hawaii and Oahu initially, later released on Molokai, Kauai and Maui. Established but effects negligible.	HDOA	9,132, 212,378, 504,722
	Lithraeus atronotatus (Pic) (previously referred to as *Bruchus atronotatus* Pic) (Coleoptera: Bruchidae)	1960	**HAWAII, U.S.A.** Ex Brazil. Released on Oahu, Maui and Hawaii. Established but effects negligible.	HDOA	212,376, 378
ARACEAE					
Pistia stratiotes Linnaeus cosmopolitan tropical, sub-tropical (water lettuce)	*Epipsammea pectinicornis* (Hampson) [previously referred to as *Namangana pectinicornis* (Hampson) and incorrectly as *Episammea pectinicornis* Hampson] (Lepidoptera: Noctuidae)	1990	**UNITED STATES OF AMERICA.** Ex Thailand. Released in FL. Establishment not confirmed. Releases continuing.	USAE USDA (3,4) State (3)	66,68

* See 'Introduction' for explanation of headings.

List A continued

Weed and its origin*	Agent and taxonomic references*	Released*	Status and degree of control*	Research organisation*	General references*
(ARACEAE continued)					
	Neohydronomus affinis Hustache (previously incorrectly referred to as *Neohydronomus pulcellus* Hustache) (Coleoptera: Curculionidae)	1982	**AUSTRALIA.** Ex Brazil. Successful control. Reduced area covered and plant size and weight within two years.	CSIRO	253,255
		1988	**BOTSWANA.** Ex Brazil via Australia. Well established and achieved control by 1989.	DWAB	193
		1985	**PAPUA NEW GUINEA.** Ex Brazil via Australia. Good control achieved. The native moth *Epipsammea pectinicornis* may have contributed to this result.	PNGDAL CSIRO	255,386
		1985	**REPUBLIC OF SOUTH AFRICA.** Ex Brazil via Australia. Well established at various sites. Successful in dams but results slower when released on fast flowing rivers.	PPRI	83,84
		1987	**UNITED STATES OF AMERICA.** Ex Brazil via Australia. Complete control within 18-30 months in FL at three of four 4 original release sites. Natural dispersal well underway. Established in LA from unknown source.	USAE USDA (3,4 13) State (3,18,19)	66,68, 177
		1988	**ZIMBABWE.** Ex Brazil via Australia. Successful control within twelve months.	PPRIZ	78
ASCLEPIADACEAE					
Cryptostegia grandiflora Madagascar (rubber vine)	*Euclasta whalleyi* Popescu-Gorj and Constantinescu (Lepidoptera: Pyralidae)	1988	**AUSTRALIA.** Ex Madagascar. Not established.	QDL	420,423

* See 'Introduction' for explanation of headings.

List A continued

Weed and its origin*	Agent and taxonomic references*	Released*	Status and degree of control*	Research organisation*	General references*
ASTERACEAE					
Acroptilon repens (Linnaeus) de Candolle (= *Centaurea repens* Linnaeus) central and western Asia, eastern Europe (Russian knapweed)	*Subanguina picridis* Kirjanova & Ivanova (previously referred to as *Paranguina picridis* Kirjanova & Ivanova) (Nematoda: Tylenchidae)	1976	**CANADA.** Ex U.S.S.R. Established in Saskatchewan, British Columbia, and Quebec field plots. Extensive galling at Saskatchewan river bank but site destroyed by erosion. Alberta site destroyed with herbicides.	CDA MU	687
		1984	**UNITED STATES OF AMERICA.** Ex U.S.S.R. via Canada. Experimental release in WA (1989); OR, MT, WA (1990). Establishment not confirmed.	USDA (7,10) State (9)	528,569, 574
Ageratina adenophora (Sprengel) R. King & H. Robinson (= *Eupatorium adenophorum* Sprengel), 351 Central America (crofton weed, Mexican devil weed, Maui pamakani)	*Phaeoramularia* sp (previously referred to as *Cercospora eupatorii* Peck, 444) (fungus: Hyphomycetes)	1988	**REPUBLIC OF SOUTH AFRICA.** Ex Central America and Australia. Limited establishment and spread. Under evaluation.	PPRI	355,444, 447
	Procecidochares utilis Stone (Diptera: Tephritidae)	1953	**AUSTRALIA.** Ex Mexico via Hawaii. Established readily and spread rapidly throughout the range of the weed. Initially large populations established but indigenous parasitic Hymenoptera caused populations to decline. Attack by *P. utilis* fluctuates as a result of this parasitism. A degree of plant suppression occurs when attack becomes heavy.	QDL	174,284, 706
		1963	**INDIA.** Ex Mexico via Hawaii via Australia via New Zealand. Established rapidly and is spreading naturally. Has given partial control of the weed in some areas, although hampered by indigenous natural enemies.	IIBC	345,544
		1958	**NEW ZEALAND.** Ex Mexico via Hawaii via Australia. Established and widespread where the weed occurs. Initially very damaging but efficiency now reduced by parasitism.	DSIR	292,304

* See 'Introduction' for explanation of headings.

6

List A continued

(ASTERACEAE continued)

Weed and its origin*	Agent and taxonomic references*	Released*	Status and degree of control*	Research organisation*	General references*
		1945	**HAWAII, U.S.A.** Ex Mexico. Released on Maui where it is responsible for control of nearly all infestations in drier areas. In the wetter lowlands and highlands the weed densities are stable and remain unchanged for the most part.	HDOA	37,38, 139,212, 504
		1985	**PEOPLE'S REPUBLIC OF CHINA.** Ex Nepalese/Chinese border. Released in Yunnan Province. Established but ineffective.	KIEC	289,683, 720
		1984	**REPUBLIC OF SOUTH AFRICA.** Ex Mexico via Hawaii via Australia. Well established and spreading. Shown to affect plants but does not control weed on its own. Incidence of parasitism often high.	PPRI	355,472
	Xanthaciura connexionis Benjamin (Diptera: Tephritidae)	1955	**HAWAII, U.S.A.** Ex Mexico. Released on Maui and Oahu. Not established.	HDOA	207,691
Ageratina riparia (Regel) R. King & H. Robinson (= *Eupatorium riparium* Regel), 351 Mexico (Hamakua pamakani, mistflower)	*Entyloma ageratinae* Barreto & Evans, 22, or *Entyloma compositarum* Farlow, 660 (previously referred to as *Cercosporella ageratina*) (fungus: Ustilaginales)	1975	**HAWAII, U.S.A.** Ex Jamaica. Established on Oahu, Hawaii, Maui. In combination with *Procecidochares alani* and *Oidaematophorus beneficus* provides substantial to complete control in all parts of the state.	UH HDOA	212,382, 465,657
		1989	**REPUBLIC OF SOUTH AFRICA.** Ex Jamaica via Hawaii. Established and spreading. Causes extensive defoliation of plants.	PPRI	446,447
	Oidaematophorus beneficus Yano & Heppner (Lepidoptera: Pterophoridae)	1973	**HAWAII, U.S.A.** Ex Mexico. Released on Hawaii and Oahu. Substantial to complete control at many localities on Hawaii.	HDOA	212,382, 463,717

* See 'Introduction' for explanation of headings.

List A continued

Weed and its origin*	Agent and taxonomic references*	Released*	Status and degree of control*	Research organisation*	General references*
(ASTERACEAE continued)					
	Procecidochares alani Steyskal (Diptera: Tephritidae)	1986	**AUSTRALIA.** Ex Mexico via Hawaii. Well established but effects negligible.	QDL	700
			Released on Norfolk Island in 1988. Established. Degree of control not assessed.	QDL	700
		1974	**HAWAII, U.S.A.** Ex Mexico. Released on Hawaii, also Maui in 1975. Substantial to complete control at many localities on Hawaii.	HDOA	212,382, 464,465
	Xanthaciura connexionis Benjamin (Diptera: Tephritidae)	1960	**HAWAII, U.S.A.** Ex Mexico. Not established.	HDOA	134,207
Ambrosia artemisiifolia Linnaeus North America (annual ragweed)	*Epiblema strenuana* (Walker) (Lepidoptera: Tortricidae)	1984	**AUSTRALIA.** Ex Mexico. Widely established. Significant reduction in plant size and vigour but control not yet adequate.	QDL IIBC	418,419
	Euaresta bella (Loew) (Diptera: Tephritidae)	1969	**UNION OF SOVIET SOCIALIST REPUBLICS.** Ex U.S.A. and Canada. Not established.	ZIAS USDA (1)	371,372
		1977	Ex U.S.A. and Canada. Not established.	ZIAS USDA (1)	371,372
		1990	Ex U.S.A. Released in the North Caucasus. Under evaluation.	ZIAS	372
	Stobaera concinna (Stål) (Hemiptera: Delphacidae)	1984	**AUSTRALIA.** Ex Mexico. Established and under evaluation.	QDL	420
	Tarachidia candefacta (Hubner) (Lepidoptera: Noctuidae)	1967	**UNION OF SOVIET SOCIALIST REPUBLICS.** Ex Canada and CA, U.S.A. Colonised in southern areas of European U.S.S.R. Effectiveness unknown.	AUPPI CDA State (5)	217,224, 369-373
	Trigonorhinus tomentosus (Say)[previously referred to as *Brachytarsus tomentosus* (Say)] (Coleoptera: Anthribidae)	1977	**UNION OF SOVIET SOCIALIST REPUBLICS.** Ex U.S.A. Not established.	ZIAS USDA (1)	117,369
		1990	Ex U.S.A. Released in the North Caucasus. Under evaluation.	ZIAS	372

* See 'Introduction' for explanation of headings.

List A continued

(ASTERACEAE continued)

Weed and its origin*	Agent and taxonomic references*	Released*	Status and degree of control*	Research organisation*	General references*
	Zygogramma bicolorata Pallister (Coleoptera: Chrysomelidae)	1982	**AUSTRALIA.** Ex Mexico. Widely established and locally abundant. Control not effective.	QDL IIBC	420
	Zygogramma disrupta Rogers (Coleoptera: Chrysomelidae)	1990	**UNION OF SOVIET SOCIALIST REPUBLICS.** Ex Kansas, Nebraska, Oklahoma, U.S.A. Released in the North Caucasus. Under evaluation.	ZIAS	372
	Zygogramma suturalis (Fabricius) (Coleoptera: Chrysomelidae)	1990	**AUSTRALIA.** Ex U.S.A. Releases in progress.	QDL	420
		1988	**PEOPLE'S REPUBLIC OF CHINA.** Ex Canada and U.S.A. via U.S.S.R. Released into field cages. Under evaluation.	CAAS	682,683
		1978	**UNION OF SOVIET SOCIALIST REPUBLICS.** Ex Canada and U.S.A. Quickly established in the North Caucasus, Caucasus, Ukraine and in the Far East. Successful control by chrysomelid beetles reared in great numbers on special plots. This species is particularly efficient in cultivation when solitary population wave is formed leading to 100% destruction of the weed. Leaf beetle efficiently influences succession process on non-cultivated lands.	ZIAS CDA USDA (1)	117,371, 372,374, 375,551, 552
		1985 1987 1990	**YUGOSLAVIA.** Ex U.S.A. Not established. Ex U.S.A. Established with low populations. Ex U.S.S.R. Under evaluation.	IPP IPP IPP	308,395 308 308,309
Ambrosia psilostachya de Candolle North America (perennial ragweed, western ragweed)	*Tarachidia candefacta* (Hübner) (Lepidoptera: Noctuidae)	1972	**UNION OF SOVIET SOCIALIST REPUBLICS.** Ex Canada and CA, U.S.A. Released in southern areas of European U.S.S.R. Not established.	AUPPI	224,369, 370,372, 373
	Zygogramma suturalis (Fabricius) (Coleoptera: Chrysomelidae)	1979	**UNION OF SOVIET SOCIALIST REPUBLICS.** Ex Canada. Established readily in the North Caucasus and Kazakhstan.	ZIAS	372,374

* See 'Introduction' for explanation of headings.

List A continued

Weed and its origin*	Agent and taxonomic references*	Released*	Status and degree of control*	Research organisation*	General references*
(ASTERACEAE continued)					
Baccharis halimifolia Linnaeus North America (groundsel bush)	*Anacassis fuscata* (Klug) (Coleoptera: Chrysomelidae)	1976	**AUSTRALIA.** Ex Brazil. Not established.	QDL	427,698
	Anacassis phaeopoda Buzzi (Coleoptera: Chrysomelidae)	1976	**AUSTRALIA.** Ex Brazil. Not established.	QDL	427,698
	Aristotelia ivae Busck (Lepidoptera: Gelechiidae)	1969	**AUSTRALIA.** Ex U.S.A. Established readily. Spread rapidly throughout most coastal groundsel bush areas. In high summer temperatures, the larvae can cause severe damage but this is not general in the field and the insect does not provide significant control.	QDL	424,698
	Bucculatrix ivella Busck (Lepidoptera: Lyonetiidae)	1989	**AUSTRALIA.** Ex U.S.A. Release program continuing. Establishment not confirmed.	QDL	655
	Heilipodus intricatus (Boheman) (Coleoptera: Curculionidae)	1983	**AUSTRALIA.** Ex Brazil. Not established.	QDL	427
	Lioplacis elliptica (Stål) (Coleoptera: Chrysomelidae)	1977	**AUSTRALIA.** Ex Brazil. Not established.	QDL	698
	Lorita baccharivora Pogue (previously incorrectly referred to as *Phalonia* sp.) (Lepidoptera: Cochylidae)	1969 1985	**AUSTRALIA.** Ex U.S.A. Not established. Ex U.S.A. Release program continuing. Establishment not yet confirmed.	QDL QDL	424,698 427
	Megacyllene mellyi (Chevrolat) (Coleoptera: Cerambycidae)	1978	**AUSTRALIA.** Ex Brazil. Established. Populations confined to host growing in or adjacent to salt marsh areas where it provides useful control. Not established in other areas.	QDL	424,425, 655
	Metallactus nigrofasciatus Suffrian (Coleoptera: Chrysomelidae)	1982	**AUSTRALIA.** Ex Brazil. Not established.	QDL	427

* See 'Introduction' for explanation of headings.

List A continued

(ASTERACEAE continued)

Weed and its origin*	Agent and taxonomic references*	Released*	Status and degree of control*	Research organisation*	General references*
	Metallactus patagonicus Suffrian (Coleoptera: Chrysomelidae)	1974	**AUSTRALIA.** Ex Brazil. Not established.	QDL	424
	Oidaematophorus balanotes (Meyrick) (Lepidoptera: Pterophoridae)	1969	**AUSTRALIA.** Ex U.S.A. Not established.	QDL	424,427, 655
		1985	Ex U.S.A. Release program completed. Established at majority of release sites. Dispersal to 30 km from release sites observed. Damage to host variable.	QDL	
		1990	**UNION OF SOVIET SOCIALIST REPUBLICS.** Ex U.S.A. via Australia. Established in the Caucasus.	ZIAS	372
	Rhopalomyia californica Felt (Diptera: Cecidomyidae)	1982	**AUSTRALIA.** Ex U.S.A. Collected from *Baccharis pilularis* DC. Widely established. Caused loss of seed production and death of many plants under shade or in upland situations. Populations have dropped to below damaging levels in most areas, probably due to attack by native Hymenoptera and a run of unfavourable dry spring seasons.	QDL	426,427, 655
		1989	**UNION OF SOVIET SOCIALIST REPUBLICS.** Ex U.S.A. via Australia. Not yet established. Release program continuing.	ZIAS	372
	Trirhabda baccharidis (Weber) (Coleoptera: Chrysomelidae)	1969	**AUSTRALIA.** Ex U.S.A. Established at many sites in coastal areas. Widespread dispersal occurring from older sites. Larvae cause annual defoliation prior to and during flowering reducing seed production.	QDL	424,427
		1990	**UNION OF SOVIET SOCIALIST REPUBLICS.** Ex Georgia, Maryland, U.S.A. Established in the Caucasus.	ZIAS	372

* See 'Introduction' for explanation of headings.

List A continued

Weed and its origin*	Agent and taxonomic references*	Released*	Status and degree of control*	Research organisation*	General references*
(ASTERACEAE continued)					
Carduus acanthoides Linnaeus Eurasia, North Africa, western Asia (plumeless thistle)	*Rhinocyllus conicus* (Frölich) (Coleoptera: Curculionidae)	1981	**ARGENTINA.** Ex France (Rhine Valley) via Canada via U.S.A. and ex France (Rhine Valley) via Canada via New Zealand. Established at one site near Buenos Aires since 1981-83. Recently established in at least two sites in Provinces of Santa Fe and Cordoba. Efforts continue to redistribute and establish elsewhere.	INTA	115,183
		1968	**CANADA.** Ex France (Rhine Valley). Established in British Columbia and in Ontario. 30-90% of seed heads attacked over 90% of the range but seed production not reduced significantly. *C. acanthoides* is not the preferred host.	CDA MU	261,273, 592
		1977	**NEW ZEALAND.** Ex France (Rhine Valley) via Canada. Established. First released against this thistle from the population introduced to attack *C. nutans*. Hybrids of *C. acanthoides* and *C. nutans* also acceptable hosts.	DSIR	326,330
		1969	**UNITED STATES OF AMERICA.** Ex France (Rhine Valley) via Canada. Established in VA where impact is increasing. Also established in ID, MD, PA and WA.	USDA (1) State (1)	291,410, 528,577, 636
	Trichosirocalus horridus (Panzer) [previously referred to as *Ceuthorhynch-idius horridus* (Panzer)] (Coleoptera: Curculionidae)	1983	**ARGENTINA.** Ex Italy via U.S.A. Not established.	INTA	115,183
		1975	**CANADA.** Ex Austria, Germany and Switzerland. Established in British Columbia where status is unknown. Established and kills rosettes in Vancouver. Establishment unknown in Ontario and Quebec.	CDA	63,261
		1974	**UNITED STATES OF AMERICA.** Ex Italy. Impacting weed and spreading rapidly in VA. Established and spreading in MD.	USDA (1) State (1)	63,291, 363,366, 368

* See 'Introduction' for explanation of headings.

List A *continued*

Weed and its origin*	Agent and taxonomic references*	Released*	Status and degree of control*	Research organisation*	General references*
(ASTERACEAE continued)					
Carduus nutans Linnaeus Europe, Asia (nodding thistle, musk thistle)	*Urophora solstitialis* (Linnaeus) (Diptera: Tephritidae)	1990	**CANADA.** Ex Germany. Bred in Ontario in 1990. Under evaluation.	CDA	593
	Rhinocyllus conicus (Frölich) (Coleoptera: Curculionidae)	1981	**ARGENTINA.** Ex France (Rhine Valley) via Canada via U.S.A. and Upper Rhine Valley via Canada via New Zealand. Established at two sites in the Provinces of Santa Fe and Cordoba. Attempts to establish colonies by redistributing adults collected from *Carduus acanthoides* in Buenos Aires continue.	INTA	115,183
		1988	**AUSTRALIA.** Ex France (Rhine Valley) via Canada via New Zealand and ex France (Le Larzac). Established at six sites. Under evaluation.	CSIRO	711
		1989	Ex Italy. Established at one site. Released in 1990 at two further sites. Under evaluation.	CSIRO	711
		1968	**CANADA.** Ex France (Rhine Valley). Established in Alberta, British Columbia, Manitoba, Ontario and Saskatchewan. Attacks 70% of plants over the weed's range, significantly damaging the weed and providing effective control. In Saskatchewan densities of 0.5-5.0 larvae/head controls thistle on well managed pasture but not on disturbed sites.	CDA	261,273, 514,592, 731
		1973	**NEW ZEALAND.** Ex France (Rhine Valley) via Canada. Widely established throughout the range of nodding thistle. Larval densities of one per mm of receptacle diameter have prevented the development of all seed. Evaluation continuing Hybrids of *C. nutans* and *C. acanthoides* also acceptable hosts. This strain of *R. conicus* is also found on *Cirsium arvense* and *C. palustre*.	DSIR	324,325, 326,329, 535

* See 'Introduction' for explanation of headings.

List A continued

Weed and its origin*	Agent and taxonomic references*	Released*	Status and degree of control*	Research organisation*	General references*
(ASTERACEAE continued)					
	Trichosirocalus horridus (Panzer) [previously referred to as *Ceuthorhynchidius horridus* (Panzer)] (Coleoptera: Curculionidae)	1983	**ARGENTINA.** Ex Italy via U.S.A. Not established.	INTA	115,183
		1975	**CANADA.** Ex Germany. Established in British Columbia and Saskatchewan but status unknown in Manitoba and Ontario. No effective control. At Regina, in Saskatchewan, most rosettes are attacked causing stunting but little mortality. May be more effective on thistles competing with grass.	CDA	63,261, 592
		1979 1985	**NEW ZEALAND.** Ex Italy. Not established. Ex Germany via Canada. Established. Redistribution continuing.	DSIR DSIR	326 326,328
	Urophora solstitialis (Linnaeus) (Diptera: Tephritidae)	1990	**NEW ZEALAND.** Ex Austria. Establishment not yet confirmed. Program continuing.	DSIR	330
Carduus pycnocephalus Linnaeus Europe, Asia (slender winged thistle, Italian thistle)	*Rhinocyllus conicus* (Frölich) (Coleoptera: Curculionidae)	1973	**NEW ZEALAND.** Ex France (Rhine Valley) via Canada. Where *Carduus pycnocephalus* is associated with *Carduus nutans*, overflow of this insect to *C. pycnocephalus* early each season results in considerable reductions in seed production. Expect good control under these circumstances.	DSIR	326,535
		1973	**UNITED STATES OF AMERICA.** Ex Italy. Established in CA and OR. Larvae directly and indirectly cause 55% seed loss in CA where weevils have been long established. Weevil race differences are being detected between *Carduus pycnocephalus*, *Carduus tenuiflorus* and *Silybum marianum*.	UDSA (7)) State (5, 14,15)	114,225, 228,229, 667
	Trichosirocalus horridus (Panzer) [previously referred to as *Ceutorhynchidius horridus* (Panzer)] (Coleoptera: Curculionidae)	1985	**NEW ZEALAND.** Ex Germany via Canada. Established. Redistribution continuing.	DSIR	326,328

* See 'Introduction' for explanation of headings.

List A continued

Weed and its origin*	Agent and taxonomic references*	Released*	Status and degree of control*	Research organisation* references*	General references*
(ASTERACEAE continued)					
Carduus tenuiflorus Curtis, western Europe (slender flower thistle, winged thistle)	*Cheilosia corydon* (Harris) [previously referred to as *Cheilosia grossa* (Fallén)] (Diptera: Syrphidae)	1990	**UNITED STATES OF AMERICA.** Ex Italy. Released in MD and NJ. Establishment not confirmed.	USDA (12) State (20)	291
	Puccinia carduorum Jacky (fungus: Uredinales)	1987	**UNITED STATES OF AMERICA.** Ex Turkey. Readily Established in VA experimental plots and spread 7 km by 2nd year. Caused accelerated senescence which reduced seed set.	USDA (2)	51
	Rhinocyllus conicus (Frölich) (Coleoptera: Curculionidae)	1973	**NEW ZEALAND.** Ex France (Rhine Valley) via Canada. Where *Carduus tenuiflorus* is associated with *Carduus nutans* overflow of this insect to *C. tenuiflorus* early each season results in considerable reduction in seed production. Expect good results under these circumstances.	DSIR	326
		1973	**UNITED STATES OF AMERICA.** Ex Italy. Strain from *Carduus pycnocephalus* attacking *C. tenuiflorus* in CA & OR.	State (15)	114,667
	Trichosirocalus horridus (Panzer) [previously referred to as *Ceutorhynchidius horridus* (Panzer)] (Coleoptera: Curculionidae)	1985	**NEW ZEALAND.** Ex Germany via Canada. Established. Redistribution continuing.	DSIR	326,328

* See 'Introduction' for explanation of headings.

List A continued

Weed and its origin*	Agent and taxonomic references*	Released*	Status and degree of control*	Research organisation*	General references*
(ASTERACEAE continued)					
Carduus thoermeri Weinmann (previously referred to as *Carduus nutans* Linnaeus) 362,367 Europe, Asia (nodding thistle, musk thistle)	*Rhinocyllus conicus* (Frölich) (Coleoptera: Curculionidae)	1969	**UNITED STATES OF AMERICA.** Ex France (Rhine Valley) via Canada. Established in AR, CA, CO, ID, IA, IL, KS, KY, MD, MN, MO, MT, ND, NE, OR, PA, SD, TN, TX, UT, WA, and WY. Weevil continues to increase and disperse to new states. Effective in KS pastures along protected wooded areas and creek bottoms; 90-99% reduction at some MT, OR, and VA sites; 80-90% reduction in south central MO. Asynchrony limits effectiveness in CA. Has transferred naturally to *Carduus arvense* in CA, MT and OR with minimal impact, and to *C. vulgare* in CA and MT with minimal impact.	USDA (1,7, 9,10,11) State (1, 13,14,15)	7,13,41, 114,291, 365,367, 540,541, 545,599, 621,636, 667
	Trichosirocalus horridus (Panzer) [previously referred to as *Ceutorhynchidius horridus* (Panzer)] (Coeoptera: Curculionidae)	1974	**UNITED STATES OF AMERICA.** Ex Italy. Established in KS, MD, MO, VA and WY. Populations widespread. Effective control at initial sites in KS; more than 99% control at sites in VA. Widespread with major weed reduction in south central MO. Ongoing redistribution to other states, but establishments unconfirmed.	USDA (1,7 9,12), State (1,7, 10,11,13)	13,41,63, 363,368, 388,393, 540,599
Centaurea diffusa Lamarck southern Europe, Asia Minor (diffuse knapweed)	*Agapeta zoegana* Linnaeus (Lepidoptera: Cochylidae)	1982	**CANADA.** Ex Austria, Hungary and Romania. Established in British Columbia but no significant effect. Most diffuse knapweed sites too dry.	CDA	267,450
	Cyphocleonus achates (Fåhraeus) (Coleoptera: Curculionidae)	1984	**UNITED STATES OF AMERICA.** Ex Austria, Hungary (IIBC). Released in ID, MT, OR and WA. Established in MT.	State (6, 7,9,15)	532,622
		1988	**UNITED STATES OF AMERICA.** Ex Austria (IIBC). Established MT.	State (7)	532,622
	Metzneria paucipunctella Zeller (Lepidoptera: Gelechiidae)	1983	**CANADA.** Ex Switzerland. Established in British Columbia. No significant effects. Not the main host, but 0.05 larvae/head persist.	CDA	267

* See 'Introduction' for explanation of headings.

List A *continued*

Weed and its origin*	Agent and taxonomic references*	Released*	Status and degree of control*	Research organisation*	General references*
(ASTERACEAE continued)					
	Pelochrista medullana (Staudinger) (Lepidoptera: Tortricidae)	1982	**CANADA.** Ex Austria, Hungary and Romania. Not established in British Columbia. Field cage colony died in cold winter of 1988-89.	CDA	267
		1984	**UNITED STATES OF AMERICA.** Ex Austria and Hungary (IIBC). Released in MT. Not established.	USDA (7,10) State (7)	532,621, 622
	Pterolonche inspersa Staudinger (Lepidoptera: Pterolonchidae)	1986	**CANADA.** Ex Hungary and Austria. Not established in British Columbia. Field cage colony died in cold winter of 1988-89.	CDA	179
		1986	**UNITED STATES OF AMERICA.** Ex Austria, Hungary. Released in ID, MT, OR and WA. Not established.	USDA (7, 10,12) State (6, 7,9,15)	532
	Sphenoptera jugoslavica Obenberger (Coleoptera: Buprestidae)	1976	**CANADA.** Ex Yugoslavia. Established in British Columbia. Widely distributed through the driest knapweed range. Adds 40% to *Urophora* spp seed reduction. Spread to *Centaurea maculosa* in British Columbia. Widespread control not provided.	UBC	267,278, 514,537
		1980	**UNITED STATES OF AMERICA.** Ex Greece. Released in CA, ID, OR and WA. Established in ID, MT, OR and WA. Redistribution underway.	USDA (7, 10) State 6,7,9,14, 15)	528,532, 621,622

* See 'Introduction' for explanation of headings.

List A continued

(**ASTERACEAE continued**)

Weed and its origin*	Agent and taxonomic references*	Released*	Status and degree of control*	Research organisation*	General references*
	Subanguina picridis Kirjanova & Ivanova (previously referred to as *Paranguina picridus* Kirjanova & Ivanova) (Nematoda: Tylenchidae)	1986	**CANADA.** Ex U.S.S.R. via Saskatchewan. Released in British Columbia. Not established.	CDA	267
	Urophora affinis (Frauenfeld) (Diptera: Tephritidae)	1970	**CANADA.** Ex France and U.S.S.R. Established in British Columbia. Forms 1.2 to 1.6 galls/head and with *U. quadrifaciata* reduces seed production by up to 95% which is population maintenance level. Many populations bivoltine. Control of weed not achieved.	CDA UBC	259,260, 265,276, 278
		1973	**UNITED STATES OF AMERICA.** Ex central and eastern Europe. Released in CA, ID, MT, OR, WA and WY. Established (except in CA) and increasing. Together with *Urophora quadrifasciata*, seed production is reduced by 75-95% at some sites; but no stand reduction results. Redistribution underway.	USDA (7,10) State (6,7, 9,13,15)	480,528, 532,619, 620,622, 625
	Urophora quadrifasciata (Meigen) (Diptera: Tephritidae)	1972	**CANADA.** Ex U.S.S.R. Established in British Columbia. Supplements attack by *U. affinis* and spreads more rapidly but does not become as dense. Mainly bivoltine. Cannot survive the winter in Saskatchewan. Control of weed not achieved.	CDA UBC	259,260, 278
		1989	**UNITED STATES OF AMERICA.** Ex U.S.S.R. via natural dispersal from established colonies in Canada. Established in ID, MT, OR and WA. Released in WY in 1989 following specificity tests. Redistribution underway. (See also List D)	USDA (10) State (6, 7,9,13,15)	388,528, 532,547, 620,621, 622
Centaurea maculosa Lamarck Europe (spotted knapweed)	*Agapeta zoegana* Linnaeus (Lepidoptera: Cochylidae)	1982	**CANADA.** Ex Austria, Rumania and Hungary. Established in British Columbia, but visible knapweed decline at only one site with 30-88 larvae/100 plants. No control achieved.	CDA	267,450

* See 'Introduction' for explanation of headings.

List A *continued*

(ASTERACEAE continued)

Weed and its origin*	Agent and taxonomic references*	Released*	Status and degree of control*	Research organisation*	General references*
		1984	**UNITED STATES OF AMERICA.** Ex Hungary and Austria (IIBC). Released in ID, OR, MT and WA. Establishment confirmed in MT.	USDA (7,10) State (6,7, 9,15)	114,623, 627
	Cyphocleonus achates (Fåhraeus) (Coleoptera: Curculionidae)	1987	**CANADA.** Ex Austria and U.S.S.R. Established in British Columbia. Kills small plants and shoots from stools of larger plants. In the north adults emerge too late for full oviposition, so does best in warm southern sites. No control so far.	CDA	618
		1988	**UNITED STATES OF AMERICA.** Ex Austria (IIBC). Establishment not confirmed.	USDA (10) State (7,9)	623
	Metzneria paucipunctella Zeller (Lepidoptera: Gelechiidae)	1973	**CANADA.** Ex Switzerland. Established in British Colombia. Attacks 50-80% of plants over 50% of the weed's range. Destroys 8 seeds/head and 2/3 of the *Urophora* larvae without reducing subsequent density. Spread 100 km in 15 years. No control.	CDA UBC	278,514, 628
		1980	**UNITED STATES OF AMERICA.** Ex Switzerland via Canada. Established in ID, MT, OR and WA. Destroyed about 6 seeds/head. In central OR, in combination with *Urophora* species, reduced seed production below level caused by *Urophora* species alone. Released in VA in 1986 but establishment not confirmed. Redistribution continues.	USDA (7) State (1, 6,7,9,15)	364,528, 569,621, 622,623
	Pelochrista medullana (Staudinger) (Lepidoptera: Tortricidae)	1984	**UNITED STATES OF AMERICA.** Ex Austria and Hungary (IIBC). Single release in MT failed to establish.	USDA (7) State (7)	623
	Pterolonche inspersa Staudinger (Lepidoptera: Pterolonchidae)	1988	**UNITED STATES OF AMERICA.** Ex Hungary (IIBC). Establishment in MT not confirmed.	USDA (7,10) State (7)	180,623

* See 'Introduction' for explanation of headings.

List A continued

Weed and its origin*	Agent and taxonomic references*	Released*	Status and degree of control*	Research organisation*	General references*
(ASTERACEAE continued)					
	Urophora affinis (Frauenfeld) (Diptera: Tephritidae)	1970	**CANADA.** Ex France. Established in British Columbia and Quebec. Status unknown in Ontario. With *Urophora quadrifasciata* forms 3.3–5.0 galls/head and reduces seed to maintenance level. Control not achieved.	CDA	259,260, 265,276, 278
		1973	**UNITED STATES OF AMERICA.** Ex France, Austria and Switzerland and ex France via Canada. Established in CA, ID, MT, NY, OR, VA, WA and WY. Together with *Urophora quadrifasciata* reduces seed production/head 36–41%.	USDA (1,7 10) State 6,7,9,13, 15)	291,364, 388,480, 528,621-626
	Urophora quadrifasciata (Meigen) (Diptera: Tephritidae)	1972	**CANADA.** Ex U.S.S.R. Established in British Columbia and Quebec. Status unknown in Ontario. Avoids capitula heavily attacked by *U. affinis* but supplements overall seed reduction. Univoltine in late flowering stands. Control not achieved.	CDA UBC MU	259,260, 266,278
			Transferred to *Centaurea debeauxii* Gren & Gordon but no control achieved.	CDA	267
Centaurea solstitialis Linnaeus Eurasia, northern Africa (yellow starthistle)	*Bangasternus orientalis* (Capimont) (Coleoptera: Curculionidae)	1985	**UNITED STATES OF AMERICA.** Ex Greece. Established in CA, ID, OR and WA. Preliminary data indicate seed reductions of 53% and 55% in infested heads at two sites in CA; insufficient to provide control.	USDA (7,12) State (6,9, 14,15)	400,401, 668
	Chaetorellia australis Héring (Diptera: Tephritidae)	1988	**UNITED STATES OF AMERICA.** Ex Greece. Released in CA, ID, OR & WA in 1989. Establishment not confirmed.	USDA (7,12) State (6,9, 14,15)	668
	Eustenopus villosus (Boheman) (Coleoptera: Curculionidae)	1990	**UNITED STATES OF AMERICA.** Ex Greece. Released in CA, ID, OR and WA. Establishment not confirmed.	USDA (7,12) State (6,9, 14,15)	190,668
	Urophora jaculata Rondani (Diptera: Tephritidae)	1969	**UNITED STATES OF AMERICA.** Ex Italy. Released (as *Urophora sirunaseva*) in CA in 1969/70/76/77. Did not establish. Does not complete development on weed populations infesting CA, ID or WA.	USDA (7,12) State (4,14)	668,696

* See 'Introduction' for explanation of headings.

List A continued

Weed and its origin*	Agent and taxonomic references*	Released*	Status and degree of control*	Research organisation* references*	General references*
(ASTERACEAE continued)					
	Urophora sirunaseva (Héring) (Diptera: Tephritidae)	1984	**UNITED STATES OF AMERICA.** Ex Greece. Released in CA in 1984. Ex Greece, released in CA, ID, OR and WA in 1985. Establishment confirmed in CA and OR.	USDA (7,12) State (6,9, 14,15)	668
		1985	Ex Turkey. Released in ID but did not establish.		668
Centaurea virgata Lamarck ssp. *squarrosa* Gugler Eurasia, Asia Minor (squarrose knapweed)	*Pterolonche inspersa* Staudinger (Lepidoptera: Pterlonchidae)	1990	**UNITED STATES OF AMERICA.** Ex Greece. Eggs released in UT. Establishment not confirmed.	USDA (10) State (21)	185
	Urophora affinis (Frauenfeld) (Diptera: Tephritidae)	1989	**UNITED STATES OF AMERICA.** Ex U.S.S.R. Released in OR, and UT via MT. Limited recovery in OR. Larval recovery in UT but establishment not confirmed.	USDA (10) State (15, 21)	185,560
	Urophora quadrifasciata (Meigen) (Diptera: Tephritidae)	1989	**UNITED STATES OF AMERICA.** Ex U.S.S.R. via MT. Released in UT. Larval recovery in UT, but establishment not confirmed. (See also List D)	USDA (10) State (9, 15,21)	114,560
Chondrilla juncea Linnaeus southern U.S.S.R., Mediterranean Europe, Asia Minor (skeleton weed)	*Cystiphora schmidti* (Rübsaamen) (Diptera: Cecidomyiidae)	1982	**ARGENTINA.** Ex Greece via Australia. Released 1982 to 1987. Not established.	INTA	115,119
		1971	**AUSTRALIA.** Ex Greece. Established readily and colonised widely until 1974. Generally common since 1975 and complementing damage by the rust *Puccinia chondrillina*. Particularly damaging to flowering stems of all forms of the weed. Parasitism first recorded in 1978 and now limiting impact.	CSIRO	120,121, 159
		1975	**UNITED STATES OF AMERICA.** Ex Greece via Australia. Established in CA, ID, OR and WA. Parasitism affects impact but seed production and biomass continue to be significantly reduced, especially in WA.	USDA (7) State (6, 9,14)	114,531, 635,693

* See 'Introduction' for explanation of headings.

List A *continued*

Weed and its origin*	Agent and taxonomic references*	Released*	Status and degree of control*	Research organisation*	General references*
(ASTERACEAE continued)					
	Bradyrrhoa gilveolella Treitschke (Lepidoptera: Pyralidae)	1974	**AUSTRALIA.** Ex Greece. Not established. Difficult to rear and culture considered weak and inbred.	CSIRO	122
		1978	Ex Greece. New colony, carefully reared. Small colonies recorded by 1980. Releases continued until 1985 but no recent recoveries.	CSIRO	122,159
	Eriophyes chondrillae (Canestrini) (previously referred to as *Aceria chondrillae*) (Acarina: Eriophyidae)	1989	**ARGENTINA.** Ex Italy via U.S.A. Established at six sites in south-western Buenos Aires Province and spreading rapidly.	INTA	115
		1971	**AUSTRALIA.** Ex Greece. Established readily but spread slowly requiring widespread colonisation. Generally distributed by 1976 but only consistently common in drier areas where it causes severe damage to the stem. Introduced strain almost specific to common form of the weed.	CSIRO	120,126, 159
		1985	Ex Greece. New strain for intermediate leaf form released widely until 1987. Established but only at very low levels.	CSIRO	123
		1977	**UNITED STATES OF AMERICA.** Ex Italy. Widely established in CA, ID, OR and WA. Most effective agent in WA, decreasing shoot and seed production and rosette regeneration. Predation by indigenous *Typhlodromus pyri* limits effectiveness in CA. Moderate seed reduction in OR.	USDA (7) State (6, 9,14)	114,531, 635
	Puccinia chondrillina Bubak & Sydenham (fungus: Uredinales)	1982	**ARGENTINA.** Ex Italy via U.S.A. Initial releases failed to establish. Established after further releases in 1984 but at very low densities.	INTA	115

* See 'Introduction' for explanation of headings.

List A *continued*

(ASTERACEAE continued)

Weed and its origin*	Agent and taxonomic references*	Released*	Status and degree of control*	Research organisation*	General references*
		1971	**AUSTRALIA.** Ex Italy (strain IT32). Established rapidly throughout distribution of weed. Strain is specific to the most widespread form of the weed only (the narrow leaf form). Providing a very high level of control.	CSIRO	120,121, 124,154
		1980	Ex Turkey (strain TU21). Released against second (intermediate leaf) form of the weed. Not established.	CSIRO	154
		1981	Ex Turkey (strain TU21). Released a second time but also failed to establish. Concluded that this strain is insufficiently virulent.	CSIRO	154
		1982	Ex Italy (strain IT36). Released against the second form of the weed. Appears to have established after further releases in 1983. Kills some leaves but does not attack the stems in summer. Has been recorded in several areas and probably generally established but ineffective.	CSIRO	123,154, 282
		1976	**UNITED STATES OF AMERICA.** Ex Italy. Established in CA, ID, OR and WA. The most damaging agent in CA, reducing plant size. Reduced density of late-flowering biotype in mesic sites in WA.	USDA (2) State 6, 9,14	531,635
Chromolaena odorata (Linnaeus) R. King & H. Robinson (= *Eupatorium odoratum* Linnaeus), 352 Caribbean, Central and South America (Siam weed, triffid weed, communist weed)	*Apion brunneonigrum* Béguin–Billecocq Coleoptera: Apionidae	1975	**GHANA.** Ex Trinidad. Not established.	IIBC	90,91,105
		1972	**INDIA.** Ex Trinidad. Introductions and releases of Trinidad material were made up to 1983. Not established.	IIBC	70,90,91, 106
		1970	**MALAYSIA.** (Sabah). Ex Trinidad. Not established.	DAMA	90,91,101, 102,494
		1984	**MARIANA ISLANDS.** Ex Trinidad to Guam. Not established.	UOG	458
		1970	**NIGERIA.** Ex Trinidad. Not established.	IIBC	90,91, 101-106

* See 'Introduction' for explanation of headings.

List A continued

Weed and its origin*	Agent and taxonomic references*	Released*	Status and degree of control*	Research organisation*	General references*
(ASTERACEAE continued)					
		1974	**SRI LANKA.** Ex Trinidad. Not established.	IIBC	90,91,105, 106
	Melanagromyza eupatoriella Spencer (Diptera: Agromyzidae)	1986	**MARIANA ISLANDS.** Ex Trinidad to Guam. Not established.	UOG	458
		1987	Ex Trinidad. Not established.	UOG	458
	Mescinia nr. *parvula* Zeller (Lepidoptera: Pyralidae)	1984	**MARIANA ISLANDS.** Ex Trinidad to Guam. Not established.	UOG	458
		1986	Ex Trinidad. Not established.	UOG	458
		1987	Ex Trinidad. Not established.	UOG	458
	Pareuchaetes aurata (Butler) (Lepidoptera: Arctiidae)	1990	**REPUBLIC OF SOUTH AFRICA.** Establishment not confirmed.	PPRI	357
	Pareuchaetes pseudoinsulata Rego Barros (previously referred to as *Ammalo insulata* Walker) (Lepidoptera: Arctiidae)	1988	**CAROLINE ISLANDS.** Ex Trinidad via Guam to Yap. Harsh climate, predators and/or parasites thought to contribute to low establishment rate. Releases and monitoring are being continued. Redistrubuted from Guam to Yap, Pohnpei and Palau in 1989. Under evaluation.	UOG	456
			Redistributed from Guam to Yap, Pohnpei and Kosrae in 1990. Under evaluation.	UOG	454,456
		1973	**GHANA.** Ex Trinidad via India. Not established.	IIBC	91,93,103, 104
		1989	Ex Trinidad via Guam. Status unknown.		454
		1973	**INDIA.** Ex Trinidad. Not established. Native predators are believed to have prevented its establishment.	IIBC	70,93
		1984	Ex Trinidad via Sri Lanka. This strain established readily in Kerala and Karnataka. In Kerala defoliation was obtained in 50% of the area, and over a 10 ha area in Karnataka.	IIHR KAU	70,321, 582

* See 'Introduction' for explanation of headings.

List A continued

Weed and its origin*	Agent and taxonomic references*	Released*	Status and degree of control*	Research organisation*	General references*
(ASTERACEAE continued)					
		1970	**MALAYSIA** (Sabah). Ex Trinidad via India. Established and dispersed widely at low density, though outbreaks causing severe damage appear at regular intervals. Weed still not under control.	DAMA	90,91,93, 101-106, 494,641
		1984	**MARIANA ISLANDS.** Ex Trinidad via India to Guam. Successful control on Guam and Rota. Established and under evaluation on Tinian, Saipan and Aguigan.	UOG	458,596
		1970	**NIGERIA.** Ex Trinidad via India via Ghana. Not established.	IIBC	91,93, 101-106
		1989	**REPUBLIC OF SOUTH AFRICA.** Ex Trinidad via Guam via Sri Lanka via India. Apparently not established in presence on heavy ant predation.	PPRI	356,357
		1972	**SRI LANKA.** Ex Trinidad via India. Established, spread widely and causes plant defoliation. Provides partial control.	IIBC	90,91,93, 168
		1986	**THAILAND.** Ex Trinidad via Guam. Failed to establish despite releases from 1986 to 1988.	NBCRC	470
		1988	**VIETNAM.** Ex Trinidad via Guam via Thailand. Released in South Vietnam. Not established.	NBCRC	469
Chrysanthemoides monilifera (Linnaeus) Norlindh South Africa (boneseed, bitou bush)	*Chrysolina* sp. (Coleoptera: Chrysomelidae)	1989	**AUSTRALIA.** Ex South Africa. Released in Victoria and New South Wales. No evidence of establishment Under evaluation.	DCE	52
	Comostolopsis germana Prout (Lepidoptera: Geometridae)	1989	**AUSTRALIA.** Ex South Africa. Established in northern New South Wales. Under evaluation.	DCE QDL	2,700

* See 'Introduction' for explanation of headings.

List A continued

Weed and its origin*	Agent and taxonomic references*	Released*	Status and degree of control*	Research organisation* references*	General references*
(ASTERACEAE continued)					
Cirsium arvense (Linnaeus) Scopoli Europe, northern Africa (Canada thistle, creeping thistle, Californian thistle)	*Altica carduorum* Guérin-Méneville (Coleoptera: Chrysomelidae)	1963	**CANADA.** Ex Switzerland and France. Not established in Alberta, British Columbia, Nova Scotia or Ontario. Slow development in cool summers exposed larvae to high predation.	CDA	258,513, 514,516
		1969	**GREAT BRITAIN.** Ex France and Switzerland. Overwinter survival in cages only. Climate too dull and wet to allow survival except locally.	IIBC IC MAFF	18,89
		1990	**NEW ZEALAND.** Ex Switzerland. Establishment not yet confirmed. Program continuing.	DSIR	330
		1966	**UNITED STATES OF AMERICA.** Ex Switzerland via Canada. Released in CA, CO, DE, ID, IN, MD, MN, MT, NV, NJ, OR, SD, WA and WI. Not established.	USDA (1,7) State (12)	291,530
		1970	Ex Atlantic Coast, France. Released in MD, NJ and SD. Not established.	USDA (1,7) State (12)	291,530
	Ceutorhynchus litura (Fabricius) (Coleoptera: Curculionidae)	1965	**CANADA.** Ex Switzerland, France, Germany. Established in Alberta,Ontario, British Columbia, New Brunswick and Saskatchewan. No significant control. Attacks early emerged shoots and some-times reduces shoot production.	CDA	514,516, 519,520, 546
		1988	**NEW ZEALAND.** Ex Great Britian. Not established. Program continuing.	DSIR	330
		1971	**UNITED STATES OF AMERICA.** Ex Germany. Released in CA, CO, ID, MD, MT, NJ, OR, SD, WA and WY. Established in ID, MD, MT, OR and WY. Populations and redistribution efforts limited.	USDA (1,7, 10) State (6, 7,9,13,15)	291,528, 619,621

* See 'Introduction' for explanation of headings.

List A *continued*

Weed and its origin*	Agent and taxonomic references*	Released*	Status and degree of control*	Research organisation*	General references*
(ASTERACEAE continued)					
	Lema cyanella (Linnaeus) (Coleoptera: Chrysomelidae)	1978	**CANADA.** Ex Switzerland. Survived in field cage tests in Saskatchewan. Not released in open field situations.	CDA	514,516
		1983	Ex Switzerland. Not established in Alberta, New Brunswick or Saskatchewan.	CDA	267,516
		1983	**NEW ZEALAND.** Ex Switzerland via Canada. Not established.	DSIR	327
		1990	Ex Switzerland. Establishment not yet confirmed. Program continuing.	DSIR	330
	Rhinocyllus conicus (Frölich) (Coleoptera: Curculionidae)	1968	**CANADA.** Ex France. Established in Saskatchewan but not in Nova Scotia. Control not achieved. Occurs in both male and female capitula.	CDA	267
	Urophora cardui (Linnaeus) (Diptera: Tephritidae)	1975	**CANADA.** Ex Germany, Austria, France and Finland. Established in New Brunswick, Nova Scotia, Ontario, Prince Edward Island, Quebec and Saskatchewan, but not in Alberta or British Columbia. Provides no effective control.	CDA UG MU	514,516, 518,521, 592
		1976	**NEW ZEALAND.** Ex France and Germany. Not established.	DSIR	330,327
		1977	**UNITED STATES OF AMERICA.** Ex Austria. Not established.	USDA (1,7) State (1,6, 7,9,13,14)	291,388, 393,621 528
		1978	Ex France and Austria, and Ex Germany, Austria and France via Canada. Released in CO, ID, IA, MD, MT, NV, OR, VA, WA and WY. Established in all states except CO, ID and IA. Released in UT in 1990. Galls on primary stem stunt plant, but otherwise impact is minimal.	USDA (1,7, 10) State (1,6,7,9, 13,14,21)	291,388, 393,528, 530,621

* See 'Introduction' for explanation of headings.

List A continued

27

Weed and its origin*	Agent and taxonomic references*	Released*	Status and degree of control*	Research organisation*	General references*
(ASTERACEAE continued)					
Cirsium palustre (Linnaeus) Eurasia (marsh thistle)	*Trichosirocalus horridus* (Panzer) (Coleoptera: Curculionidae)	1985	**NEW ZEALAND.** Ex Germany via Canada. Established. Redistribution continuing.	DSIR	326,328
Cirsium vulgare (Savi) Tenore Eurasia, northern Africa (bull thistle, spear thistle)	*Rhinocyllus conicus* (Frölich) (Coleoptera: Curculionidae)	1990	**AUSTRALIA** (Victoria). Ex France. Released at one site in Victoria. Under evaluation.	DCE	52
		1985	**CANADA.** Ex France. Released in British Columbia. Not established.	CDA	267
		1989	**REPUBLIC OF SOUTH AFRICA.** Ex France. Established and spreading at a release site at Pietermaritzburg.	PPRI	357,724
	Trichosirocalus horridus (Panzer) (Coleoptera: Curculionidae)	1984	**NEW ZEALAND.** Ex Germany via Canada. Established. Redistribution continuing.	DSIR	326,328
	Urophora stylata (Fabricius) (Diptera: Tephritidae)	1973	**CANADA.** Ex Germany and Switzerland. Established in British Columbia, Nova Scotia and Quebec but not in Ontario. No control achieved. Reduced seed by up to 65% at some sites. Dies out in sparse stands. Occasionally attacks *C. arvense* with no significant control.	CDA MU	105,279, 514
		1983	**REPUBLIC OF SOUTH AFRICA.** Ex Germany. Established and spreading, but main population accidentally destroyed by herbicidal application.	PPRI	724,725
		1989	Ex Germany. Survived at least one year since release.	PPRI	724,725
		1983	**UNITED STATES OF AMERICA.** Ex Germany and Switzerland via Canada. Established in CO, MD and OR. Establishment in MT not confirmed.	USDA (1,7) State (9,15)	114,291, 528,573

* See 'Introduction' for explanation of headings.

List A continued

Weed and its origin*	Agent and taxonomic references*	Released*	Status and degree of control*	Research organisation*	General references*
(ASTERACEAE continued)					
Elephantopus mollis Humboldt, Bonplaud & Kunth (= *Elephantopus scaber* Linnaeus) Central America, West Indies (elephant's foot, tobacco weed, tavoko ni veikau)	*Tetreuaresta obscuriventris* (Loew) (Diptera: Tephritidae)	1957	**FIJI.** Ex Trinidad. Established quickly. Status unknown.	DAF	485,543, 604
		1961	**HAWAII, U.S.A.** Ex Trinidad via Fiji. Released on Hawaii and Kauai. Effects negligible. Weed slowly spreading.	HDOA	141,142, 143,290
Gutierrezia microcephala (de Candolle) Gray [also referred to as *Xanthocephalum microcephalum* (de Candolle) Shinners] North America and warm western South America (threadleaf snakeweed)	*Heilipodus ventralis* Kuschel (Coleoptera: Curculionidae)	1988	**UNITED STATES OF AMERICA.** Ex Argentina. *H. ventralis* was collected in the extended (exotic) range of the weed, ie. Argentina, and released into the native range of the weed in NM and TX. Establishment not confirmed.	USDA (9)	161
Gutierrezia sarothrae (Pursh) Britton & Rusby [also referred to as *Xanthocephalum sarothrae* (Pursh) Shinners] North America and warm western South America (broom snakeweed)	*Heilipodus ventralis* Kuschel (Coleoptera: Curculionidae)	1988	**UNITED STATES OF AMERICA.** Ex Argentina. *H. ventralis* was collected in the extended (exotic) range of the weed, ie. Argentina, and released into the native range of the weed in NM and TX. Establishment not confirmed.	USDA (9)	161
Mikania micrantha Kunth Central and South America (mile-a-minute weed)	*Liothrips mikaniae* (Priesner) (Thysanoptera: Phloethripidae)	1990	**MALAYSIA.** Ex Trinidad and Tobago via United Kingdom. Not yet established.	IIBC AP	240
		1988	**SOLOMON ISLANDS.** Ex Trinidad. Not established. Further importation from Trinidad and release in 1989. Not established.	MAL	241

* See 'Introduction' for explanation of headings.

List A continued

Weed and its origin*	Agent and taxonomic references*	Released*	Status and degree of control*	Research organisation*	General references*
(ASTERACEAE continued)					
Onopordum acanthium Linnaeus Europe (Scotch thistle)	*Rhinocyllus conicus* (Frölich) (Coleoptera: Curculionidae)	1973	**UNITED STATES OF AMERICA.** Ex *Carduus pycnocephalus* Italy. Released in eastern OR. No establishment.	State (15)	114
Parthenium hysterophorus Linnaeus Mexico (Parthenium weed, whitetop, congress grass)	*Bucculatrix parthenica* Bradley (Lepidoptera: Lyonetidae)	1984	**AUSTRALIA.** Ex Mexico. Widely established throughout range of the weed. In favourable conditions up to 50% of total leaf area destroyed. Partial control achieved. Under evaluation.	QDL IIBC	413,418
	Epiblema strenuana (Walker) (Lepidoptera: Tortricidae)	1982	**AUSTRALIA.** Ex Mexico. Widely established. Reducing weed vigour and competitiveness but control not adequate.	QDL IIBC	418,419
	Listronotus setosipennis (Hustache) (Coleoptera: Curculionidae)	1983	**AUSTRALIA.** Ex Brazil. Established at several sites but populations low. No control.	QDL	418,420
	Smicronyx lutulentus Dietz (Coleoptera: Curculionidae)	1980	**AUSTRALIA.** Ex Mexico. Not established.	QDL	418,420, 421
	Stobaera concinna (Stål) (Hemiptera: Delphacidae)	1983	**AUSTRALIA.** Ex Mexico. Not established.	QDL	412,420
	Zygogramma bicolorata Pallister (Coleoptera: Chrysomelidae)	1980	**AUSTRALIA.** Ex Mexico. Established at one site. Population very low. No control.	QDL IIBC	418,420, 421
		1984	**INDIA.** Ex Mexico. Released in Bangalore. Developed damaging populations after four years. By 1990, dispersed naturally over 10,000 sq km around Bangalore. Caused defoliation, reduced flower production and reduced weed density in many areas. Promises to be an effective agent.	IIBC IIHR	317,321

* See 'Introduction' for explanation of headings.

List A continued

Weed and its origin*	Agent and taxonomic references*	Released*	Status and degree of control*	Research organisation*	General references*
(ASTERACEAE continued)					
Pluchea odorata (Linnaeus) Cassini tropical America (sour bush, hairy fleabane)	*Acinia picturata* (Snow) (Diptera: Tephritidae)	1959	**HAWAII, U.S.A.** Ex Guatemala. Established throughout state and attacking up to 90% of seedheads, but ineffective in reducing density of plants.	HDOA	9,133,140, 212,312, 380
	Trichotaphe aenigmatica Clarke (Lepidoptera: Gelechiidae)	1957	**HAWAII, U.S.A.** Ex Mexico. Established on Oahu and Kauai. Populations low and ineffective.	HDOA	9,140,212, 380
Senecio jacobaeae Linnaeus Eurasia, northern Africa (ragwort, tansy ragwort)	*Botanophila jacobaeae* (Hardy) [formerly *Pegohylemyia jacobaeae* (Hardy); also refered to as *Hylemyia jacobaeae* Meade] (Diptera: Anthomyiidae)	1936	**NEW ZEALAND.** Ex England. Established over much of Central North Island. Has minor effect on seed production.	DSIR	181,301, 348,642, 643
	Botanophila seneciella (Meade) (formerly *Pegohylemyia seneciella* Meade; also referred to as *Hylemyia seneciella* Meade) (Diptera: Anthomyiidae)	1959	**AUSTRALIA.** Ex England via New Zealand. No establishment.	CSIRO	159
		1968	**CANADA.** Ex Italy via U.S.A. Established in British Columbia but not on Prince Edward Island or Nova Scotia. Disperses well but no control achieved.	CDA	272,280, 514
		1936	**NEW ZEALAND.** Ex England. Not established.	DSIR	301,434
		1966	**UNITED STATES OF AMERICA.** Ex France. Established in CA, OR and WA. Destroys approximately 30% of seed heads in WA.	USDA (7,12) State (8,9, 15)	201,416, 528
	Cochylis atricapitana (Stephens) (Lepidoptera: Cochylidae)	1987	**AUSTRALIA.** Ex France. Established at some sites in Victoria. Spread up to 450 m from release. Number of plants attacked is increasing. No control.	DCE	428
		1990	**CANADA.** Ex France via Australia. Released in New Brunswick. Establishment unknown.	CDA	267

* See 'Introduction' for explanation of headings.

List A *continued*

Weed and its origin*	Agent and taxonomic references*	Released*	Status and degree of control*	Research organisation*	General references*
(ASTERACEAE continued)					
	Longitarsus flavicornis (Stephens) (Coleoptera: Chrysomelidae)	1985	**AUSTRALIA.** Ex Spain. Well established in Victoria and Tasmania and acheived good control. Redistributions continuing.	DCE DPIT	188,310
		1971	**CANADA.** Ex Britain. Established in British Columbia. No control. Only 10% as abundant as *L. jacobaeae* on Vancouver Island. Maritimes probably too cool.	CDA	267
	Longitarsus jacobaeae (Waterhouse) (Coleoptera: Chrysomelidae)	1988	**AUSTRALIA.** Ex Italy via U.S.A. via New Zealand. Established at several sites in Victoria and completed two generations in the field in Tasmania. No assessable impact.	DCE TDA	188,203, 428
		1971	**CANADA.** Ex Italy via U.S.A. Established in British Columbia, Prince Edward Island and bred in New Brunswick in 1990. Not established in Ontario. Controls weed and disperses well in British Columbia but in Maritimes may start oviposition too late in the fall. Overall no control.	CDA	280
		1983	**NEW ZEALAND.** Ex Italy via U.S.A. Well established at sites throughout New Zealand. Reduced plant density at some sites.	DSIR	256,643, 644,645
		1969	**UNITED STATES OF AMERICA.** Ex Italy. Released CA, OR and WA. Reduced weed by more than 99% at CA and OR sites with sustained excellent control. Compliments effect of *Tyria jacobaeae.*	USDA (7,12) State (8,9, 15)	114,286, 287,415, 416,511, 528
	Longitarsus sp. (Coleoptera: Chrysomelidae) (released as *L. jacobaeae;* more closely resembles *L. flavicornis* 188, 310)	1979	**AUSTRALIA.** Ex France. Established and spreading. Causing high reduction in weed density at some sites.	CSIRO DCE DPIT	125,187, 188

* See 'Introduction' for explanation of headings.

List A continued

Weed and its origin*	Agent and taxonomic references*	Released*	Status and degree of control*	Research organisation*	General references*
(ASTERACEAE continued)					
	Tyria jacobaeae (Linnaeus) (also referred to as *Callimorpha jacobaeae* (Linnaeus)) (Lepidoptera: Arctiidae)	1930	**AUSTRALIA.** Ex England via New Zealand. No establishment. Heavy predation of larvae by scorpion flies.	CSIR	127,159
		1936	Ex England. No establishment. Heavy predation of larvae by scorpion flies.	CSIR	127,159
		1955	Ex Italy and England. No establishment. Predation plus disease problems in larvae.	CSIRO / DCE	43,159, / 587
		1956	Ex England. No establishment. Predation of larvae by various insects and birds and polyhedrosis caused heavy larval mortality.	DCE	159,587
		1962	Ex Switzerland and Austria. No establishment.	DCE	159,587
		1978	Ex France via U.S.A. via Canada, and ex Switzerland and Sweden via Canada. Not established. Project terminated in 1982.	DCE	187,588
		1963	**CANADA.** Ex France via U.S.A. and ex Switzerland and Sweden. Established in British Columbia, Nova Scotia, Prince Edward Island, New Brunswick but not in Ontario. Variable attack over most of the weed's range. Periodically defoliates to control weed in Maritimes on well drained pasture and reduces weed biomass in British Columbia. Weed problem increased in Prince Edward Island with decreased herbicide use. Overall no control.	CDA	274,275, 280,457, 514
		1928	**NEW ZEALAND.** Ex England. Established initially at a number of sites but dispersal and persistence was poor. During 1970s large populations emerged in southern North Island and although numbers are rarely sufficient to markedly affect the weed, the moth is well established. Redistribution to other areas is continuing.	CI	256,434, 642,643, 644,654

* See 'Introduction' for explanation of headings.

List A continued

Weed and its origin*	Agent and taxonomic references*	Released*	Status and degree of control*	Research organisation*	General references*
(ASTERACEAE continued)		1959	**UNITED STATES OF AMERICA**. Ex France. Released in CA, OR and WA. Defoliates the weed annually at sites in CA, OR and WA causing some mortality, but effect on plant density is limited. Shoot consumption reduces seed production. Complements effect of *Longitarsus jacobaeae*.	USDA (7,12) State (8,9, 15)	114,285, 286,287, 415,416, 511,528,
Silybum marianum (Linnaeus) Gaertner Mediterranean, south-west Europe (milk thistle, variegated thistle)	*Rhinocyllus conicus* (Frölich) (Coleoptera: Curculionidae)	1988	**AUSTRALIA**. Ex France. Released at two site in Victoria. Not established.	DCE	52
		1969	**UNITED STATES OF AMERICA**. Ex France (Rhine Valley) via Canada. Collected from *Carduus macrocephalus*. Failed to establish.	USDA (7,9) State (5,14, 15)	42,114, 222,229, 661,667
		1971	Ex Italy. Collected from *Silybum marianum*. Established in CA, TX and OR. Up to 98% capitula attacked with estimated 50-80% seed reduction. No control.	USDA (7,9) State (5,14, 15)	42,114, 222,229, 661,667
Sonchus arvensis Linnaeus Eurasia (perennial sow-thistle)	*Cystiphora sonchi* (Bremi) (Diptera: Cecidomyiidae)	1981	**CANADA**. Ex Austria. Established in Alberta, Manitoba, Nova Scotia and Saskatchewan but not in British Columbia or Quebec. Parasitism 30-60% and higher. No control.	CDA	517,523
	Liriomyza sonchi Hendel (Diptera: Agromyzidae)	1987	**CANADA**. Ex Austria. Established in Nova Scotia but not in Saskatchewan. Under evaluation.	CDA	267,522
	Tephritis dilacerata (Loew) (Diptera: Tephritidae)	1979	**CANADA**. Ex Austria. Not established in Alberta, Nova Scotia, Prince Edward Island, Quebec or Saskatchewan.	CDA	267,515

* See 'Introduction' for explanation of headings.

List A continued

Weed and its origin*	Agent and taxonomic references*	Released*	Status and degree of control*	Research organisation*	General references*
(ASTERACEAE: continued)					
Xanthium strumarium Linnaeus (= *Xanthium pungens* Wallroth) cosmopolitan (noogoora burr, cockleburr)	*Epiblema strenuana* (Walker) (Lepidoptera: Tortricidae)	1984	**AUSTRALIA.** Ex Mexico. Widely established. Reducing weed vigour and competitiveness.	QDL IIBC	418,419
	Euaresta aequalis (Loew) (Diptera: Tephritidae)	1932	**AUSTRALIA.** Ex Kansas, Texas and California, U.S.A. Established at low levels. No control.	CSIR CPPB QDAS	284,654, 706
		1951	**FIJI.** Ex U.S.A. via Australia. Not established.	KRS	483,485
	Mecas saturnina LeConte (Coleoptera: Cerambycidae)	1963	**AUSTRALIA.** Ex North America. Previously established at one site. No recent recoveries, thought to have died out.	QDL CSIRO	175,284, 684,706
	Nupserha vexator (Pascoe) (previously referred to as *Nupserha antennata* Gahan) (Coleoptera: Cerambycidae)	1964	**AUSTRALIA.** Ex India. Widely established populations have declined since the establishment of *Epiblema strenuana*. Provides little control.	QDL CSIRO	684,706
		1971	**FIJI.** Ex India and ex India via Australia. Not established.	KRS	343
BORAGINACEAE					
Echium plantagineum Linnaeus Spain, Portugal, Canary Islands (Paterson's curse, salvation Jane)	*Ceutorhynchus larvatus* Schultze (Coleoptera: Curculionidae)	1989	**AUSTRALIA.** Ex France. Released in low numbers. No recovery so far. Under evaluation.	CSIRO	438
	Dialectica scalariella (Zeller) (Lepidoptera: Gracillariidae)	1980	**AUSTRALIA.** Ex Portugal and France. Not established. Further releases prevented by High Court injunction. Two subsequent government inquiries found that control of the weed would be in the national interest.	CSIRO	157,160
		1988	Ex France and Portugal. Established widely. Spread up to 25 km from release points. Commonly attacks *Echium vulgare*. Under evaluation.	DCE,QDL DANSW	52,700

* See 'Introduction' for explanation of headings.

List A continued

Weed and its origin*	Agent and taxonomic references*	Released*	Status and degree of control*	Research organisation*	General references*
(BORAGINACEAE continued)					
Heliotropium europaeum Linnaeus Mediterranean Europe, northern Africa (common heliotrope)	*Longitarsus albineus* (Foudras) (Coleoptera: Chrysomelidae)	1979 1981	**AUSTRALIA.** Ex Greece. Establishment prevented due to drought eliminating host. Ex Greece and France. Establishment prevented due to drought eliminating host.	CSIRO CSIRO	154,156, 159 154
CACTACEAE					
Acanthocereus pentagonus (Linnaeus) Britton & Rose Central and North Americas (sword pear)	*Alcidion cereicola* Fisher (Coleoptera: Cerambycidae)	1979	**AUSTRALIA.** Ex Argentina. Not established.	QDL	655
	Hypogeococcus festerianus (Lizer y Trelles) (Hemiptera: Pseudococcidae)	1979	**AUSTRALIA.** Ex Argentina. Established. Causes deformed growth. Spreads slowly. Long term effects not yet determined.	QDL	655
Eriocereus bonplandii (Parmentier) Riccobono South America (Harrisia cactus)	*Hypogeococcus festerianus* (Lizer y Trelles) (Hemiptera: Pseudococcidae)	1982	**AUSTRALIA.** Ex Argentina. Well established. Provides effective control.	QDL	420
Eriocereus martinii (Labouret) Riccobono Argentina and Paraguay (Harrisia cactus)	*Alcidion cereicola* Fisher (Coleoptera: Cerambycidae)	1974	**AUSTRALIA.** Ex Argentina. Widely established. Only attacks older growth of mature plants. Very effective in killing top growth. Regrowth is then a target for *Hypogeococcus festerianus*. Population density is low due to activity by *Hypogeococcus festerianus*.	QDL	420,422
	Cactoblastis sp. (Lepidoptera: Pyralidae)	1978	**AUSTRALIA.** Ex Argentina. Not established.	QDL	417,422
	Eriocereophaga humeridens O'Brien (Coleoptera: Curculionidae)	1976	**AUSTRALIA.** Ex Brazil. Initially established readily but did not persist due to destruction of host by *Hypogeococcus festerianus*.	QDL	420,422

* See 'Introduction' for explanation of headings.

List A continued

Weed and its origin*	Agent and taxonomic references*	Released*	Status and degree of control*	Research organisation* references	General references*
(CACTACEAE continued)					
	Hypogeococcus festerianus (Lizer y Trelles) (Hemiptera: Pseudococcidae)	1975	**AUSTRALIA.** Ex Argentina. Established rapidly. Attack is concentrated around growing points causing grossly distorted growth. Prolonged attack causes death of plants. Highly effective against shoots, regrowth and flower buds. Also effective against mature plants. Manual distribution of field collected material has been undertaken on a large scale. Successful control is being achieved. Continued and follow-up distribution is necessary in many areas.	QDL	420,422, 655,656
		1983	**REPUBLIC OF SOUTH AFRICA.** Ex Argentina via Australia. Established, killing patches of the weed effectively, but poor dispersal in sparse infestations limits effectiveness.	PPRI	441,725
Eriocereus tortuosus (Forbes) Riccobono South America (Millmerran Harrisia cactus)	*Alcidion cereicola* Fisher (Coleoptera: Cerambycidae)	1976	**AUSTRALIA.** Ex Argentina. Establishment difficult A field colony exists but it is unlikely to assist control.	QDL	417,420
	Cactoblastis sp. (Lepidoptera: Pyralidae)	1980	**AUSTRALIA.** Ex Argentina. Not established.	QDL	175,420
	Hypogeococcus festerianus (Lizer y Trelles) (Hemiptera: Pseudococcidae)	1976	**AUSTRALIA.** Ex Argentina. Established readily and provides good control.	QDL	420,422, 655
Opuntia aurantiaca Lindley Argentina, Uruguay (tiger pear, South African jointed cactus)	*Cactoblastis cactorum* (Bergroth) (Lepidoptera: Pyralidae)	1926	**AUSTRALIA.** Ex Argentina. Released on other *Opuntias*. Colonies soon attacked *Opuntia aurantiaca* but gives little effective control.	CPPB	170-173, 284,706

* See 'Introduction' for explanation of headings.

List A *continued*

37

Weed and its origin*	Agent and taxonomic references*	Released*	Status and degree of control*	Research organisation*	General references*
(CACTACEAE continued)					
		1933	**REPUBLIC OF SOUTH AFRICA.** Ex Argentina via Australia. Released on *Opuntia megacantha* and spread to *Opuntia aurantiaca*. Attacks above ground parts, killing small plants only. Generally not effective. Effects restricted by the disease *Nosema cactoblastis*.	PPRI	442,524
	Dactylopius austrinus De Lotto, 150 (Hemiptera: Dactylopiidae)	1933	**AUSTRALIA.** Ex Argentina. Established readily. Destroyed widespread infestations of the weed. Keeps the weed to a scattered distribution. Now requires manual distribution to control scattered infestations.	CPPB	172,173, 284,302
		1935	**REPUBLIC OF SOUTH AFRICA.** Ex Argentina. Established but increase slow as a result of predation. Material sent to warmer, drier areas resulting in spectacular initial control. Now responsible for checking infestation, especially in drier areas.	PPRI	524,439, 442,473
	Dactylopius ceyloncus (Green), 150 (Hemiptera: Dactyopiidae)	1935	**AUSTRALIA.** Ex Argentina. Not established.	CPPB	173
	Melitara prodenialis Walker (Lepidoptera: Pyralidae)	1928	**AUSTRALIA.** Ex Florida, U.S.A. Not established.	CPPB	173
	Mimorista pulchellalis (Dyar) (Lepidoptera: Pyralidae)	1979	**REPUBLIC OF SOUTH AFRICA.** Ex Argentina. Established at low levels. May have died out.	PPRI RU	442,472, 476
	Nanaia sp. (Lepidoptera: Pyralidae)	1983	**REPUBLIC OF SOUTH AFRICA.** Ex Peru. Numerous releases until 1985 but not established.	PPRI	442,725

* See 'Introduction' for explanation of headings.

List A continued

(CACTACEAE continued)

Weed and its origin*	Agent and taxonomic references*	Released*	Status and degree of control*	Research organisation*	General references*
	Tucumania tapiacola Dyar (Lepidoptera: Pyralidae)	1935	**AUSTRALIA.** Ex Argentina. Slow to establish. Provides no effective control. Rare in the field. Has been found on *Opuntia inermis* and *Eriocereus martinii* in Australia.	CPPB	173
		1976	**REPUBLIC OF SOUTH AFRICA.** Ex Argentina. Survived some years and then disappeared. Not established.	PPRI RU	439,442, 725
Opuntia cordobensis Spegazzini Argentina	*Dactylopius opuntiae* (Cockerell) (Hemiptera: Dactylopiidae)	1949	**HAWAII, U.S.A.** Ex California, U.S.A. Plant originally found near shore of northwest side of island of Hawaii, heavy attack by *D. opuntiae* and other introduced agents may have exterminated plant. It has not been seen or reported in over 30 years.	BAF	312,688
Opuntia elatior Miller Curacao, Venezuela Columbia, Panama	*Dactylopius opuntiae* (Cockerell) (Hemiptera: Dactylopiidae)	1926	**INDIA.** Ex U.S.A. via Sri Lanka via Australia. Widely established giving complete control.		220,544
		1935	**INDONESIA.** Ex U.S.A. via Australia. Established rapidly throughout Sulawesi Island, providing complete control by 1939.	DAI	173,544
Opuntia ficus-indica (Linnaeus) Miller (= *Opuntia megacantha* Salm-Dyck) Central and North America (Indian fig)	*Archlagocheirus funestus* (Thomson) (Coleoptera: Cerambycidae)	1951	**HAWAII, U.S.A.** Ex Mexico via Australia. Established but distribution is limited.	HDOA	133,205, 212,504
		1943	**REPUBLIC OF SOUTH AFRICA.** Ex Mexico via Australia. Established in very localised areas but insect is rare.	PPRI	15,16, 473,524

* See 'Introduction' for explanation of headings.

List A continued

Weed and its origin*	Agent and taxonomic references*	Released*	Status and degree of control*	Research organisation*	General references*
(CACTACEAE continued)					
	Cactoblastis cactorum (Bergroth) (Lepidoptera: Pyralidae)	1950	**HAWAII, U.S.A.** Ex Argentina via Australia. Lowland and coastal regions under excellent control by *Cactoblastis cactorum* and *Dactylopius opuntiae*. Following initial control there is indication of resurgence at certain mid-range elevations (e.g. Waimea). Infestations at higher elevations (914+m) remain unaffected.	HDOA	205,504
		1933	**REPUBLIC OF SOUTH AFRICA.** Ex Argentina via Australia. Established readily in inland areas Mostly destroys small plants, preventing re-infestation of cleared areas. Also colonises other *Opuntia* species (e.g. *O. tardospina, O. spinulifera, O. imbricata, O. vulgaris* and *O. aurantiaca*) but does not control them. Redistributed to *Opuntia stricta* in 1982. Established and killing patches and single plants of this weed. Not as effective as on *Opuntia inermis* in Australia.	PPRI	15,16, 473,524, 725,726
	Dactylopius confusus (Cockerell), 150 (Hemiptera: Dactylopiidae)	1832	**REPUBLIC OF SOUTH AFRICA.** Ex South America via Germany. Little effect on the weed. According to De Lotto (150) it is likely that the *Dactylopius* sp. introduced by Baron Ludowigne in 1832 was *Dactylopius confusus*. However Annecke and Moran (16) suggest it may have been *Dactylopius coccus* Costa.		16,150
	Dactylopius opuntiae (Cockerell) (Hemiptera: Dactylopiidae)	1949	**HAWAII, U.S.A.** Ex Mexico via Australia. Lowland and coastal regions under excellent control by *Cactoblastis cactorum* and *Dactylopius opuntiae*. Following initial control there is indication of resurgence at certain mid-range elevations (e.g. Waimea). Infestations at higher elevations (914+m) remain unaffected.	HDOA	205,504

* See 'Introduction' for explanation of headings.

List A continued

Weed and its origin*	Agent and taxonomic references*	Released*	Status and degree of control*	Research organisation*	General references*
(CACTACEAE continued)					
		1938	**REPUBLIC OF SOUTH AFRICA.** Ex Texas and Arizona via Australia. Established readily and responsible for clearing most areas when aided by felling. Also responsible for control of *Opuntia tardospina* Griffiths. Redistributed to *Opuntia stricta* in 1982. Established but damage not sufficient to reduce density of this weed.	PPRI	14,15,16, 524,725, 726
	Dactylopius sp. (Hemiptera: Dactylopiidae)	1949	**HAWAII, U.S.A.** Ex California, U.S.A. Distinct species separate from *D. opuntiae*. Failed to become established.	HDOA	149
	Melitara dentata (Grote) [previously referred to as *Melitara doddalis* (Dyar)] (Lepidoptera: Pyralidae)	1949	**HAWAII, U.S.A.** Ex Texas, U.S.A. Failed to establish.	HDOA	205,220, 688
		1951	Ex Texas, U.S.A. Not established.	HDOA	205,220
	Melitara prodenialis Walker (Lepidoptera: Pyralidae)	1949	**HAWAII, U.S.A.** Ex Texas, U.S.A. Not established.	HDOA	205,220, 688
		1951	Ex Texas, U.S.A. Not established.	HDOA	205,220
	Metamasius spinolae (Gyllenhal) (Coleoptera: Curculionidae)	1948	**REPUBLIC OF SOUTH AFRICA.** Ex Mexico. Very local distribution. Abundant and destructive at two localities only.	PPRI	15,16, 473
	Moneilema armatum LeConte (Coleoptera: Cerambycidae)	1950	**HAWAII, U.S.A.** Ex Texas. Not established.	HDOA	205
	Moneilema crassum LeConte (Coleoptera: Cerambycidae)	1950	**HAWAII, U.S.A.** Ex Texas, U.S.A. Not established.	HDOA	205,688

* See 'Introduction' for explanation of headings.

List A continued

Weed and its origin*	Agent and taxonomic references*	Released*	Status and degree of control*	Research organisation*	General references*
(CACTACEAE continued)					
Opuntia imbricata (Haworth) de Candolle [= *Cylindropuntia imbricata* (Haworth) Knuth] Mexico, south-western U.S.A. (devil's rope)	*Dactylopius tomentosus* (Lamarck), 150 (Hemiptera: Dactylopiidae)	1925	**AUSTRALIA.** Ex Texas, U.S.A. Rapid establishment and destruction of infestations of the weed. Controls the weed to a very low distribution, killing any seedlings around established plants.	CPPB	169,170, 173,284
		1970	**REPUBLIC OF SOUTH AFRICA.** Ex Texas, U.S.A. via Australia. Very good control. Also attacks *Opuntia rosea* DC. and *Opuntia leptocaulis* DC.	PPRI	472,473
Opuntia inermis de Candolle Mexico (common pest pear, common prickly pear)	*Cactoblastis cactorum* (Bergroth) (Lepidoptera: Pyralidae)	1926	**AUSTRALIA.** Ex Argentina. Rapid establishment and destruction of primary growth by 1934 and regrowth by 1935. In most areas where small outbreaks of pear occur, control is affected within a few years. Spread naturally to *Opuntia tomentosa* but due to poor oviposition on this there is no control.	CPPB	169-173, 284,706
	Chelinidea tabulata (Burmeister) (Hemiptera: Coreidae)	1922	**AUSTRALIA.** Ex Texas, U.S.A. Rapid establishment, population increase and dispersal. Heavy destruction of new shoots and fruit. Had a significant controlling effect prior to extensive control by *Cactoblastis cactorum*. The populations of *Chelinidea tabulata* are now very low. Spread naturally to *Opuntia tomentosa* but provided no control.	CPPB	4,169-173 284
	Chelinidea vittiger Uhler (Hemiptera: Coreidae)	1925	**AUSTRALIA.** Ex Florida and Texas, U.S.A. Slow establishment; the population then declined and no bugs have been found since 1940.	CPPB	169,170, 172,173

* See 'Introduction' for explanation of headings.

List A continued

Weed and its origin*	Agent and taxonomic references*	Released*	Status and degree of control*	Research organisation*	General references*
(CACTACEAE continued)					
	Dactylopius opuntiae (Cockerell), 150 (Hemiptera: Dactylopiidae)	1921	**AUSTRALIA.** Ex California, U.S.A. Rapidly established. Provided good control of dense pear prior to control by *Cactoblastis cactorum*. Destroyed young regrowth after initial *Cactoblastis cactorum* attack. Not efficient in open forest. Now a minor control factor, killing fruit and young growth, especially in dry years. Redistributed and established in northeastern Victoria during 1985. Ongoing program in New South Wales of mass rearing and releasing.	QDL CPPB	4,169, 172,173
	Melitara doddalis Dyar (Lepidoptera: Pyralidae)	1926	**AUSTRALIA.** Ex Texas and Arizona, U.S.A. No establishment.	CPPB	169,173, 706
	Melitara prodenialis Walker (Lepidoptera: Pyralidae)	1928	**AUSTRALIA.** Ex Texas, U.S.A. Not established.	CPPB	173
	Melitara sp. (Lepidoptera: Pyralidae)	1925	**AUSTRALIA.** Ex Texas, U.S.A. Not established.	CPPB	706
	Mimorista flavidissimalis (Grote) (Lepidoptera: Pyralidae)	1925	**AUSTRALIA.** Ex Texas, U.S.A. Not established.	CPPB	173
	Moneilema ulkei Horn (Coleoptera: Cerambycidae)0	1926 1932	**AUSTRALIA.** Ex Texas, U.S.A. Not established. Ex Texas, U.S.A. Established in New South Wales and causes occasional destruction of larger plants but does not give effective control. Not established in Queensland.	CPPB CPPB	173,706 173,706
	Moneilema variolare Thomson (Coleoptera: Cerambycidae)	1932	**AUSTRALIA.** Ex Mexico. Established in New South Wales. Provides no control.	CPPB	173

* See 'Introduction' for explanation of headings.

List A continued

Weed and its origin*	Agent and taxonomic references*	Released*	Status and degree of control*	Research organisation*	General references*
(CACTACEAE continued)					
	Olycella junctolineella (Hulst) (Lepidoptera: Pyralidae)	1924	**AUSTRALIA.** Ex Texas, U.S.A. Established and abundant in 1928. Populations then declined following destruction of the pear by *Cactoblastis cactorum*. Low populations were observed until 1938. Survival has not been confirmed since.	CPPB	173
Opuntia lindheimeri Engelmann Mexico, southern U.S.A. (prickly pear)	*Cactoblastis cactorum* (Bergroth) (Lepidoptera: Pyralidae)	1960	**ANTIGUA.** Ex Argentina via South Africa and Nevis. Control is occurring but not as effectively as occurred for *Opuntia tricantha*.	DAA	27,91, 607
		1957	**NEVIS.** Ex Argentina via South Africa. Rapidly provided control in pastures. Weed persists along roadsides.	IIBC	27,91, 607
	Dactylopius austrinus De Lotto (Hemiptera: Dactylopiidae)	1957	**NEVIS.** Ex U.S.A. via South Africa. Not established.	IIBC	27,91, 607
	Dactylopius opuntiae (Cockerell) (Hemiptera: Dactylopiidae)	1957	**NEVIS.** Ex U.S.A. via South Africa. Not established.	IIBC	27,91, 607
Opuntia aff. *lindheimeri* Engelmann, 575 (also referred to as *Opuntia tardospina* Griffiths) Texas, U.S.A.	*Dactylopius opuntiae* (Cockerell) (Hemiptera: Dactylopiidae)	1938	**REPUBLIC OF SOUTH AFRICA.** Ex Texas and Arizona, U.S.A. via Australia. Successful control.	PPRI	441,472, 473

* See 'Introduction' for explanation of headings.

List A *continued*

(CACTACEAE continued)

Weed and its origin*	Agent and taxonomic references*	Released*	Status and degree of control*	Research organisation*	General references*
Opuntia littoralis (Engelmann) Cockerell south-west coast U.S.A. including Santa Cruz Island (prickly pear)	*Dactylopius opuntiae* (Cockerell) (Hemiptera: Dactylopiidae)	1940 1951	**UNITED STATES OF AMERICA.** Ex California, U.S.A. Not established on Santa Cruz Island. Ex Mexico via Australia via Hawaii. Main agent for control on Santa Cruz Island; reduced cactus by 75% by 1979. Predation by *Laetilia coccidivara* (Comstock) slowed the rate of destruction on Santa Cruz Island.	State (5) State (4,5)	220,223 223,227
Opuntia oricola Philbrick south-west coast U.S.A. including Santa Cruz Island (prickly pear)	*Dactylopius opuntiae* (Cockerell) (Hemiptera: Dactylopiidae)	1940 1951	**UNITED STATES OF AMERICA.** Ex California, U.S.A. Not established on Santa Cruz Island. Ex Mexico via Australia via Hawaii. Main agent for control on Santa Cruz Island; reduced cactus by 75% by 1979. *Opuntia oricola* is less susceptible to *Dactylopius opuntiae* than *Opuntia littoralis*. This and predation by *Laetilia coccidivara* (Comstock) slowed the rate of destruction.	State (4,5) State (4,5)	220,223 223,227
Opuntia streptacantha Lemaire Mexico (cardona, Westwood pear, white spine prickly pear)	*Archlagocheirus funestus* (Thomson) (Coleoptera: Cerambycidae)	1936	**AUSTRALIA.** Ex Mexico. Established readily. The gregarious larvae feed in the heavy woody stems causing collapse of even very large plants. Where present it gives a reasonable degree of control. The larvae and pupae are subject to predation by crows, rodents and lizards.	CPPB	173,706
	Cactoblastis cactorum (Bergroth) (Lepidoptera: Pyralidae)	1926	**AUSTRALIA.** Ex Argentina. Released onto *Opuntia inermis* and *Opuntia stricta* this insect readily attacked this cactus. The larvae develops in young plants, frequently destroying them. Old stems are too woody for larval development. The weed serves as a reservoir of the moth in Central Queensland.	CPPB	173,706

* See 'Introduction' for explanation of headings.

List A *continued*

Weed and its origin*	Agent and taxonomic references*	Released*	Status and degree of control*	Research organisation*	General references*
(CACTACEAE continued)					
	Chelinidea tabulata (Burmeister) (Hemiptera: Coreidae)	1922	**AUSTRALIA.** Ex Texas, U.S.A. Released onto *Opuntia inermis* and *Opuntia stricta* the insect readily attacked this weed without providing any degree of control. The plant remains an important host for the bug.	CPPB	173
	Chelinidea vittiger Uhler (Hemiptera: Coreidae)	1925	**AUSTRALIA.** Ex Florida, U.S.A. Established with difficulty. Last record of this bug from *Opuntia streptacantha* was in 1934.	CPPB	173
	Dactylopius opuntiae (Cockerell), 150 (Hemiptera: Dactylopiidae)	1928	**AUSTRALIA.** Ex Mexico. Established readily giving useful control in heavy weed infestations by destroying young plants. After mechanical clearing regrowth was effectively controlled. Remains a significant factor in control of this pear.	CPPB	170,172, 173,706
	Moneilema ulkei Horn (Coleoptera: Cerambycidae)	1926	**AUSTRALIA.** Ex Texas, U.S.A. Established readily. Destroyed large plants but due to small isolated populations did not provide effective control. Has not been recovered for many years.	CPPB	173,706
Opuntia stricta (Haworth) Haworth Florida, Texas, U.S.A., Cuba (spiny pest pear, common prickly pear)	*Cactoblastis cactorum* (Bergroth) (Lepidoptera: Pyralidae)	1926	**AUSTRALIA.** Ex Argentina. Rapid establishment and destruction of the weed by 1934 and of re-growth by 1935 especially in scrubs. In more open areas the results were variable. In most areas where small outbreaks of pear occur the moth controls them within a few years. Spread naturally to *Opuntia tomentosa* but due to poor oviposition on this weed there is no control.	CPPB	169-173, 284,706

* See 'Introduction' for explanation of headings.

List A continued

(CACTACEAE continued)

Weed and its origin*	Agent and taxonomic references*	Released*	Status and degree of control*	Research organisation*	General references*
	Chelinidea tabulata (Burmeister) (Hemiptera: Coreidae)	1924	**AUSTRALIA.** Ex Texas, U.S.A. Rapid establishment, increase and dispersal causing heavy destruction of fruit and new shoots. However the degree of control it achieved over this pear was not as great as that it achieved over *Opuntia inermis*. Due to population decline, *Chelinidea tabulata* now has no importance in the control of the weed. Spread naturally to *Opuntia tomentosa* but provided no control.	CPPB	173,706
	Dactylopius confusus (Cockerell), 150 (Hemiptera: Dactylopiidae)	1933	**AUSTRALIA.** Ex Florida, U.S.A. Initial establishment was rapid but population declined and was thought to have become extinct. Rediscovered in Central Queensland in 1967. It provides no appreciable control.	CPPB	173,175
	Dactylopius opuntiae (Cockerell), 150 (Hemiptera: Dactylopiidae)	1921	**AUSTRALIA.** Ex Texas and Arizona, U.S.A. Rapidly established. Provided excellent control of dense pear in brigalow scrubs. By mid 1928 there was a rapid decrease in cochineal populations prior to the major destruction of this pear by *Cactoblastis cactorum* and it never became an effective control agent again.	CPPB	4,169,170, 172,173, 706
	Melitara prodenialis Walker (Lepidoptera: Pyralidae)	1926	**AUSTRALIA.** Ex Florida, U.S.A. Not established.	CPPB	173
	Mimorista flavidissimalis (Grote) (Lepidoptera: Pyralidae)	1925	**AUSTRALIA.** Ex Texas, U.S.A. Not established.	CPPB	173
	Moneilema ulkei Horn (Coleoptera: Cerambycidae)	1926	**AUSTRALIA.** Ex Texas, U.S.A. Not established.	CPPB	173

* See 'Introduction' for explanation of headings.

List A *continued*

Weed and its origin*	Agent and taxonomic references*	Released*	Status and degree of control*	Research organisation*	General references*
(CACTACEAE continued)					
	Olycella junctolineella (Hulst) (Lepidoptera: Pyralidae)	1924	**AUSTRALIA.** Ex Texas, U.S.A. Established readily but never became a factor in the control of the weed. After the destruction of the pear by *Cactoblastis cactorum* this insect declined, and it is doubtful if the insect now occurs on *Opuntia stricta*.	CPPB	173,175
Opuntia stricta (Haworth) Haworth *dillenii* (Ker-Gawler) L. Benson [previously referred to as *Opuntia dillenii* (Ker-Gawler) Haworth], 670,671 Florida and West Indies (prickly pear)	*Cactoblastis cactorum* (Bergroth) (Lepidoptera: Pyralidae)	1970	**CAYMAN ISLANDS.** Ex Argentina via South Africa via Nevis and Antigua. Well established in 1971. No further report. The weed is native to Cayman Islands.	IIBC	26,27,31, 91
		1933	**NEW CALEDONIA.** Ex Argentina via Australia. Successful control.	NCC	173,544, 638
		1957	**NEVIS.** Ex Argentina via South Africa. Rapidly provided control in pastures. Weed persists along roadsides.	IIBC	91,607
	Dactylopius austrinus De Lotto (Hemiptera: Dactylopiidae)	1957	**NEVIS.** Ex U.S.A. via South Africa. Not established.	IIBC	91,607
	Dactylopius opuntiae (Cockerell) (Hemiptera: Dactylopiidae)	1926	**INDIA.** Ex U.S.A. via Australia via Sri Lanka. Privately imported by merchants. Widely established, giving complete control. Heavily infested areas became fit for cultivation within five or six years.		220,544
		1957	**NEVIS.** Ex U.S.A. via South Africa. Not established.	IIBC	91,607
		1925	**SRI LANKA.** Ex U.S.A. via Australia. Widely established, giving complete control.	DASL	544

* See 'Introduction' for explanation of headings.

List A continued

Weed and its origin*	Agent and taxonomic references*	Released*	Status and degree of control*	Research organisation*	General references*
(CACTACEAE continued)					
Opuntia tomentosa Salm-Dyck Mexico (velvet tree pear)	*Archlagocheirus funestus* (Thomson) (Coleoptera: Cerambycidae)	1936	**AUSTRALIA.** Ex Mexico. Rapid establishment. Gregarious larvae feed down the stems causing collapse of plants. The initial control of the weed was good but the population of the insects declined and control is sporadic. The larvae and pupae are subject to predation by crows, rodents and lizards.	CPPB	173,284, 706
	Cactoblastis doddi Heinrich (Lepidoptera: Pyralidae)	1935	**AUSTRALIA.** Ex Argentina. No establishment.	CPPB	173
	Dactylopius coccus Costa (Hemiptera: Dactylopiidae)	1926	**AUSTRALIA.** Ex Central America via South Africa. No establishment.	CPPB	173
	Dactylopius opuntiae (Cockerell) (Hemiptera: Dactylopiidae)	1922	**AUSTRALIA.** Ex Texas and Arizona, U.S.A. Established readily. Effective in killing young seedlings, small older plants, and large plants in dense stands in scrubs. Less effective on large plants in the open. Currently, effectiveness is limited by inefficient dispersal.	CPPB	4,169,170, 172,173, 706
	Moneilema ulkei Horn (Coleoptera: Cerambycidae)	1926	**AUSTRALIA.** Ex Texas, U.S.A. Establishment slow. It is capable of causing collapse of large plants but this rarely occurs. Populations are small and isolated.	CPPB	173,284, 706
Opuntia triacantha (Willdenow) Sweet, 670, 671 Caribbean Islands	*Cactoblastis cactorum* (Bergroth) (Lepidoptera: Pyralidae)	1960	**ANTIGUA.** Ex Argentina via South Africa and Nevis. Well established and provided effective control. The weed is native to Antigua.	DAA	27,91, 607
		1960	**MONTSERRAT.** Ex Argentina via South Africa and Nevis. Well established and provided good control The weed is native to Montserrat.	DAM	27,91, 607

* See 'Introduction' for explanation of headings.

List A continued

Weed and its origin*	Agent and taxonomic references*	Released*	Status and degree of control*	Research organisation*	General references*
(CACTACEAE continued)					
		1957	**NEVIS.** Ex Argentina via South Africa. Rapidly provided very good control. The weed is native to Nevis.	IIBC	27,91, 607
	Dactylopius austrinus De Lotto (Hemiptera: Dactylopiidae)	1957	**NEVIS.** Ex U.S.A. via South Africa. Not established. The weed is native to Nevis.	IIBC	27,91, 607
	Dactylopius opuntiae (Cockerell) (Hemiptera: Dactylopiidae)	1957	**NEVIS.** Ex U.S.A. via South Africa. Not established. The weed is native to Nevis.	IIBC	27,91, 607
Opuntia tuna (Linnaeus) Miller West Indies	*Cactoblastis cactorum* (Bergroth) (Lepidoptera: Pyralidae)	1950	**MAURITIUS.** Ex Argentina via South Africa. Re-established control that was lost when predation restricted effects of *Dactylopius opuntiae*.	MAM	237
	Dactylopius ceylonicus (Green) (Hemiptera: Dactylopiidae)	1914	**MAURITIUS.** Ex Brazil via South Africa. Not established.	MAM	237,449
	Dactylopius opuntiae (Cockerell) (Hemiptera: Dactylopiidae)	1928	**MAURITIUS.** Ex U.S.A. via Sri Lanka. Effective control occurred followed by slow increase in the weed probably as a result of predation on *Dactylopius opuntiae* by *Cryptolaemus montrouzieri* Mulsant.	MAM	237,449
Opuntia vulgaris Miller Argentina, Brazil, Paraguay, Uraguay (drooping prickly pear, Barbary fig)	*Cactoblastis cactorum* (Bergroth) (Lepidoptera: Pyralidae)	1950	**MAURITIUS.** Ex Argentina via South Africa. Re-established control that was lost when predation restricted effects of *Dactylopius opuntiae*.	MAM	237
	Dactylopius ceylonicus (Green) (Hemiptera: Dactylopiidae)	1914	**AUSTRALIA.** Ex Brazil via India via Sri Lanka. Established rapidly and readily controlled the weed in all areas. This cochineal generally keeps the weed under control. Outbreaks of *Opuntia vulgaris* are rare and are controlled by manual distribution of the cochineal.	PPTC QDL	169,170, 171,173, 706

* See 'Introduction' for explanation of headings.

List A continued

(CACTACEAE continued)

Weed and its origin*	Agent and taxonomic references*	Released*	Status and degree of control*	Research organisation*	General references*
		1795	**INDIA.** Ex Brazil. Introduced for commercial purposes in the mistaken belief that it was *Dactylopius coccus* Costa. Established on *Opuntia vulgaris* and provided control of the weed. Subsequently the insect was spread to southern India in 1836 and Sri Lanka in 1865 (see below) as the first attempt at deliberate biological control of a weed. Complete control was achieved in India.		220,221, 544,662
		1958	**KENYA.** Ex Brazil via India via South Africa via Tanzania. Some control in coastal areas and Lake Victoria areas.	DAK	237
		1914	**MAURITIUS.** Ex Brazil via South Africa. Almost cleared island of *Opuntia vulgaris* but predation by *Cryptolaemus montrouzieri* Mulsant now limits effectiveness.	MAM	237
		1913	**REPUBLIC OF SOUTH AFRICA.** Ex Brazil via Sri Lanka. Complete control of the weed.	PPRI	15,441, 473
		1865	**SRI LANKA.** Ex Brazil via India. Widely established and completely controlled the weed over vast areas.		220,221
		1957	**TANZANIA.** Ex Brazil via India via South Africa. Substantial control in the Lake Victoria area.	DAT	237
		1915	**AUSTRALIA.** Ex South America via South Africa. Rapid establishment at one site causing destruction of the weed. But there is no record of the survival at this site after the destruction of the weed.	PPTC QDL	169,173
	Dactylopius confusus (Cockerell) (Hemiptera: Dactylopiidae)	1926	Ex South America via South Africa. Failed to establish.	CPPB	173

* See 'Introduction' for explanation of headings.

List A continued

(CACTACEAE continued)

Weed and its origin*	Agent and taxonomic references*	Released*	Status and degree of control*	Research organisation*	General references*
Opuntia spp. (prickly pear)		1836	**INDIA.** Ex South America via South Africa. Not established.		220,662
		1838	Ex South America via South Africa. Not established.		220,662
		1832	**REPUBLIC OF SOUTH AFRICA.** Ex South America via Germany. According to De Lotto (150) it is likely that the *Dactylopius* sp. introduced by Baron Ludowigne in 1832 was *Dactylopius confusus*. However, Annecke and Moran (16) suggested that it may have been *Dactylopius coccus* Costa. Not recorded recently probably as a result of the destruction of *Opuntia vulgaris* by *Dactylopius ceylonicus*.		16,150
Dactylopius opuntiae (Cockerell) (Hemiptera: Dactylopiidae)		1928	**MAURITIUS.** Ex U.S.A. via Sri Lanka. Effective control occurred followed by slow increase in the weed probably as a result of predation on *Dactylopius opuntiae* by *Cryptolaemus montrouzieri* Mulsant	MAM	237
Cactoblastis cactorum (Bergroth) (Lepidoptera: Pyralidae)		1965	**KENYA.** Ex Brazil via South Africa via Antigua. Not established.	IIBC	237,240
		1971	Passed through two generations at one site near Nairobi, may have died out as release area was cleared. No recent surveys.	IIBC	240
Dactylopius opuntiae (Cockerell) (Hemiptera: Dactylopiidae)		1923	**MADAGASCAR.** Ex U.S.A. Complete control of all *Opuntia* spp. present.	MAMA	196,237

* See 'Introduction' for explanation of headings.

List A continued

Weed and its origin*	Agent and taxonomic references*	Released*	Status and degree of control*	Research organisation*	General references*
CAESALPINIACEAE					
Parkinsonia aculeata Linnaeus tropical America (retama, Jerusalem thorn, palo verde, parkinsonia)	*Rhinacloa callicrates* Herring (Hemiptera: Miridae)	1989	**AUSTRALIA.** Ex Arizona, U.S.A. Established at two sites in Queensland but not in Western Australia or Northern Territory. Under evaluation.	DPIF,QDL DAW	175,701
CARYOPHYLLACEAE					
Silene vulgaris (Moench) Garcke	*Cassida azurea* Fabricius (Coleoptera: Chrysomelidae)	1989	**CANADA.** Ex Europe. Bred in the field in Manitoba and Saskatchewan and may be established. Under evaluation.	CDA	518
CHENOPODIACEAE					
Halogeton glomeratus (M. Beib) C. Meyer Central Asia (halogeton)	*Coleophora parthenica* Meyrick (Lepidoptera: Coleophoridae)	1975	**UNITED STATES OF AMERICA.** Ex Egypt and Pakistan. Released CA, ID and NV. Not established.	USDA (7)	288,506
	Coleophora klimeschiella Toll (Lepidoptera: Coleophoridae)	1977	**CANADA.** Ex Pakistan via U.S.A. Released in Saskatchewan but not established. Survived one year but not 1979 flooding.	CDA	264
Salsola australis R. Brown (= S. *iberica* Sennen & Pau; = S. *kali* var. *tenuifolia* Tausch; = S. *pestifera* A. Nelson) Eurasia, Africa, (Russian thistle, tumbleweed)		1980	**HAWAII, U.S.A.** Ex Pakistan via U.S.A. Not established.	HDOA	382,383
		1981	Ex Pakistan via U.S.A. Not established.	HDOA	382,383
		1977	**UNITED STATES OF AMERICA.** Ex Pakistan. Released in CA, CO, ID, KS, MN, MT, NE, NV, SD, TX, WA and WY. Established in CA and ID but effect on weed is negligible. Parasites and predators hindered establishment in southern CA.	USDA (7) State (5)	230,231, 288

* See 'Introduction' for explanation of headings.

List A continued

Weed and its origin*	Agent and taxonomic references*	Released*	Status and degree of control*	Research organisation*	General references*
(CHENOPODIACEAE continued)					
	Coleophora parthenica Meyrick (Lepidoptera: Coleophoridae)	1975	**CANADA.** Ex Egypt and Pakistan via U.S.A. Released in Saskatchewan but not established. Summer too cool for breeding.	CDA	226,264
		1980	**HAWAII, U.S.A.** Ex Egypt and Pakistan via U.S.A. Not established.	HDOA	207,383
		1973	**UNITED STATES OF AMERICA.** Ex Egypt,Pakistan and Turkey. Released in AZ, CA, CO, ID, MN, NE, NV, SD, TX, UT, WA and WY. Established in AZ, CA and TX where three generations are produced annually. Moth spreading in TX. Little or no impact on weed in CA at any site, primarily due to poor host-plant synchronization and generalist predators and parasitoids which limit population sizes, and the limited impact of larval stem tunnelling on plants. Not established in more northern states.	USDA (7,9) State (5)	161,231, 388,451, 452,507
CLUSIACEAE					
Hypericum androsaemum Linnaeus Asia Minor, Europe, northern Africa	*Chrysolina hyperici* (Forster) [previously referred to as *Chrysomela hyperici* (Forster)] (Coleoptera: Chrysomelidae)	1947	**NEW ZEALAND.** Ex England. Not established. Released for control of *Hypericum perforatum* but found to attack this weed. Despite some early damage the insect has not persisted on this weed.	DSIR	247,434
Hypericum perforatum Linnaeus Asia, Europe, northern Africa (St John's wort, klamath weed)	*Actinotia hyperici (Denis & Schiffermüller)* (Lepidoptera: Noctuidae)	1986	**AUSTRALIA.** Ex southern France. Not established. Predation and drought suspected as major reasons.	CSIRO	49,342
	Agrilus hyperici (Creutzer) (Coleoptera: Buprestidae)	1939	**AUSTRALIA.** Ex France. Established but in very restricted area. Only one remaining population known. No contribution to control.	CSIR	123,158, 501,705
		1981	Ex France. Not established.	CSIRO	49
		1989	Ex France. No establishment. Adults failed to lay eggs in the field.	CSIRO	342

* See 'Introduction' for explanation of headings.

List A continued

Weed and its origin*	Agent and taxonomic references*	Released*	Status and degree of control*	Research organisation*	General references*
(CLUSIACEAE continued)					
		1955	**CANADA.** Ex Austria via U.S.A. Established in British Columbia. No control.	CDA	268,271, 277
		1964	Ex France via U.S.A. Not established.	CDA	268
		1977	Ex France via U.S.A. Not established.	CDA	107,277
		1974	**REPUBLIC OF SOUTH AFRICA.** Ex France via California and Australia. Small releases, but plants killed by *Chrysolina quadrigemina*. Not established.	PPRI	235
		1978	Ex France via U.S.A. Not established.	PPRI	235,472
		1982	Ex France via Australia. Not established.	PPRI	235,472
		1950	**UNITED STATES OF AMERICA.** Ex France. Established in CA, ID, OR and WA. Not established in MT. Up to 87% infestation rate recorded in WA. Redistribution ongoing.	USDA (7,10) State (4,6 7,9,15)	62,114, 411,528, 621
	Aphis chloris Koch (Hemiptera: Aphididae)	1986	**AUSTRALIA.** Ex southern France. Widely established but impact is limited to isolated small patches. Currently being released in Victoria.	CSIRO	47,48
		1979	**CANADA.** Ex Germany. Not established in British Columbia.	CDA	277
		1990	Ex Germany. Establishment not yet confirmed.	CDA	277
		1983	**REPUBLIC OF SOUTH AFRICA.** Ex France and Germany via Canada. Not established. Failed to overwinter.	PPRI	235,357
	Aplocera efformata (Guenée) (previously referred to as *Anaitis efformata* Guenée) (Lepidoptera: Geometridae)	1936	**AUSTRALIA.** Ex England. Not established. Predation and climate probable cause. Both *Anaitis efformata* and *Anaitis plagiata* were released together and not distinguished.	CSIR	127,705, 706
		1981	Ex France. Not established, due to losses to generalist predators, parasitoides and pathogens.	CSIRO	46

* See 'Introduction' for explanation of headings.

List A continued

Weed and its origin*	Agent and taxonomic references*	Released*	Status and degree of control*	Research organisation*	General references*
(CLUSIACEAE continued)					
	Aplocera plagiata (Linnaeus) (previously referred to as *Anaitis plagiata* Linnaeus) (Lepidoptera: Geometridae)	1983	**REPUBLIC OF SOUTH AFRICA.** Ex France via Australia. Small number released. Not established.	PPRI	235,357
		1936	**AUSTRALIA.** Ex England. Not established. Predation and climate probable cause. Both *Anaitis efformata* and *Anaitis plagiata* were released together and not distinguished.	CSIR	127,159, 705,706
		1976	**CANADA.** Ex France, Germany and Switzerland. Established in British Columbia. Not effective.	CDA	268,271, 277
		1977	Ex Switzerland. Not established.	CDA	277
		1980	Ex France. Established. No control.	CDA	277,
		1989	**UNITED STATES OF AMERICA.** Ex Europe via Canada. Released in MT and OR. Establishment not confirmed.	USDA (10) State (7,15)	114,547
	Chrysolina brunsvicensis (Gravenhorst) (previously referred to as *Chrysomela brunsvicensis* Gravenhorst) (Coleoptera: Chrysomelidae)	1930	**AUSTRALIA.** Ex England. Not established. Considered to have suffered from heavy predation and unfavourable climate.	CSIR	127,654, 705,706
	Chrysolina hyperici (Forster) [previously referred to as *Chrysomela hyperici* (Forster)] (Coleoptera: Chrysomelidae)	1930	**AUSTRALIA.** Ex England. Not recovered until five years after release and became abundant. Now relatively rare compared with *Chrysolina quadrigemina* but in combination with this species helped to provide good control in open areas. Avoids shade.	CSIR	127,501, 705
		1980	Ex France. Population selected as better adapted climatically and to shady areas. Status uncertain.	CSIRO	158,159
		1951	**CANADA.** Ex England via Australia via U.S.A. Established in British Columbia, New Brunswick, Nova Scotia and Ontario. Together with *Chrysolina quadrigemina* controls weed in most sites. The most effective species in the Maritimes.	CDA	268,271, 277

* See 'Introduction' for explanation of headings.

List A continued

Weed and its origin*	Agent and taxonomic references*	Released*	Status and degree of control*	Research organisation*	General references*
(CLUSIACEAE continued)					
		1953	**CHILE.** Ex England via Australia via U.S.A. Ready establishment and spread. Effective control.	MOA	232,675
		1943	**NEW ZEALAND.** Ex England via Australia. Good establishment and significant control in some localities.	DSIR	247,433, 646
		1960	**REPUBLIC OF SOUTH AFRICA.** Ex England via Australia. Formed part of *Chrysolina quadrigemina* release. Not recovered in later years.	PPRI	235,472, 473
		1973	Ex England via Australia via U.S.A. via Canada. Small release. Establishment doubtful.	PPRI	15,235
		1945	**UNITED STATES OF AMERICA.** Ex England via Australia. Not established in CA. Initially recovered in MT but status is unknown. Provides significant control in OR and WA. Also established in ID and NV. Best in mesic sites in ID.	USDA (7) State (4, 6,7,9,15)	62,114, 411,528, 621
	Chrysolina quadrigemina (Suffrian) [previously referred to as *Chrysolina gemellata* (Rossi), *Chrysomela quadrigemina* Suffrian and *Chrysomela gemellata* Rossi] (Coleoptera: Chrysomelidae)	1939	**AUSTRALIA.** Ex France. Recovered in 1942 and became very common. Has greatly assisted control in open areas but avoids shade and is not well adapted to summer rainfall. It is also affected by variability in winter rainfall.	CSIR	45,501, 705
		1980	Ex France. Selected as better adapted climatically and to shady areas. Status uncertain.	CSIRO	158,159
		1952	**CANADA.** Ex France via Australia via U.S.A. Established in British Columbia, New Brunswick, Nova Scotia and Ontario. More effective than *Chrysolina hyperici* unless site has early frost. Forage production increased four-fold in Ontario. Successful control.	CDA	268,271, 277

* See 'Introduction' for explanation of headings.

List A continued

(CLUSIACEAE continued)

Weed and its origin*	Agent and taxonomic references*	Released*	Status and degree of control*	Research organisation*	General references*
		1953	**CHILE.** Ex France via Australia via U.S.A. Ready establishment and spread. Most effective control agent with substantial control. Ineffectiveness in some areas is probably due to lack of soil moisture.	MOA	232,675
		1965	**HAWAII, U.S.A.** Ex France via Australia via California, U.S.A. Well established. In combination with *Zeuxidiplosis giardi* gives excellent control.	HDOA	135,145, 148,212
		1963	**NEW ZEALAND.** Ex France via Australia. Well established by 1990. Substantial populations over last few years at Clyde, Central Otago, have, in mixed populations with *Chrysolina hyperici*, caused high levels of defoliation.	DSIR	197,323, 644
		1961	**REPUBLIC OF SOUTH AFRICA.** Ex France via Australia Established readily causing general defoliation and giving good control locally. Required reintroduction into some areas.	PPRI	235,472, 473
		1946	**UNITED STATES OF AMERICA.** Ex France via Australia. Main factor in controlling the weed in CA and OR and probably in ID where it is the dominant agent in grassland areas. High populations in central and south-eastern WA provide excellent control. Not effective in most areas of MT.	USDA (7) State (4, 6,7,9)	62,306, 411,528, 621
	Chrysolina varians (Schaller) [previously referred to as *Chrysomela varians* (Schaller)] (Coleoptera: Chrysomelidae)	1930	**AUSTRALIA.** Ex England. Not established. Considered to have suffered from heavy predation and unfavourable climate.	CSIR	127,705, 706
		1957	**CANADA.** Ex Sweden. Not established in British Columbia. Release sites too dry in summer.	CDA	268,271, 514

* See 'Introduction' for explanation of headings.

List A continued

(CLUSIACEAE continued)

Weed and its origin*	Agent and taxonomic references*	Released*	Status and degree of control*	Research organisation*	General references*
		1950	**UNITED STATES OF AMERICA.** Ex Europe. Not established.	USDA (7) State (4)	7
	Zeuxidiplosis giardi (Kieffer) (Diptera: Cecidomyiidae)	1953	**AUSTRALIA.** Ex France and California, U.S.A. Established and generally distributed but ineffective.	CSIRO	158,159, 706
		1955	**CANADA.** Ex France via U.S.A. Not established in British Columbia.	CDA	268,271
		1965	**HAWAII, U.S.A.** Ex France via Australia and New Zealand. Released on Hawaii. Well established. In combination with *Chrysolina quadrigemina* gives excellent control.	HDOA	135,145, 148,212
		1961	**NEW ZEALAND.** Ex France via Australia. Well established in northern South Island particularly in shingle beds. Kills seedlings.	DSIR	219,247, 323
		1972	**REPUBLIC OF SOUTH AFRICA.** Ex France via Australia. Established readily and thriving in most infestations. Causes death of seedlings and reduces growth and flowering. In conjunction with *Chrysolina quadrigemmina* gives good control.	PPRI	15,233, 234,235, 473
		1950	**UNITED STATES OF AMERICA.** Ex France. Established in CA but of little consequence. Redistributed to ID, MT, OR and WA during 1980's. Not established.	USDA (7) State (4, 6,7,9)	411,528, 621

* See 'Introduction' for explanation of headings.

List A continued

Weed and its origin*	Agent and taxonomic references*	Released*	Status and degree of control*	Research organisation*	General references*
CONVOLVULACEAE					
Convolvulus arvensis	*Aceria convolvuli* Nalepa 1989 (Acarina: Eriophyidae)		**CANADA.** Ex Italy. Not established in Saskatchewan.	CDA	267
Linnaeus Eurasia (field bindweed)	*Aceria malherbe* Nuzzaci (Acarina: Eriophyidae)	1989	**UNITED STATES OF AMERICA.** Ex Greece. Released in NJ and TX. Established in TX.	USDA (7,10 12)	41,568, 570,572
	Tyta luctuosa (Denis & Schiffermüller) (Lepidoptera: Noctuidae)	1989	**CANADA.** Ex Italy. Not established in Saskatchewan. Released in Alberta during 1990.	CDA	571
		1987	**UNITED STATES OF AMERICA.** Ex Italy. Released in AR, IA, MO, OK and TX. Establishment not confirmed.	USDA (7,10, 12) State (25,26)	41,540, 570,571
CUSCUTACEAE					
Cuscuta americana Linnaeus North America (love vine)	*Melanagromyza cuscutae* Héring (Diptera: Agromyzidae)	1967	**BARBADOS.** Ex Pakistan. Collected from *Cuscuta reflexa.* Not established.	IIBC	91,97,98, 218
	Smicronyx roridus Marshall (Coleoptera: Curculionidae)	1967	**BARBADOS.** Ex Pakistan. Collected from *Cuscuta refexa.* Not established. Shipped under the name *Smicronyx cuscutae.*	IIBC	91,98,218
	Smicronyx rufovittatus Anderson (Coleoptera: Curculionidae)	1971	**BARBADOS.** Ex Pakistan. Collected from *Cuscuta campestris.* Not established.	IIBC	91,101, 102,218
Cuscuta indecora Choisy tropical America (love vine, dodder)	*Melanagromyza cuscutae* Héring (Diptera: Agromyzidae)	1967	**BARBADOS.** Ex Pakistan. Collected from *Cuscuta reflexa.* Not established.	IIBC	91,97,98, 218
	Smicronyx roridus Marshall (Coleoptera: Curculionidae)	1967	**BARBADOS.** Ex Pakistan. Collected from *Cuscuta reflexa.* Not established. Shipped under the name *Smicronyx cuscutae.*	IIBC	91,98, 218

* See 'Introduction' for explanation of headings.

List A continued

Weed and its origin*	Agent and taxonomic references*	Released*	Status and degree of control*	Research organisation*	General references*
(CUSCUTACEAE continued)					
	Smicronyx rufovittatus Anderson (Coleoptera: Curculionidae)	1971	**BARBADOS.** Ex Pakistan. Collected from *Cuscuta campestris*. Not established.	IIBC	91,101, 102
Cuscuta reflexa Roxburgh (dodder)	*Smicronyx roridus* Marshall (Coleoptera: Curculionidae)	1968	**BANGLADESH.** Ex Pakistan. Initially established but did not persist. Shipped under the name *Smicronyx cuscutae*.	IIBC	98,218, 544
Cuscuta spp. (dodder)	*Melanagromyza cuscutae* Héring (Diptera: Agromyzidae)	1966 1968	**BAHAMAS.** Ex Pakistan. Probably established. Ex Pakistan. Released onto *Cassytha* sp. that had been misidentified as *Cuscuta filiformis* Linnaeus. Not established.	IIBC	91 91,98
	Smicronyx roridus Marshall (Coleoptera: Curculionidae)	1968	**BAHAMAS.** Ex Pakistan. Released onto *Cassytha* sp. that had been misidentified as *Cassytha filiformis* Linnaeus. Not established.	IIBC	91,98
CYPERACEAE					
Cyperus rotundus Linnaeus India (nut grass, purple nut sedge)	*Athesapeuta cyperi* Marshall (Coleoptera: Curculionidae)	1974	**BARBADOS.** Ex Pakistan. Not established.	IIBC	103
		1971 1973	**COOK ISLANDS.** Ex India. Not established. Ex India. Not established.	IIBC DAC	104 539
		1936 1971	**FIJI.** Ex Philippines via Hawaii. No establishment. Ex Pakistan. No establishment.	KRS	482 101,343
		1925	**HAWAII, U.S.A.** Ex Philippines. Established. Effects negated by parasitoids.	HDOA	9,290, 534,640
		1982	**MAURITIUS.** Ex India. Status unknown.	IIBC	109,110, 111
		1971	**TONGA.** Ex Pakistan. Established.	IIBC	101,686

* See 'Introduction' for explanation of headings.

List A *continued*

61

Weed and its origin*	Agent and taxonomic references*	Released*	Status and degree of control*	Research organisation*	General references*
(CYPERACEAE continued)					
	Bactra minima Meyrick (Lepidoptera: Tortricidae)	1974	**BARBADOS.** Ex Pakistan. Not established.	IIBC	91
		1973	**COOK ISLANDS.** Ex Pakistan. Not established.	IIBC	101,539
		1971	**FIJI.** Ex Pakistan. No establishment.	KRS	101,343
		1971	**TONGA.** Ex Pakistan and India. Established. Status unknown.	IIBC	101,686
	Bactra venosana (Zeller) (previously referred to as *Bactra truculenta* Meyrick (Lepidoptera: Tortricidae)	1974	**BARBADOS.** Ex Pakistan. Not established.	IIBC	91,103
		1971	**COOK ISLANDS.** Ex Pakistan. Not established.	IIBC	101,539, 686
		1936	**FIJI.** Ex Philippines via Hawaii. Established but ineffective. Prone to attack by indigenous parasites.	KRS	482
		1971	Ex Pakistan. Effect negligible.	KRS	101,343
		1925	**HAWAII, U.S.A.** Ex Philippines. Established but effect negated by parasitoids.	HDOA	9,290, 534,640
		1978	**SUDAN.** Ex Pakistan. Status unknown.	UKS	107
EHRETIACEAE					
Cordia curassavica (Jacquin) Roemer & Schultes [= *Cordia macrostachya* (Jacquin) Roemer & Schultes] South and Central America, West Indies (black sage)	*Eurytoma attiva* Burks Hymenoptera: Eurytomidae)	1977	**MALAYSIA.** Ex Trinidad via Mauritius. Spread and attacking 33 to 81% of fruits. Status unknown.	DAMA	91,107, 491,605, 669
		1950	**MAURITIUS.** Ex Trinidad. Destruction of fruit prevented recolonisation by the weed resulting in effective control.	IIBC	91,237

* See 'Introduction' for explanation of headings.

List A *continued*

(EHRETIACEAE continued)

Weed and its origin*	Agent and taxonomic references*	Released*	Status and degree of control*	Research organisation*	General references*
		1978	**SRI LANKA.** Ex Trinidad via Malaysia. Established and spreading. Up to 80% of seed destroyed. Successful control is likely.	IIBC DASL	91,606
	Metrogaleruca obscura (Degeer) (previously referred to as *Schematiza cordiae* Barber) (Coleoptera: Chrysomelidae)	1977	**MALAYSIA.** Ex Trinidad. Spreading and causing extensive defoliation. Status unknown.	DAMA	91,107, 605,669
		1948	**MAURITIUS.** Ex Trinidad. Complete defoliation and substantial control.	IIBC	91,237, 603,697
		1978	**SRI LANKA.** Ex Trinidad via Malaysia. Established, spreading and causing extensive defoliation. Successful control is likely.	IIBC DASL	91,606
	Physonota alutacea Boheman (Coleoptera: Chrysomelidae)	1947	**MAURITIUS.** Ex Trinidad. Not established owing to interference by ants.	IIBC	91,237, 603,697
EUPHORBIACEAE					
Euphorbia cyparissias Linnaeus Eurasia (Cypress spurge)	*Aphthona cyparissiae* (Koch) (Coleoptera: Chrysomelidae)	1982	**CANADA.** Ex Austria, Hungary and Switzerland. Established in Ontario. No control.	CDA	614
	Aphthona czwalinai (Weise) (Coleoptera: Chrysomelidae)	1987	**CANADA.** Ex Hungary. Not established in Ontario.	CDA	214
	Aphthona flava Guillebeau (Coleoptera: Chrysomelidae)	1982	**CANADA.** Ex Hungary and Italy. Not established in Ontario.	CDA	614
	Aphthona nigriscutis Foudras (Coleoptera: Chrysomelidae)	1983	**CANADA.** Ex Hungary via Manitoba. Established in Ontario. No control. (Accidentally released with *Aphthona cyparissiae* in 1982. This site was treated with herbicide and insecticide).	CDA	214,407

* See 'Introduction' for explanation of headings.

List A continued

Weed and its origin*	Agent and taxonomic references*	Released*	Status and degree of control*	Research organisation*	General references*
(EUPHORBIACEAE continued)					
	Chamaesphecia empiformis Esper (Lepidoptera: Aegeriidae)	1970	**CANADA.** Ex Switzerland, Austria and Germany. Not established in Ontario.	CDA	262,593
		1989	Ex Switzerland, Austria and Germany. Status unknown.	CDA	267
	Hyles euphorbiae (Linnaeus) (Lepidoptera: Sphingidae)	1965	**CANADA.** Ex Germany. Established in Ontario, but establishment unknown in Quebec. Spread through southern Ontario but control not achieved.	CDA	262,269
		1976	**UNITED STATES OF AMERICA.** Ex *Euphorbia cyparissiae* in Germany and *Euphorbia seguieriana* Necker in Switzerland via Braeside, Canada. Released in MD, NY and VA. Established on the fertile tetraploid form of weed in NY with total defoliation of *E. cyparissiae* and *E. x pseudoesula* Schur in some areas.	USDA (1)	23,291, 509
	Oberea erythrocephala (Schrank) (Coleoptera: Cerambycidae)	1990	**CANADA.** Ex Switzerland. Released in Ontario. Status unknown.	CDA	593
	Pegomya euphorbiae (Kieffer) (Diptera: Anthomyiidae)	1989	**CANADA.** Ex Hungary. Released in Ontario, Status unknown.	CDA	214,430
	Spurgia capitigena (Bremi) (Diptera: Cecidomyiidae)	1990	**CANADA.** Ex Italy from *E. esula* via U.S.A. Trivoltine and attacks most shoots in Saskatchewan field cage. Increasing in Ontario in moist sites.	CDA	211,267

* See 'Introduction' for explanation of headings.

List A continued

Weed and its origin*	Agent and taxonomic references*	Released*	Status and degree of control*	Research organisation*	General references*
(EUPHORBIACEAE continued)					
Euphorbia x pseudovirgata (Schur) Soo, a hybrid of *E. esula* sensu stricto and *E. waldstein* (= *E. virgata* Waldstein & Kitaibel), 505 (previously referred to as *E. esula* Linnaeus) Eurasia (*E. esula*) Europe (*E. waldsteinii*) (leafy spurge)	*Aphthona cyparissiae* (Koch) (Coleoptera: Chrysomelidae)	1982	**CANADA.** Ex Austria, Hungary and Switzerland. Established in Saskatchewan and Alberta. Released in Manitoba during 1990. Spurge controlled in open, dry mesic sites in Saskatchewan, but overall no control.	CDA	614
		1986	**UNITED STATES OF AMERICA.** Ex Austria and Hungary. Released MT, ND, OR, WA and WY. Establishment confirmed except in WY.	USDA (7,10) State (7,9, 11,13,15)	114,509, 529
	Aphthona czwalinai (Weise) (Coleoptera: Chrysomelidae)	1985	**CANADA.** Ex Austria and Hungary. Not established in Alberta, Manitoba or Saskatchewan. Further releases made in 1989 and 1990. Under evaluation.	CDA	214
		1987	**UNITED STATES OF AMERICA.** Ex Austria. Released in MT. Establishment confirmed.	USDA (7,10, 12) State (7)	478,509
	Aphthona flava Guillebeau (Coleoptera: Chrysomelidae)	1982	**CANADA.** Ex Hungary and Italy. Established in Alberta and Saskatchewan. Causes over 65% damage to the weed and reduced spurge at two sites in Alberta on coarse soil with high water table. Accepts light shade.	CDA	614
		1988	Ex Inner Mongolia. Released in Manitoba and recovered in 1989.	CDA	614
		1985	**UNITED STATES OF AMERICA.** Ex *Euphorbia esula* and *E. cyparissiae* in Italy, and ex Hungary, via Canada. Released in ID, MT, ND, OR, WA and WY. Established in MT, ND and OR.	USDA (7,10, 12) State (6,7, 9,11,13,15)	114,509, 510,529

* See 'Introduction' for explanation of headings.

List A continued

Weed and its origin*	Agent and taxonomic references*	Released*	Status and degree of control*	Research organisation* references*	General references*
(EUPHORBIACEAE continued)					
	Aphthona nigriscutis Foudras (Coleoptera: Chrysomelidae)	1983	**CANADA.** Ex Hungary. Established in Alberta, British Columbia, Manitoba and Saskatchewan. Controls spurge in the open on coarse dry prairie, but not in shaded or mesic sites. (Accidentally released with *Aphthona cyparissiae* in 1982. This site was treated with herbicide and insecticide).	CDA	214,407
		1989	**UNITED STATES OF AMERICA.** Ex Hungary via Canada. Released in ID, MT, ND, NE, OR, WA and WY. Established in MT, OR and WA.	USDA (10) State (6,7, 9,11,13,15)	114,509, 478
	Chamaesphecia tenthredini-formis (Denis & Schiffermüller) (Lepidoptera: Aegeriidae)	1972	**CANADA.** Ex Yugoslavia and Austria. Not established in Saskatchewan. Spurge latex toxic to the larvae.	CDA	262,267, 593
		1975	**UNITED STATES OF AMERICA.** Ex *Euphorbia esula* in Austria. Released under the name *Chamaespecia empiformis* Esper in ID and MT. Not established.	USDA (7,10) State (6,7 15)	509,621
	Hyles euphorbiae (Linnaeus) (Lepidoptera: Sphingidae)	1966	**CANADA.** Ex Germany, France and Switzerland. Not established in Alberta, British Columbia, Manitoba, Ontario and Saskatchewan. High larval predation by ants.	CDA	262,269
		1964	**UNITED STATES OF AMERICA.** Ex *Euphorbia cyparissiae* Germany and *E. seguieriana* Necker Switzerland via Braeside, Canada. Released in 1973-80 in CA, ID, NE, NV, OR and MT. Established in MT only. Redistributed to CO, ND, WA, WY and other sites in MT. Established in WY. Heavy vertebrate and invertebrate predation may limit establishment and buildup.	USDA (7,10) State (6,7, 9,13)	23,478, 509,621
		1980	Ex *Euphorbia virgata* (*Euphorbia esula* complex) in Hungary. Released in MT 1980-85 and established.		7,509

* See 'Introduction' for explanation of headings.

List A *continued*

Weed and its origin*	Agent and taxonomic references*	Released*	Status and degree of control*	Research organisation*	General references*
(EUPHORBIACEAE continued)					
	Lobesia euphorbiana (Freyer) (Lepidoptera: Tortricidae)	1983	**CANADA.** Ex Italy. Not established in Manitoba or Saskatchewan. Released in Alberta, British Columbia, Manitoba and Saskatchewan in 1990, ex Saskatchewan field cage colony. Status unknown.	CDA	267
	Oberea erythrocephala (Schrank) (Coleoptera: Cerambycidae)	1979	**CANADA.** Ex Switzerland. Established in Alberta but not in Manitoba or Saskatchewan. Additional releases were made in Saskatchewan during 1990 from a Saskatchewan cage colony.	CDA	593
		1980	**UNITED STATES OF AMERICA.** Ex *Euphorbia esula* and *E. cyparissiae*, Italy. Released but not established in OR and WY.	USDA (7,10) State (7, 13,15)	509,548, 621
		1983	Ex Italy and ex *Euphorbia virgata*, Hungary. Established in MT. Adults ex Italy established in ND. Persisting in low numbers.	USDA (7,10) State (7, 13,15)	509,548, 621
	Pegomya curticornis (Stein) (Diptera: Anthomyiidae)	1988	**CANADA.** Ex Hungary. Established in Saskatchewan but not in Alberta or Manitoba. No control.	CDA	214,430
	Pegomya euphorbiae (Kieffer) (Diptera: Anthomyiidae)	1988	**CANADA.** Ex Hungary. Not established in Alberta, Manitoba or Saskatchewan.	CDA	214,430
	Spurgia capitigena (Bremi) [also referred to as *Bayeria capitigena* (Bremi) and *Dasineura capitigena*] (Diptera: Cecidomyiidae)	1987	**CANADA.** Ex Italy via U.S.A. Surviving in Saskatchewan in field cages and in low numbers where it was released with *Spurgia esulae*.	CDA	211,267
		1985	**UNITED STATES OF AMERICA.** Ex *Euphorbia esula* Italy. Released in MT, ND, OR and WY. Establishment confirmed in MT and ND.	USDA (7,10, 12) State (7,11, 13,15)	478,503, 509
	Spurgia esulae Gagné (Diptera: Cecidomyiidae)	1987	**CANADA.** Ex Italy via U.S.A. Established in Alberta, Manitoba and Saskatchewan in field cages. No control achieved.	CDA	508

* See 'Introduction' for explanation of headings.

List A continued

Weed and its origin*	Agent and taxonomic references*	Released*	Status and degree of control*	Research organisation* references*	General references*
FABACEAE					
Cytisus scoparius (Linnaeus) Link central and southern Europe (Scotch broom)	*Apion fuscirostre* Fabricius (Coleoptera: Apionidae)	1964	**UNITED STATES OF AMERICA.** Ex Italy. Released in CA. High populations in coastal mountains with up to 60% seed destruction. Only low populations occur in the Sierra foothills due to mortality of immatures in pods from high temperatures. No noticeable control of plants in either area. Released in OR (1983) and WA (1989). Well established in western OR with average of 85% seeds destroyed.	USDA (7,12) State (9,15)	8,10
	Bruchidius villosus Fabricius (Coleoptera: Bruchidae)	1988	**NEW ZEALAND.** Ex England. Not established.	DSIR	644,647
	Leucoptera spartifoliella Hübner (Lepidoptera: Lyonetiidae)	1960	**UNITED STATES OF AMERICA.** Ex France. Established on CA coastal and Sierra foothill infestations. Impact negligible. Was found to be already present in OR and WA, probably as a result of accidental introduction, (see List D).	USDA (7) State (9,15)	10,200
Galega officinalis Linnaeus Asia Minor, southern Europe (goat's rue)	*Uromyces galegae* (Opiz) Saccardo (fungus: Uredinales)	1973	**CHILE.** Ex France via Switzerland. Established and still spreading.	UAC	488
Sesbania punicea (Cavanille) Bentham Argentina, Brazil, Uruguay	*Neodiplogrammus quadrivittatus* (Olivier) (Coleoptera: Curculionidae)	1984	**REPUBLIC OF SOUTH AFRICA.** Ex Argentina. Established from small numbers. Extensive destruction of plants and striking reduction in density of weed around release sites.	PPRI	297,300
	Rhyssomatus marginatus Fåhraeus (Coleoptera: Curculionidae)	1984	**REPUBLIC OF SOUTH AFRICA.** Ex Argentina. Established, becoming abundant and spreading. Destroys developing seeds.	PPRI	297,300

* See 'Introduction' for explanation of headings.

List A continued

Weed and its origin*	Agent and taxonomic references*	Released*	Status and degree of control*	Research organisation*	General references*
(FABACEAE continued)					
	Trichapion lativentre (Béguin-Billecocq) (Coleoptera: Apionidae)	1984	**REPUBLIC OF SOUTH AFRICA.** Ex Argentina. Established and abundant. Prevents seed production and stunts growth of plants (see List D).	PPRI	296,297, 299,300, 440
Ulex europaeus Linnaeus western Europe (gorse, furze)	*Agonopterix ulicetella* (Stainton) (Lepidoptera: Oecophoridae)	1988	**HAWAII, U.S.A.** Ex England. Established on Maui and Hawaii. Rapidly dispersing but heavily parasitised.	HDOA	718
		1990	**NEW ZEALAND.** Ex England. Too early to assess establishment.	DSIR	293
	Apion scutellare Kirby (Coleoptera: Apionidae)	1961	**HAWAII, U.S.A.** Ex Portugal. Released on Maui. Not established.	HDOA	212,403
		1989	Ex Spain. Released on Hawaii. Status unknown.	HDOA	718
	Apion (*Exapion*) *ulicis* (Forster) (Coleoptera: Apionidae)	1939	**AUSTRALIA.** Ex England via New Zealand. Rapidly established in Tasmania but has not significantly affected the spread of gorse. Has also been recorded in Victoria.	TDA	184,706
		1981	**CHILE.** Ex England via New Zealand. Well established and consumes high percentages of seed but dispersal is slow. Not yet providing control.	INIA UAC	477
		1926	**HAWAII, U.S.A.** Ex England. Not established.	HDOA	220,403
		1949	Ex England via New Zealand. Not established.	HDOA	220,403
		1955	Ex France. Established on Maui. Ineffective, populations sporadic, supressed by fungus *Hirsutello* sp. Introduced from Maui to island of Hawaii in 1984. Expanding rapidly and attacking 21% of pods in 1990.	HDOA	220,403

* See 'Introduction' for explanation of headings.

List A continued

(FABACEAE continued)

Weed and its origin*	Agent and taxonomic references*	Released*	Status and degree of control*	Research organisation*	General references*
		1931	**NEW ZEALAND.** Ex England. Established readily in almost all areas. High levels of seed reduction in spring but many seeds are produced at other times of the year.	DSIR	118,293, 294,434
		1953	**UNITED STATES OF AMERICA.** Ex France. Established in CA, OR and WA. Seed reductions up to 95% at some sites in WA, 90% in OR. No detectable impact in CA except at one site at San Rafael.	USDA (7) State (9, 15)	114,404, 528
	Apion sp. (possibly *A. uliciperda* Pandelle) (Coleoptera: Apionidae)	1958	**HAWAII, U.S.A.** Ex Spain and Portugal. Released on Maui. Not established.	HDOA	403
	Sericothrips staphylinus Haliday (Thysanoptera: Thripidae)	1990	**NEW ZEALAND.** Ex England. Too early to assess establishment.		DSIR293
	Tetranychus lintearius Dufour (Acari: Tetranychidae)	1989	**NEW ZEALAND.** Ex England. Established at over 100 sites and beginning to spread. Difficult to establish in warmer climates. Causing heavy damage to foliage at release sites.	DSIR	293,295
HYDROCHARITACEAE					
Hydrilla verticillata (Linnaeus f) Royle Africa, Asia, Australia (hydrilla)	*Bagous affinis* Hustache (Coleoptera: Curculionidae)	1987	**UNITED STATES OF AMERICA.** Ex India. Released at numerous sites in FL. Establishment not confirmed.	IIBC, USAE, USDA (3,4) State (3)	56,66,68
	Hydrellia balciunasi Bock (Diptera: Ephydridae)	1989	**UNITED STATES OF AMERICA.** Ex Australia. Apparently established at one site in FL.	USAE, USDA (3,4) State (3)	68,114

* See 'Introduction' for explanation of headings.

List A continued

Weed and its origin*	Agent and taxonomic references*	Released*	Status and degree of control*	Research organisation*	General references*
(HYDROCHARITACEAE continued)					
	Hydrellia pakistanae Deonier (Diptera: Ephydridae)	1987	**UNITED STATES OF AMERICA.** Ex India and Pakistan. Established in FL and being redistributed.	USAE, USDA (3,4) State (3,18)	56,68
LAMIACEAE					
Salvia aethiopis Linnaeus Europe, northern Africa, western Asia (Mediterranean sage)	*Phrydiuchus spilmani* Klarner (Coleoptera: Curculionidae)	1969	**UNITED STATES OF AMERICA.** Ex Italy. Not established.	USDA (7,12) State (15)	11
	Phrydiuchus tau Warner (Coleoptera: Curculionidae)	1971	**UNITED STATES OF AMERICA.** Ex Yugoslavia. Widespread in OR. Plant density reduced at several sites. Recolonized and established in CA in 1977 and ID in 1979.	USDA (7,12) State (6, 14,15)	11
LORANTHACEAE					
Phthirusa adunca (Meyer) Maquire (bird vine)	*Ceratitella asiatica* Hardy (Diptera: Tephritidae)	1978	**TRINIDAD.** Ex Pakistan. Not established.	IIBC	31,91,107, 108,218
MALVACEAE					
Sida acuta Burman f. tropical America (spinyhead sida)	*Calligrapha pantherina* Stål (Coleoptera: Chrysomelidae)	1989	**AUSTRALIA.** Ex Mexico. Established in Northern Territory. Excellent control at some sites. Under evaluation.	CSIRO DPIF	216,701
Sida rhombifolia Linnaeus tropical America (Paddy's lucerne, sida ratusa, common sida)	*Calligrapha pantherina* Stål (Coleoptera: Chrysomelidae)	1989	**AUSTRALIA.** Ex Mexico. Established in coastal northern Queensland. Not established in south-eastern Queensland. Under evaluation.	QDL	1,216

* See 'Introduction' for explanation of headings.

List A continued

Weed and its origin*	Agent and taxonomic references*	Released*	Status and degree of control*	Research organisation*	General references*
MELASTOMATACEAE					
Clidemia hirta (Linnaeus) D. Don tropical Central and South America, West Indies (Koster's curse)	*Ategumia atulinalis* (Guenée) (previously referred to as *Blepharomastix ebulealis* Guenée) (Lepidoptera: Pyralidae)	1970	**HAWAII, U.S.A.** Ex Puerto Rico. Released on Hawii, Oahu and Kauai. Established but ineffective.	HDOA	91,136, 212,695
	Colletotrichum gloeosporioides (Penzig) Penzig & Saccardo f. sp. *clidemiae* (fungus: Coelomycetes)	1986	**HAWAII, U.S.A.** Ex Panama. Released on Oahu. Well established and locally causing leaf fall and dieback. Released on Kauai in 1987, and on Hawaii and Maui in 1990. Established and under evaluation.	HDOA	658,659
	Liothrips urichi Karny (Thysanoptera: Phlaeothripidae)	1930	**FIJI.** Established and spread rapidly. Excellent control in most areas by reducing the weed's competitive ability. Largely able to check succulent regrowth. Little effect in wet and shady habitats. Generally reduced weeding costs by 75%.	DAF	91,210, 543,600, 601,602, 609,610
		1953	**HAWAII, U.S.A.** Ex Trinidad via Fiji. Well established on Oahu. Provides excellent control in open pastureland but ineffective in shaded, forested areas. Introduced to Hawaii and Maui in 1990. Established and under evaluation.	HDOA	91,148, 212,504 549,689
		1938	**SOLOMON ISLANDS.** Ex Trinidad via Fiji. Not established	MAL	390,544
		1973	Ex Trinidad via Fiji. Not established.	MAL	396
		1975	Ex Trinidad via Fiji. Not established.	MAL	396
	Lius poseidon Napp (Coleoptera: Buprestidae)	1988	**HAWAII, U.S.A.** Ex Trinidad. Well established on Oahu and population increasing. Released on Kauai and Maui in 1989, and on Hawaii in 1990. Established and under evaluation.	HDOA	312

* See 'Introduction' for explanation of headings.

List A *continued*

72

Weed and its origin*	Agent and taxonomic references*	Released*	Status and degree of control*	Research organisation* references*	General references*
(MELASTOMATACEAE continued)					
Melastoma malabathricum Linnaeus India, south-east Asia, Australia (Indian rhododendron, Malabar melastome)	*Ategumia adepalis* Lederer [previously referred to as *Bocchoris adipalis* (Lederer)] Lepidoptera: Pyralidae	1965	**HAWAII, U.S.A.** Ex Malaysia. Established with low populations but not effective.	HDOA	145,148
	Ategumia fatualis (Lederer) [previously referred to as *Bocchoris fatualis* (Lederer)] (Lepidoptera: Pyralidae)	1958	**HAWAII, U.S.A.** Ex Philippines. Established with low populations but not effective.	HDOA	133,140, 145,148, 380
	Selca brunella Hampson (Lepidoptera: Arctiidae)	1965	**HAWAII, U.S.A.** Ex Singapore and mainland Malaysia. Released on Hawaii and Kauai. Causes foliar damage and dieback providing partial control.	HDOA	145,148, 212,379
MIMOSACEAE					
Acacia longifolia (Andrews) Willdenow south-eastern Australia (long-leaved wattle)	*Melanterius ventralis* Lea (Coleoptera: Curculionidae)	1985	**REPUBLIC OF SOUTH AFRICA.** Ex Australia. Established, destroying large proportions of seeds that may still form on plants affected by *Trichilogaster acaciaelongifoliae.*	PPRI	166
	Trichilogaster acaciaelong- ifoliae (Froggatt) (Hymenoptera: Pteromalidae)	1982	**REPUBLIC OF SOUTH AFRICA.** Ex Australia. Established widely and multiplied exponentially. Largely to totally prevents seed-set and stunts affected plants at study sites. Too soon to determine effect.	PPRI	163,164, 166,471
Acacia melanoxylon R. Brown Australia (blackwood)	*Melanterius acaciae* Lea (Coleoptera: Curculionidae)	1986	**REPUBLIC OF SOUTH AFRICA.** Ex Australia. Established, spreading slowly. Under evaluation for effects on seeding.	PPRI	166
Acacia nilotica indica (Bentham) Brenan Indian sub-continent (prickly acacia)	*Bruchidius sahlbergi* Schilsky (Coleoptera: Bruchidae)	1982	**AUSTRALIA.** Ex Pakistan. Established throughout most areas of the weed with up to 80% of seeds infested in non-grazed areas.	QDL IIBC	699,700

* See 'Introduction' for explanation of headings.

List A continued

Weed and its origin*	Agent and taxonomic references*	Released*	Status and degree of control*	Research organisation*	General references*
(MIMOSACEAE continued)					
	Cuphodes profluens Meyrick (Lepidoptera: Gracillaridae)	1983	**AUSTRALIA.** Ex Pakistan. Not established.	QDL IIBC	699,700
Acacia saligna (Labillardiére) Wendland Australia (Port Jackson willow)	*Uromycladium tepperianum* (Saccardo) McAlpine (fungus: Uredinales)	1987	**REPUBLIC OF SOUTH AFRICA.** Ex Australia. Established and spreading.	PPRI	443,447
Mimosa invisa Martius Brazil (giant sensitive plant)	*Heteropsylla* sp (Hemiptera: Psyllidae)	1988	**AUSTRALIA.** Ex Brazil. Established widely. Plants severely stunted and killed. Seed set largely to totally prevented.	QDL	700
		1988	**WESTERN SAMOA.** Ex Brazil via Australia. Established but no evidence of reduced seed set. Under evaluation.	DAFF QDL	391,700
	Scamurius sp (Hemiptera: Coreidae)	1987	**AUSTRALIA.** Ex Brazil. Not Established.	QDL	700
		1988	**WESTERN SAMOA.** Ex Brazil via Australia. Not established.	DAFF QDL	391,700
Mimosa pigra Linnaeus var. *pigra* tropical America. (giant sensitive plant, mimosa)	*Acanthoscelides puniceus* Johnson (Coleoptera: Bruchidae)	1983	**AUSTRALIA.** Ex Mexico. Widely established. These beetles are unlikely, on their own, to have any significant effect on *Mimosa pigra* populations wherever seed production is strongly seasonal.	CSIRO DPIF	254,347 394,701, 703
		1984	**THAILAND.** Ex Mexico via Australia. Established and widespread in all infested areas. With *Acanthoscelides quadridentatus* up to 25% of seed destroyed. Under evaluation.	NBCRC	194,254, 469
		1987	**VIETNAM.** Ex Mexico via Australia via Thailand. Establishment not yet confirmed.	NBCRC	469

* See 'Introduction' for explanation of headings.

List A continued

List A continued

Weed and its origin*	Agent and taxonomic references*	Released*	Status and degree of control*	Research organisation*	General references*
(MIMOSACEAE continued)					
	Acanthoscelides quadridentatus (Schaeffer) (Coleoptera: Bruchidae)	1983	**AUSTRALIA.** Ex Mexico. Widely established. These beetles are unlikely, on their own, to have any significant effect on *Mimosa pigra* populations wherever seed production is strongly seasonal.	CSIRO DPIF.	189,194, 254,347, 394,701, 703
		1984	**THAILAND.** Ex Mexico via Australia. Established and widespread in all infested areas. With *Acanthoscelides puniceus* up to 25% of seed destroyed. Under evaluation.	NBCRC	194,254, 469
		1987	**VIETNAM.** Ex Mexico via Australia via Thailand. Establishment not confirmed.	NBCRC	469
	Carmenta mimosa Eichlin & Passoa (Lepidoptera: Sesiidae)	1989	**AUSTRALIA.** Ex Mexico. Released at several sites in the Northern Territory. Established and under evaluation.	CSIRO DPIF	193,701
	Chlamisus mimosae Karren (Coleoptera: Chrysomelidae)	1985	**AUSTRALIA.** Ex Brazil. Established and spreading but ineffective.	CSIRO DPIF	701
		1986	**THAILAND.** Ex Brazil via Australia. Established at a few locations. Not spreading. Under evaluation.	NBCRC	469
		1990	**VIETNAM.** Ex Brazil via Australia via Thailand. Establishment not yet confirmed.	NBCRC	469
	Neurostrota gunniella Busck (Lepidoptera: Gracillariidae)	1989	**AUSTRALIA.** Ex Mexico. Established and spread rapidly at least 160 km from release sites. Extremely abundant. Under evaluation.	CSIRO DPIF	701,702
	Scamurius sp (Hemiptera; Coreidae)	1988	**AUSTRALIA.** Ex Brazil. Normal host *Mimosa invisa*. Released onto *M. pigra* in the Northern Territory but failed to become established.	QDL DPIF	701

* See 'Introduction' for explanation of headings.

List A continued

Weed and its origin*	Agent and taxonomic references*	Released*	Status and degree of control*	Research organisation*	General references*
(MIMOSACEAE continued)					
Paraserianthes lophantha (Willdenow) Nielsen [previously *Albizia lophantha* (Willdenow) Bentham] Australia	*Melanterius servulus* Pascoe (Coleoptera: Curculionidae)	1989	**REPUBLIC OF SOUTH AFRICA.** Ex Australia. Established and under evaluation for effect on seeding.	PPRI	166
Prosopis glandulosa Torrey var. *torreyana* (Benson) Johnston North America (mesquite)	*Algarobius bottimeri* Kingsolver (Coleoptera: Bruchidae)	1990	**REPUBLIC OF SOUTH AFRICA.** Ex Texas, U.S.A. Field population established.	PPRI	723
Prosopis velutina Wooten North America (mesquite)	*Algarobius prosopis* (LeConte) (Coleoptera: Bruchidae)	1987	**REPUBLIC OF SOUTH AFRICA.** Ex Arizona, U.S.A. Field populations spreading well and causing seed damage.	PPRI	723
MYRICACEAE					
Myrica faya Aiton Azores, Madeira and Canary Islands (firebush, firetree)	*Strepsicrates smithiana* Walsingham (Lepidoptera: Tortricidae)	1956	**HAWAII, U.S.A.** Ex Florida and Georgia, U.S.A. Released on Hawaii. Not established on *Myrica faya* but became established on southern wax myrtle, *Myrica cerifera*, on Hawaii.	HDOA	9,140, 212,722
PASSIFLORACEAE					
Passiflora tripartita (C. Jussieu) Poir var. *triparita* [also reported as *P. mollissima* (Kunth) L.H. Bailey] Andes of South America (banana poka)	*Cyanotricha necyria* Felder (Lepidoptera: Dioptidae)	1988	**HAWAII, U.S.A.** Ex Colombia. Released on Hawaii and Kauai. Not established.	HDOA	65,402

* See 'Introduction' for explanation of headings.

List A continued

Weed and its origin*	Agent and taxonomic references*	Released*	Status and degree of control*	Research organisation*	General references*
POLYGONACEAE					
Emex australis Steinheil South Africa (three cornered Jack(s), doublegee, spiny emex)	*Lixus cribricollis* Boheman (Coleoptera: Curculionidae)	1979	**AUSTRALIA.** Ex Morocco. Not established.	CSIRO DAV,DAW	54,208, 336,553
	Perapion antiquum (Gyllenhal) (previously referred to as *Apion antiquum* Gyllenhal) (Coleoptera: Apionidae)	1974	**AUSTRALIA.** Ex South Africa. Established at three sites only. Large numbers released using colonies collected from three ecoclimatically selected areas, Franskraal, Ladismith and Grahamstown. No control of the weed.	CSIRO	336
		1975	Ex South Africa via Hawaii. Small number released. Not established.	CSIRO	339
		1984	Ex Olifants River, South Africa. Established at release sites in Victoria but not in South Australia. No control.	DAV DAW	54,208, 497,553
		1957	**HAWAII, U.S.A.** Ex South Africa. Released on Hawaii and Molokai. Release on Oahu and Maui in 1961. Substantial to complete control from 600 to 1200 m elevation. Occasional reinfestations in these zones are readily controlled by the weevil. No control below 150 m.	HDOA	9,134, 139,140, 212,378
	Perapion neofallax (Warner) (previously referred to as *Apion neofallax* Warner) (Coleoptera: Apionidae)	1962	**HAWAII, U.S.A.** Ex Morocco. Not established.	HDOA	142,212, 378
	Perapion violaceum (Kirby) (previously referred to as *Apion violaceum* Kirby) (Coleoptera: Apionidae)	1962	**HAWAII, U.S.A.** Ex Portugal. Not established.	HDOA	142,212, 378
Emex spinosa (Linnaeus) Campdera northern Africa, western Europe (lesser Jacks)	*Perapion antiquum* (Gyllenhal) (previously referred to as *Apion antiquum* Gyllenhal) (Coleoptera: Apionidae)	1974	**AUSTRALIA.** Ex South Africa. Established at one site only. Large numbers released at numerous sites using colonies collected from three ecoclimatically selected areas. No control of the weed.	CSIRO	336

* See 'Introduction' for explanation of headings.

List A continued

Weed and its origin*	Agent and taxonomic references*	Released*	Status and degree of control*	Research organisation*	General references*
(POLYGONACEAE continued)					
		1957	**HAWAII, U.S.A.** Ex South Africa. Released on Hawaii and Molokai. Release on Oahu and Maui in 1960. Substantial to complete control from 600 to 1200 m elevation. Occasional reinfestations in these zones are readily controlled by the weevil. Chemical control has been abandoned in favour of biological control in most ranchlands. No control below 150m.	HDOA	206,212, 378
	Perapion neofallax (Warner) (previously referred to as *Apion neofallax* Warner) (Coleoptera: Apionidae)	1962	**HAWAII, U.S.A.** Ex Morocco. Not established.	HDOA	142,212, 378
	Perapion violaceum (Kirby) (previously referred to as *Apion violaceum* Kirby) (Coleoptera: Apionidae)	1962	**HAWAII, U.S.A.** Ex Portugal. Not established.	HDOA	142,212, 378
Rumex crispus Linnaeus Asia, Africa, Europe (curled dock)	*Chamaesphecia doryliformis* (Ochsenheimer) (Lepidoptera: Sesiidae)	1989	**AUSTRALIA.** Ex Europe. Released in Western Australia, Victoria and New South Wales. Under evaluation.	CSIRO DAW	594,595
Rumex sp. (docks)	*Chamaesphecia doryliformis* (Ochsenheimer) (Lepidoptera: Sesiidae)	1989	**AUSTRALIA.** Ex Europe. Released in Western Australia, Victoria and New South Wales. Under evaluation.	CSIRO DAW	594,595
PONTEDERIACEAE					
Eichhornia crassipes (Martius) Solms-Laubach South America (water hyacinth)	*Acigona infusella* (Walker) (Lepidoptera: Pyralidae)	1981	**AUSTRALIA.** Ex Brazil. Recoveries made over a period of 13 months but not thereafter. Not established.	CSIRO	579,713

* See 'Introduction' for explanation of headings.

List A *continued*

Weed and its origin*	Agent and taxonomic references*	Released*	Status and degree of control*	Research organisation*	General references*
(PONTEDERIACEAE continued)					
	Neochetina bruchi Hustache (Coleoptera: Curculionidae)	1990	**AUSTRALIA.** Ex South America via Florida, U.S.A. Limited releases, but mass rearing underway for widespread liberations in Australia and to supply starter colonies to Thailand and Malaysia.	CSIRO	714
		1990	**HONDURAS.** Ex South America via Florida. Established and under evaluation.	EAP	193,533
		1984	**INDIA.** Ex Argentina via Florida, U.S.A. Established readily. Brought about 90% control of water hyacinth in three years in one tank and in combination with *N. eichhorniae* in two other tanks. Release with *N. eichhorniae* into Loktak Lake in 1987 resulted in successful control by 1990.	IIHR	316,319, 333,502
		1977	**PANAMA.** Ex South America via U.S.A. Status unknown.	PCC	32,500
		1989	**REPUBLIC OF SOUTH AFRICA.** Ex Argentina via Florida, U.S.A. Established. Under evaluation.	PPRI	87
		1979	**SUDAN.** Ex Argentina via U.S.A. Established but least effective of the agents released.	UKS	34,35,36, 311
		1974	**UNITED STATES OF AMERICA.** Ex Argentina. Established throughout FL. Usually dominated by *Neochetina eichhorniae*. Similarity of mature stages and damage makes effects of the two species difficult to distinguish. Established in TX, LA and CA.	USAE, USDA (4,7,13) State (14)	39,67,68
	Neochetina eichhorniae Warner (Coleoptera: Curculionidae)	1975	**AUSTRALIA.** Ex Argentina via Florida, U.S.A. Widely established. Good control at large infestations and infestations on permanent waters. Less effective were pesticide use continues and in cool temperate regions. Released on Norfolk Island in 1982. Establishment not confirmed.	CSIRO	712 714

* See 'Introduction' for explanation of headings.

List A continued

(PONTEDERIACEAE continued)

Weed and its origin*	Agent and taxonomic references*	Released*	Status and degree of control*	Research organisation*	General references*
		1980	**EGYPT.** Ex Argentina via Florida, U.S.A. Establishment not yet confirmed.		32
		1977	**FIJI.** Ex Argentina via U.S.A. via Australia. Established and spread throughout but no significant control.	KRS	343,611
		1990	**HONDURAS.** Ex Argentina via Florida, U.S.A. Established and under evaluation.	EAP	193,533
		1983	**INDIA.** Ex Argentina via Florida, U.S.A. and ex Argentina via Australia. Established readily. In 3–4 years 95% weed reduction achieved in six tanks covering 1000 ha in and around Bangalore, either alone (in three tanks) or in combination with *N. bruchi*. Releases with *N. bruchi* into Loktak Lake in 1987 resulted in control by 1990.	IIHR	316,318, 319,320, 502
		1979	**INDONESIA.** Ex Argentina via U.S.A. Established at one site at Bogor. Status unknown.	BIOTROP	346
		1983	**MALAYSIA.** Ex Argentina via U.S.A. via Thailand. Established and widely spread throughout the Malaysian Peninsular.		339
		1985	**PAPUA NEW GUINEA.** Ex Argentina via Australia. Established and increasing slowly.	PNGDAL	385,387
		1974	**REPUBLIC OF SOUTH AFRICA.** Ex Argentina via U.S.A. Released at five localities. Established and increased readily, but no effective control.	PPRI	28,32, 87
		1985	Ex Argentina via Australia via U.S.A. Released in Natal and Transvaal. Established and becoming abundant at various release sites. Main cause for slower increase of the weed's populations, and probably already contributing significantly to control.	PPRI	83,87

* See 'Introduction' for explanation of headings.

List A continued

(PONTEDERIACEAE continued)

Weed and its origin*	Agent and taxonomic references*	Released*	Status and degree of control*	Research organisation*	General references*
		1982	**SOLOMON ISLANDS.** Ex Argentina via Australia. Not established.		686
		1988	Ex Argentina via U.S.A. via Australia via Fiji. Established. Status unknown.	MAL	241,652
		1988	**SRI LANKA.** Ex Argentina via U.S.A. via Australia. Established but not yet providing control.	NBCRC	566
		1978	**SUDAN.** Ex Argentina via U.S.A. Established and now distributed throughout White Nile system in Sudan. Successful control attributed to this insect.	UKS	34-36, 311,686
		1979	**THAILAND.** Ex Argentina via U.S.A. Established and widespread in almost all areas of the country. Good control in many locations.	NBCRC	466,467, 469
		1980	**UNION OF MYANMAR (Burma).** Ex Argentina via U.S.A. via Thailand. Establishment to be confirmed.	NBCRC	469
		1972	**UNITED STATES OF AMERICA.** Ex Argentina. Established throughout the weed's range in south-eastern U.S.A. Major reductions of the weed in FL, LA and TX probably due primarily to this agent. Effects may be gradual attrition, loss of competitive ability and replacement by other plants; or faster, more dramatic weed population collapse. Effects negated in many sites due to herbicidal control. Also established in CA.	USAE, USDA (4,7,13) State (14)	39,67,68
		1985	**VIETNAM.** Ex Argentina via U.S.A. via Thailand. Establishment to be confirmed in southern Vietnam.	NBCRC	469
		1971	**ZAMBIA.** Ex Brazil via Trinidad. Establishment not confirmed.	IIBC	28,32,101

* See 'Introduction' for explanation of headings.

List A continued

(PONTEDERIACEAE continued)

Weed and its origin*	Released*	Status and degree of control*	Research organisation*	General references*	Agent and taxonomic references*
	Approx. 1971	**ZIMBABWE.** Ex South America. Establishment not confirmed.	IIBC	28	*Orthogalumna terebrantis* Wallwork (previously referred to as *Leptogalumna* sp.) (Acarina: Galumnidae)
	Approx. 1976	**EGYPT.** Ex South America. Establishment not confirmed.		31	
	1986	**INDIA.** Ex South America via Florida, U.S.A. Established readily. High populations caused browning of leaves in all release areas, but dose not control the weed by itself.	IIHR	316,322, 333	
	1971	**ZAMBIA.** Ex South America via India. Established temporarily only. Current status unknown.	IIBC	28,32	
	1977	**AUSTRALIA.** Ex Argentina via Florida, U.S.A. Widely established. Has the potential to inflict severe damage on expanding infestations and luxuriant growths of mature plants, however, effects often temporary and patchy.	CSIRO	712,714	*Sameodes albiguttalis* (Warren) [also referred to as *Epipagis albiguttalis* (Warren)] (Lepidoptera: Pyralidae)
	1977	**PANAMA.** Ex Argentina via U.S.A. Establishment not confirmed.	PCC	500	
	1990	**REPUBLIC OF SOUTH AFRICA.** Ex Argentina via Australia via Florida U.S.A. Established and being redistributed.	PPRI	83,87	
	1980	**SUDAN.** Ex Argentina via U.S.A. Well established and extending its distribution. Successful control of the weed attributed to *Neochetina eichhorniae*.	UKS	34,35,36, 311	

* See 'Introduction' for explanation of headings.

List A continued

Weed and its origin*	Agent and taxonomic references*	Released*	Status and degree of control*	Research organisation*	General references*
(PONTEDERIACEAE continued)					
		1977	**UNITED STATES OF AMERICA.** Ex Argentina. Significant impact on developing colonies of the weed but effects lost when plants become large. Probably retards growth in early stages of mat development. Generally sporadic and patchy. Established in FL, LA and MS. Establishment not confirmed in CA.	USAE,USDA (4,7,13) State (14)	39,68
		1971	**ZAMBIA.** Ex Trinidad via India. Establishment not confirmed.	IIBC	28,32
PROTEACEAE					
Hakea gibbosa (Smith) Cavanilles Australia (rock hakea)	*Erytenna consputa* Pascoe (Coleoptera: Curculionidae)	1972	**REPUBLIC OF SOUTH AFRICA.** Ex Australia. Established but consistent large scale fruit destruction not acheived. More suitable genetic stock probably needed.	PPRI	15,359, 472,473
Hakea sericea Schrader Australia (silky hakea)	*Carposina autologa* Meyrick (Lepidoptera: Carposinidae)	1972	**REPUBLIC OF SOUTH AFRICA.** Ex Australia. Dispersed and destroying significant proportions of seed accumulated on plants. Contributed towards limiting regeneration of the weed after fires.	PPRI	165,359, 472
	Cydmaea binotata Lea (Coleoptera: Curculionidae)	1980	**REPUBLIC OF SOUTH AFRICA.** Ex Australia. Widely redistributed but only a few colonies surviving. Damage probably insignificant.	PPRI	357,359, 472
	Erytenna consputa Pascoe (Coleoptera: Curculionidae)	1972	**REPUBLIC OF SOUTH AFRICA.** Ex Australia. Poor establishment and poor results. Need for more suitable genetic stock.	PPRI	15,359, 472-474
		1974	Ex Australia. Larger colonies from inland localities in Australia and from better matched host plant forms. Established and causing significant seed destruction. With *Colletotricum gloeosporioides*, the insect is implicated in the decline of weed densities.	PPRI	358,359, 472,474

* See 'Introduction' for explanation of headings.

List A continued

Weed and its origin*	Agent and taxonomic references*	Released*	Status and degree of control*	Research organisation*	General references*
ROSACEAE					
Acaena anserinifolia (Forster & G. Forster) Druce New Zealand (piripiri)	*Ucona acaenae* Smith (previously referred to as *Antholcus varinervis* Spinola) (Hymenoptera: Tenthredinidae)	1936	**NEW ZEALAND.** Ex Chile. Not established. Species persisted in two localities for four years. No further field recoveries since 1940. The weed is native to New Zealand.	CI DSIR	434
Rubus argutus Link (previously referred to as *R. penetrans* Bailey and *R. lucidus*) eastern U.S.A. (prickly Florida blackberry)	*Chlamisus gibbosa* (Fabricius) (Coleoptera: Chrysomelidae)	1969	**HAWAII, U.S.A.** Ex Missouri, U.S.A. Not established.	HDOA	135,212, 459
	Croesia zimmermani Clarke (previously referred to as *Apotoforma* sp.) (Lepidoptera: Tortricidae)	1964	**HAWAII, U.S.A.** Ex Mexico. Well established throughout the state, in combination with *Priophorus morio* and *Schreckensteinia festaliella*, gives good control in pasture and open areas, but of limited effect in forests.	HDOA	135,144, 145,147, 212,459
	Pennisetia marginata (Harris) [previously referred to as *Bembecia marginata* (Harris)] (Lepidoptera: Sesiidae)	1963 1966	**HAWAII, U.S.A.** Ex Oregon, U.S.A. Not established. Ex Oregon, U.S.A. Not established.	HDOA HDOA	143,147, 212,459
	Priophorus morio (Lepeletier) (Hymenoptera: Tenthredinidae)	1966	**HAWAII, U.S.A.** Ex Oregon, Washington and California, U.S.A. Established on Maui and Hawaii but not on Oahu. Released on Kauai in 1988. Well established on all islands except Oahu. Effectiveness there limited by presence of a virus.	HDOA	147,212, 459,462
	Schreckensteinia festaliella Hübner (Lepidoptera: Heliodinidae)	1963	**HAWAII, U.S.A.** Ex California, U.S.A. Well established throughout the state and in combination with the other two agents, gives good control in pasture and open areas, but of limited effect in forests.	HDOA	135,143, 144,145, 147,212, 459

* See 'Introduction' for explanation of headings.

List A continued

Weed and its origin*	Agent and taxonomic references*	Released*	Status and degree of control*	Research organisation*	General references*
(ROSACEAE continued)					
Rubus constrictus Lefevre & P.J. Mueller Asia, Europe (black berry)	*Phragmidium violaceum* (Schultz) Winter (fungus: Uredinales)	1973	**CHILE.** Ex Germany. Readily established with rapid dispersal. *Rubus constrictus* more susceptible than *Rubus ulmifolius*. Hastens normal defoliation and stems do not lignify properly thereby facilitating invasion by secondary pathogens and frost damage. Weed density decreasing.	UAC	486,487, 489
Rubus ulmifolius Schott Asia, Europe (black berry)	*Phragmidium violaceum* (Schultz) Winter (fungus: Uredinales)	1973	**CHILE.** Ex Germany. Readily established with rapid dispersal. *Rubus constrictus* more susceptible than *Rubus ulmifolius*. Hastens normal defoliation and stems do not lignify properly thereby facilitating invasion by secondary pathogens and frost damage. Weed density decreasing.	UAC	486,487, 489
SALVINIACEAE					
Salvinia molesta D.S. Mitchell Brazil (water fern, salvinia, Kariba weed)	*Cyrtobagous salviniae* Calder & Sands (Coleoptera: Curculionidae)	1980	**AUSTRALIA.** Ex Brazil. Very successful control in tropical and sub-tropical areas. Control in some temperate areas.	CSIRO	191,192, 339,562
			BOTSWANA. Spread naturally to Botswana from releases made in Namibia in 1983. Manually distributed during 1984. Very successful control.		193,215
		1983	**INDIA.** Ex Brazil via Australia. Established readily and successfully controlled the weed in Bangalore. Releases in Kerala in 1984 resulted in spectacular control within 3 years.	IIHR KAU	315,335
		1990	**KENYA.** Ex Brazil via Australia. Released on Lake Nairasha but died out when water level dropped. Further releases planned for 1991.	CSIRO	561

* See 'Introduction' for explanation of headings.

List A continued

Weed and its origin*	Agent and taxonomic references*	Released*	Status and degree of control*	Research organisation*	General references*
(SALVINIACEAE continued)					
		1989	**MALAYSIA.** Ex Brazil via Australia. Established and being distributed. Control at one site.	MARDI AP	339
		1983	**NAMIBIA (South West Africa).** Ex Brazil via Australia. Rapid establishment and successful control of salvinia on the border of Namibia and Botswana-within 1 to 2 years.	DWAN	215,586
		1982	**PAPUA NEW GUINEA.** Ex Brazil via Australia. Complete control achieved by August 1985.	CSIRO FAO	564,653
		1985	**REPUBLIC OF SOUTH AFRICA.** Ex Brazil via Australia via Namibia. Rapid establishment and successful control at various release sites within 1-2 years of release.	PPRI	83,86
		1987	**SRI LANKA.** Ex Brazil via Australia. Successful control in most areas where it has been released.	KU, DASL CSIRO	565,566
		1990	**ZAMBIA.** Ex Brazil via Australia. Released at Ndola. Established and beginning to damage the weed.	CSIRO	561
	Cyrtobagous singularis Hustache (Coleoptera: Curculionidae)	1971 1976	**BOTSWANA.** Ex Trinidad. Not established. Ex Trinidad. Found established in eastern Caprivi in 1981. No significant control.	IIBC PPRI	28,29 182,538, 585
		1979	**FIJI.** Ex Trinidad. Established but not effective.	KRS	339,384
		1971	**ZAMBIA.** Ex Trinidad. Released on Zambian side of Lake Kariba. Established though earlier reports suggest not established. Although the weed has declined evidence suggests that other factors were responsible. Established along the Zambezi River.	IIBC	406,436, 585

* See 'Introduction' for explanation of headings.

List A continued

(SALVINIACEAE continued)

Weed and its origin*	Agent and taxonomic references*	Released*	Status and degree of control*	Research organisation*	General references*
	Paulinia acuminata (De Geer) (Orthoptera: Pauliniidae)	1971	**BOTSWANA.** Ex Trinidad via Zimbabwe. Not established.	IIBC	28,29
		1975	Ex Trinidad and Ex Trinidad via Lake Kariba, Zimbabwe. Established but giving no control.	PPRI	182,193
		1976	**FIJI.** Ex Trinidad via India. Established but not effective.	KRS	339,384, 343
		1974	**INDIA.** Ex Trinidad. Established at one site only. No control.	IIBC KAU	29,104, 334
		1970	**KENYA.** Ex Trinidad. Not established on Lake Naivasha.	IIBC	28,29,100
		1973	**SRI LANKA.** Ex Trinidad via India. Not established.	DASL	29
		1978	Ex Trinidad. Not established.	IIBC	581
		1970	**ZAMBIA.** Ex Trinidad. Established on Lake Kariba. Although the weed has declined evidence suggests that other factors were responsible.	IIBC	28,29,31, 406,567
		1969	**ZIMBABWE.** Ex Trinidad. Established on Lake Kariba following escapes from cage experiments. Deliberate release made in 1970.	IIBC	28,29
		1971	Ex Uruguay. Established but Trinidad strain spread further and is better adapted. Although the weed has declined evidence suggests that other factors were responsible.		28,29,406, 436
	Samea multiplicalis (Guenée) (Lepidoptera: Pyralidae)	1981	**AUSTRALIA.** Ex Brazil. Established and spread rapidly but has not controlled the weed in tropical and sub-tropical areas. Is currently spreading into temperate areas.	CSIRO	191,192, 338,563

* See 'Introduction' for explanation of headings.

List A continued

Weed and its origin*	Agent and taxonomic references*	Released*	Status and degree of control*	Research organisation*	General references*
(SALVINIACEAE continued)					
		1972	**BOTSWANA.** Ex Trinidad. Not established.	IIBC	31,215
		1976	**FIJI.** Ex Trinidad via India. Established and is widespread, but not effective.	KRS	339,343, 384
		1970	**ZAMBIA.** Ex Trinidad. Not established.	IIBC	29,579
SCROPHULARIACEAE					
Linaria dalmatica (Linnaeus) Miller [also referred to as *Linaria genistifolia* (Linnaeus) Miller ssp. *dalmatica* (Linnaeus) Marie & Petitmengin] Europe (Dalmation toadflax)	*Calophasia lunula* (Hufnagel) (Lepidoptera: Noctuidae)	1962	**CANADA.** Ex Switzerland. Established in Ontario.	CDA	263,270
		1989	Ex Yugoslavia. Released in British Columbia. Status unknown.	CDA	267
		1967	**UNITED STATES OF AMERICA.** Multiple releases in 1960s, 1970s and 1980s in CO, ID, OR, MT, WA and WY. Establishment confirmed at one site in MT (1989) and another in WA (1990).	USDA (7) State (6, 7,9,13,15)	388,414, 479,528, 621
	Gymnetron antirrhini (Paykull) (Coleoptera: Curculionidae)	1986	**UNITED STATES OF AMERICA.** Ex Europe via Canada. Released in WY. Establishment not confirmed. (See also List D)	State (13)	388,612
Linaria vulgaris Miller Europe (common toadflax, butter-and-eggs)	*Calophasia lunula* (Hufnagel) (Lepidoptera: Noctuidae)	1962	**CANADA.** Ex Switzerland and Yugoslavia. Established in Ontario but not in Alberta, British Columbia, Nova Scotia or Saskatchewan. Defoliates 20% of stems in Ontario and has spread 300 km. No control.	CDA	263,270
		1968	**UNITED STATES OF AMERICA.** Established in ID but not elsewhere.	State (6)	479

* See 'Introduction' for explanation of headings.

List A continued

Weed and its origin*	Agent and taxonomic references*	Released*	Status and degree of control*	Research organisation*	General references*
(SCROPHULARIACEAE continued)					
Striga hermontheca Bentham Africa (witchweed)	*Eulocastra argentisparsa* Hampson (Lepidoptera: Noctuidae)	1974	**ETHIOPIA.** Ex India. Collected from *Striga asiatica*. Released at Humera on the Setit River. Status unknown.	IIBC FAO	239
	Smicronyx albovariegatus Faust (Coleoptera: Curculionidae)	1974	**ETHIOPIA.** Ex India. Collected from *Striga asiatica*. Released at Humera on the Setit River. Status unknown.	IIBC FAO	239
		1978	Ex India. Collected from *Striga asiatic*. Released at Kobbo in Welo Province. Recovered in 1979 but current status is unknown.	IIBC FAO	239
SOLANACEAE					
Solanum elaeagnifolium Cavanilles North and South America (silverleaf nightshade)	*Frumenta nephelomicta* (Meyrick) (Lepidoptera: Gelechiidae)	1979	**REPUBLIC OF SOUTH AFRICA.** Ex Mexico. Small numbers of eggs released but lost during subsequent drought.	PPRI	490
		1984	Ex Mexico. Small releases of eggs. Establishment doubtful.	PPRI	490
		1985	Ex Mexico. Large release of eggs but no establishment due to drought.	PPRI	475,490
VERBENACEAE					
Clerodendrum philippinum Sweet China, south east Asia (Honolulu rose)	*Phyllocharis undulata* (Linnaeus) (Coleoptera: Chrysomelidae)	1990	**THAILAND.** Ex Vietnam. Established at some sites and providing local damage.	NBCRC	339,469

* See 'Introduction' for explanation of headings.

List A continued

Weed and its origin*	Agent and taxonomic references*	Released*	Status and degree of control*	Research organisation*	General references*
(VERBENACEAE continued)					
Lantana camara Linnaeus tropical America (lantana) (talamoa, Tonga) (latana, Samoa) (te kaibuaka, Kiribati) (tataromo, Rarotonga) (kauboica, Fiji)	*Aerenicopsis championi* Bates (Coleoptera: Cerambycidae)	1902 1955	**HAWAII, U.S.A.** Ex Mexico. Failed to establish. Ex Mexico. Not established despite numerous releases between 1955 to 1967.	HDOA HDOA	512,691 141,143, 147,220
	Alagoasa parana Samuelson (Coleoptera: Chrysomelidae)	1981	**AUSTRALIA.** Ex Brazil. Not established.	CSIRO	709
		1985	**REPUBLIC OF SOUTH AFRICA.** Ex Brazil, and ex Brazil via Australia. Small number released. Not established.	PPRI	88
	Apion species A (Coleoptera: Apionidae)	1902	**HAWAII, U.S.A.** Ex Mexico. Not established.	HDOA	512
	Apion species B (Coleoptera: Apionidae)	1902	**HAWAII, U.S.A.** Ex Mexico. Not established.	HDOA	512
	Autoplusia illustrata Guenée (Lepidoptera: Noctuidae)	1976	**AUSTRALIA.** Ex Colombia. Not established.	QDL,FCN	698
		1978	**REPUBLIC OF SOUTH AFRICA.** Ex Colombia via Hawaii via Australia. Not established.	PPRI	88
		1984	Ex Colombia via Hawaii via Australia. Not established	PPRI	88
	Calcomyza lantanae Frick (previously referred to as *Phytobia lantanae*) (Diptera: Agromyzidae)	1974	**AUSTRALIA.** Ex Trinidad. Established well, spread rapidly and produced important damage by 1978. Since then populations have declined except in lower rainfall areas where the leaf mining beetles, *Uroplata girardi* and *Octotoma scabripennis*, are unable to survive. Unable to survive sub-tropical winter. No control.	CSIRO	103,250, 686

* See 'Introduction' for explanation of headings.

List A continued

Weed and its origin*	Agent and taxonomic references*	Released*	Status and degree of control*	Research organisation*	General references*
(VERBENACEAE continued)					
		1982	**REPUBLIC OF SOUTH AFRICA.** Ex Trinidad via Australia. Readily established in sub-tropical Natal coastal areas (on pink flowering plants). Still increasing and expanding range.	PPRI	83
		1989	Ex Texas and Florida U.S.A. Released to increase genetic diversity. Believed to have established at low density around Pretoria.	PPRI	472
	Cremastobombycia lantanella Busck (Lepidoptera: Gracillariidae)	1902	**HAWAII, U.S.A.** Ex Mexico. Established on all major islands. Provides partial control in dry areas.	HDOA	207,512, 639,686
	Diastema tigris Guenée (Lepidoptera: Noctuidae)	1965	**AUSTRALIA.** Ex Panama via Hawaii. No establishment.	QDL	249,706
		1955	**CAROLINE ISLANDS.** Ex Panama via Hawaii to Pohnpei. Establishment unknown.	UOG	167,591
		1971	**INDIA.** Ex Trinidad. Not established.	CPPTI	455,580
		1954	**FIJI.** Ex Panama via Hawaii. No establishment.	KRS	484,485, 543
		1971	Ex Trinidad via India. No establishment.	KRS	343,344
		1971	**GHANA.** Ex Trinidad via India. Not established.	IIBC	101,584
		1954	**HAWAII, U.S.A.** Ex Panama. Failed to establish.	HDOA	377,690
		1962	Ex Mexico. Not established.	HDOA	142,220
		1967	**MAURITIUS.** Ex Trinidad. Established near release site.	IIBC	237
		1967	**TANZANIA.** Ex Trinidad. Not established.	IIBC	97,237
		1968	Ex Trinidad via Uganda. Not established.	IIBC	98

* See 'Introduction' for explanation of headings.

List A continued

(VERBENACEAE continued)

Weed and its origin*	Agent and taxonomic references*	Released*	Status and degree of control*	Research organisation*	General references*
		1963	**UGANDA.** Ex Trinidad. Not established.	IIBC	97,236, 237
		1970	**ZAMBIA.** Ex Trinidad. Not established.	IIBC	100,240
	Epinotia lantana (Busck) [= *Crocidosema lantana* (Busck)] (Lepidoptera: Tortricidae)	1914	**AUSTRALIA.** Ex Mexico via Hawaii. Established in Queensland and northern New South Wales. Causes minor reduction in seed production. Spread naturally to Norfolk Island where it was recorded in 1971.	QDAS	249,284, 706
		1948	**CAROLINE ISLANDS.** Ex Mexico via Hawaii. Established on Pohnpei and Yap and exerting some control. Spread to Palau.		167
		1902	**HAWAII, U.S.A.** Ex Mexico. Present on all islands and contributes usefully to control.	HDOA	212,512, 639,686
		1948	**MARSHALL ISLANDS.** Ex Mexico via Hawaii. Established but effect unknown.		243
	Eutreta xanthochaeta Aldrich (previously referred to as *Eutreta sparsa*) (Diptera: Tephritidae)	1914	**AUSTRALIA.** Ex Mexico via Hawaii. No establishment.	QDAS	249,706
		1971	Ex Mexico via Hawaii. No establishment.	CSIRO	249
		1977	Ex Mexico via Hawaii. No establishment.	CSIRO	579
		1902	**HAWAII, U.S.A.** Ex Mexico. Established on all islands but of minor importance.	HDOA	212,512, 639,686
		1983	**REPUBLIC OF SOUTH AFRICA.** Ex Mexico via Hawaii. Not established.	PPRI	88
	Hepialus sp. (Lepidoptera: Hepialidae)	1902	**HAWAII, U.S.A.** Not established.	HDOA	212,686

* See 'Introduction' for explanation of headings.

List A continued

(VERBENACEAE continued)

Weed and its origin*	Agent and taxonomic references*	Released*	Status and degree of control*	Research organisation*	General references*
	Hypena strigata (Fabricius) (Lepidoptera: Noctuidae)	1965	**AUSTRALIA.** Ex Kenya and Zimbabwe via Hawaii. Indistinguishable from the Australian strain with which it interbreeds. Probably established. Released on Norfolk Island in 1968 and probably established. Australian strain was found to be present immediately prior to releasing the African strain.	QDL CSIRO	249 339
		1958	**CAROLINE ISLANDS.** Ex Kenya and Zimbabwe via Hawaii. Released on Pohnpei and Yap. Established on Yap. Establishment unknown on Pohnpei.	UOG	167,591
		1960	**FIJI.** Ex Kenya and Zimbabwe via Hawaii. Established but no marked effects.	KRS	344,543
		1957	**HAWAII, U.S.A.** Ex Kenya and Zimbabwe. Established and caused foliar devastation in 1959 to 1961. Populations of *Hypena strigata* declined in some areas and lantana regeneration occurred while in others defoliation occurred.	HDOA	132,140, 290,377
		1964	Ex Philippines. Released on Hawaii, Kauai, Maui and Oahu. One of the complex of agents introduced that provides partial to substantial control in dry areas (under 1270 mm annual rainfall).	HDOA	212,220, 290
		1967	**MARIANA ISLANDS.** Ex Kenya and Zimbabwe via Hawaii. Released on Guam, not effective. Present on Aguijan, Saipan and Tinian. Effects unknown.	UOG	167,686
		1961	**REPUBLIC OF SOUTH AFRICA.** Ex Kenya and Zimbabwe via Hawaii. In 1962 it was found to be indigenous to South Africa. Plentiful in some summers. Does not exert any noticeable control.	PPRI	88,495

* See 'Introduction' for explanation of headings.

List A *continued*

(**VERBENACEAE** continued)

Weed and its origin* / Agent and taxonomic references*	Released*	Status and degree of control*	Research organisation*	General references*
Lantanophaga pusillidactyla (Walker) (previously referred to as *Platyptilia pusillidactyla* Walker) (Lepidoptera: Pterophoridae)	1948	**CAROLINE ISLANDS.** Ex Mexico via Hawaii. Released on Pohnpei, and on Palau in 1960. Established on both islands and exerting some control on Pohnpei. Also present on Truk and Yap.		167,544, 591
	1902	**HAWAII, U.S.A.** Ex Mexico. First released on Hawaii, now established on all islands.	HDOA	212,512, 639,686
	1933	**HONG KONG.** Ex Mexico probably via Hawaii. Found to be already established (see List D).		220
	1984	**REPUBLIC OF SOUTH AFRICA.** Ex Mexico via Hawaii. Small numbers released. Not established.	PPRI	88
Leptobyrsa decora Drake (Hemiptera: Tingidae)	1969	**AUSTRALIA.** Ex Peru and Columbia. Established at restricted localities. Seasonal heavy defoliation. Released on Norfolk Island in 1971. Established but exerting no control.	CSIRO QDL FCN	698,700 339
	1977	**CAROLINE ISLANDS.** Ex Peru and Columbia via Australia via Hawaii. Released on Palau. Establishment unknown.	UOG	167,591
	1972	**COOK ISLANDS.** Ex Peru and Columbia via Australia Released into field cages. Establishment not confirmed.	DAC	332
	1971 1976	**FIJI.** Ex Peru via Hawaii. No establishment. Ex Peru via Australia. No establishment.	KRS KRS	101,343 343,384
	1971	**GHANA.** Ex Peru and Columbia probably via Australia. Not established.	IIBC	101,584
	1970	**HAWAII, U.S.A.** Ex Peru and Columbia via Australia. Released on Kauai, Oahu and Maui. Established and spreading slowly.	HDOA	136,137, 212,686

* See 'Introduction' for explanation of headings.

List A continued

(VERBENACEAE continued)

Weed and its origin*	Agent and taxonomic references*	Released*	Status and degree of control*	Research organisation*	General references*
		1971	MARIANA ISLANDS. Ex Peru and Columbia via Australia via Hawaii. Not established.	UOG	453
		1972	REPUBLIC OF SOUTH AFRICA. Ex Peru and Columbia via Australia. Not established.	PPRI	80,81
		1978	Ex Peru and Columbia via Australia. Not established.	PPRI	81,83
		1981	Ex Peru and Columbia via Australia. Not established.	PPRI	88
		1970	ZAMBIA. Ex Peru and Columbia via Australia. Not established.	CSIRO	100,240
	Neogalea esula (Druce) (previously referred to as *Catabena esula*) (Lepidoptera: Noctuidae)	1957	AUSTRALIA. Ex California, U.S.A. via Hawaii. Established. Ineffective due to low population levels. Heavily parasitised. Released on Norfolk Island in 1962 and 1964.	QDL	249,284, 706
				QDL	339
		1955	CAROLINE ISLANDS. Ex U.S.A. via Hawaii. Released on Pohnpei. Establishment unknown.	UOG	167,591
		1955	HAWAII, U.S.A. Ex California, U.S.A. Released on Kauai, Oahu, Maui and Hawaii. Causes widespread seasonal defoliation. Heavily parasitised by an ichneumonid, *Echthromorpha fuscator* (F.).	HDOA	136,140, 141,212, 686
		1962	REPUBLIC OF SOUTH AFRICA. Ex California, U.S.A. via Hawaii via Trinidad. No establishment.	PPRI	80,495
		1968	Ex California, U.S.A. via Hawaii via Australia. No establishment.	PPRI	81,473
	Octotoma championi Baly (Coleoptera: Chrysomelidae)	1975	AUSTRALIA. Ex Costa Rica. Established at one site. Not effective.	QDL FCN	698,700
		1988	Released on Norfolk Island. Status unknown.	QDL	579

* See 'Introduction' for explanation of headings.

List A continued

Weed and its origin*	Agent and taxonomic references*	Released*	Status and degree of control*	Research organisation*	General references*
(VERBENACEAE continued)					
		1976	**FIJI.** Ex Central America via Australia. Not established.	KRS	384
		1978	**REPUBLIC OF SOUTH AFRICA.** Ex Central America via Australia. Not established.	PPRI	80,81 88
	Octotoma plicatula (Fabricius) (Coleoptera: Chrysomelidae)	1954	**HAWAII, U.S.A.** Not established.	HDOA	212,686
	Octotoma scabripennis Guérin-Méneville (Coleoptera: Chrysomelidae)	1966	**AUSTRALIA.** Ex Mexico via Hawaii. Readily established in southern Queensland with slower establishment in northern Queensland and New South Wales. Now present in large numbers throughout lantana areas in favourable seasons. Causes significant damage in some districts. Released on Norfolk Island in 1971 where it established but is exerting no control.	CSIRO QDL FCN	248,249
		1974	Ex El Salvador. Not distinguishable from material previously released and now common.	CSIRO	250
		1973	**COOK ISLANDS.** Ex Mexico via Hawaii via Australia via India. Not established.	DAC	539
		1971 1976	**FIJI.** Ex Mexico via Australia. Not established. Ex Mexico via Australia. Not established.	KRS	101,343 343,384
		1971	**GHANA.** Ex Mexico via Hawaii via Australia. Established but ineffective probably as a result of predation and parasitism.	IIBC	101,102, 584
		1973	Ex Mexico via Hawaii via Australia. Established, but no marked control.	IIBC	102-107

* See 'Introduction' for explanation of headings.

List A continued

Weed and its origin*	Agent and taxonomic references*	Released*	Status and degree of control*	Research organisation*	General references*
(VERBENACEAE continued)					
		1902	**HAWAII, U.S.A.** Ex Mexico. Failed to establish.	HDOA	220,512
		1954	Ex Mexico. Established on Kauai, Maui, Oahu and Hawaii. One of the complex of agents that provides partial to substantial control in dry areas (under 1270 mm annual rainfall).	HDOA	143,290
		1972	**INDIA.** Ex Mexico via Hawaii via Australia. Established in North India but not effective.	FRI	455,597
		1971	**MARIANA ISLANDS.** Ex Mexico via Hawaii. Released on Guam. Not established.	UOG	453
		1977	**NEW CALEDONIA.** Ex Mexico via Hawaii via Australia. Established. Works with other agents to reduce spread.	RSTO	243
		1971	**REPUBLIC OF SOUTH AFRICA.** Ex Mexico via Hawaii via Australia. Established.	PPRI	81,82,85,88
		1974	Ex Mexico via Hawaii via Australia. Established.	PPRI	81,82,85,88
		1981	Ex Mexico via Hawaii via Australia. Established on the Natal coastal belt and Transvaal lowveld. Numbers still increasing and in Natal together with other established agents, is retarding growth and vigour of a pink flowering form of the weed.	PPRI	81,82,85,88
	Ophiomyia lantanae Froggatt (Diptera: Agromyzidae)	1914	**AUSTRALIA.** Ex Mexico via Hawaii. Not established.	QDAS	706
		1917	Ex Mexico via Hawaii via Fiji. Established and spread throughout Queensland and New South Wales. Insignificant reductions of seed viability.	QDAS	249,284, 706
			Released on Norfolk Island in 1959, 1960 and established.		339

* See 'Introduction' for explanation of headings.

List A continued

Weed and its origin*	Agent and taxonomic references*	Released*	Status and degree of control*	Research organisation*	General references*
(VERBENACEAE continued)					
		1948	**CAROLINE ISLANDS.** Ex Mexico via Hawaii. Released on Pohnpei. Establishment doubtful. Present on Palau.	UOG	167,591
		1972	**COOK ISLANDS.** Ex Mexico via Hawaii via Australia. Status unknown.	DAC	332
		1911	**FIJI.** Ex Mexico via Hawaii. Well established. Weed reported to have been eliminated within several miles of Suva but unlikely to have been due to this insect.	DAF	349,482, 600,686
		1902	**HAWAII, U.S.A.** Ex Mexico. Common but not effective.	HDOA	512,639, 686
		1933	**HONG KONG.** Probably ex Hawaii. Establishment not confirmed.		220,615
		1921	**INDIA.** Ex Mexico via Hawaii. Considered not to have established from this release. Recovered in 1933 probably from accidental introduction (see List D). Not effective.	DAIN	455,544, 580,633
		1958	**KENYA.** Ex Mexico via Hawaii. Was then found to be already present and well established (see List D).		236,237
		1971	**MARIANA ISLANDS.** Ex Mexico via Hawaii. Released on Guam. Established and effective. Spread to Saipan and Tinian.	UOG	167,453
		1911	**NEW CALEDONIA.** Ex Mexico via Hawaii. Well established. Limits spread of the weed in conjunction with *Teleonemia scrupulosa*.		512,544, 663

* See 'Introduction' for explanation of headings.

List A continued

Weed and its origin*	Agent and taxonomic references*	Released*	Status and degree of control*	Research organisation*	General references*
(VERBENACEAE continued)					
		1961	**REPUBLIC OF SOUTH AFRICA.** Ex Mexico via Hawaii. Already present prior to release (see List D). Widely spread. Contributes towards seed destruction.	PPRI	80,85,88,
	Parevander xanthomelas (Guérin-Méneville) [previously referred to as *Evander xanthomelas* (Guérin-Méneville)] (Coleoptera: Cerambycidae)	1902	**HAWAII, U.S.A.** Ex Mexico. Not established.	HDOA	212,512, 686
	Plagiohammus spinipennis (Thomson) (Coleoptera: Cerambycidae)	1967	**AUSTRALIA.** Ex Mexico via Hawaii. Established at one site only. Not effective.	CSIRO QDL FCN	249,251, 579
		1977	**CAROLINE ISLANDS.** Ex Mexico via Hawaii. Released on Palau, not established.	UOG	591
		1960	**HAWAII, U.S.A.** Ex Mexico. Established on Hawaii. Partial control in some high rainfall areas. Not adapted to drier areas.	HDOA	134,135, 145,212, 686
		1973	**MARIANA ISLANDS.** Ex Mexico via Hawaii via Australia. Released on Guam. Not established.	UOG	453
		1970	**REPUBLIC OF SOUTH AFRICA.** Ex Mexico via Hawaii via Australia. Limited establishment in a garden only. Disappeared by 1990.	PPRI	80,81
		1973	Ex Mexico via Hawaii via Australia. Limited, temporary establishment.	PPRI	81,88
		1979	Ex Mexico via Hawaii via Australia. Limited, temporary establishment.	PPRI	81,88

* See 'Introduction' for explanation of headings.

List A continued

(VERBENACEAE continued)

Weed and its origin*	Agent and taxonomic references*	Released*	Status and degree of control*	Research organisation*	General references*
	Pseudopyrausta acutangulalis (Sneller) (previously referred to as *Blepharomastix acutangulalis*) (Lepidoptera: Pyralidae)	1955	**CAROLINE ISLANDS.** Ex Mexico via Hawaii. Released on Pohnpei. Establishment unknown.	UOG	167,591
		1954	**FIJI.** Ex Mexico via Hawaii. No establishment.	KRS	484,485, 543
		1953	**HAWAII, U.S.A.** Ex Mexico. No establishment.	HDOA	140,689
	Salbia haemorrhoidalis Guenée [previously referred to as *Syngamia haemorrhoidalis* (Guenée) or *Anania haemorrhoidalis*] (Lepidoptera: Pyralidae)	1958	**AUSTRALIA.** Ex Florida and Cuba via Hawaii. Established well in northern Queensland and with difficulty in southern Queensland. Population fluctuations result in varying degrees of plant damage. In combination with other insects it can sometimes be a factor in reduction of plant vigour in some areas. Released and established on Norfolk Island in 1959 to 1960.	QDL	175,284
				QDL	339
		1958	**CAROLINE ISLANDS.** Ex Florida and Cuba via Hawaii. Released and established on Pohnpei. Released on Palau in 1960 and on Yap in 1962 but establishment doubtful.	UOG	167,591
		1958	**FIJI.** Ex Florida and Cuba via Hawaii. Well established. No marked effect.	KRS	485,543
		1956	**HAWAII, U.S.A.** Ex Florida and Cuba. Released on Hawaii, Kauai, Maui and Oahu. Widespread and causes severe foliar destruction. Together with other agents it provides partial to substantial control in dry areas (under 1270 mm annual rainfall).	HDOA	132,139, 140,212, 290
		1971	**INDIA.** Ex Trinidad. Not established.	CPPTI	455

* See 'Introduction' for explanation of headings.

List A continued

Weed and its origin*	Agent and taxonomic references*	Released*	Status and degree of control*	Research organisation*	General references*
(VERBENACEAE continued)					
		approx. 1958	KENYA. Ex Florida and Cuba via Hawaii. Not established. Only four individuals released. Ex Trinidad via Uganda. Not established.	IIBC	236,237
		1965		IIBC	237,240
		1958	MARIANA ISLANDS. Ex Florida and Cuba via Hawaii. Released on Guam. Not established.		453
		1965	MAURITIUS. Ex Trinidad. Established. Weed no longer spreading.	IIBC	237
		1958	REPUBLIC OF SOUTH AFRICA. Ex Florida and Cuba via Hawaii. Establishment confirmed in 1985. Not effective.	PPRI	88,495
		1967	TANZANIA. Ex Trinidad via Uganda. Not established.	IIBC	98,237
		1964	UGANDA. Ex Trinidad. Recovered but rare. Parasitised by indigenous braconid.	IIBC	236,237
		1970	ZAMBIA. Ex Trinidad via India and Pakistan. Observed breeding in field. Establishment not confirmed.	IIBC	100
	Teleonemia elata Drake (Hemiptera: Tingidae)	1969	AUSTRALIA. Ex Brazil. No establishment.	CSIRO QDL	249,698
		1973	COOK ISLANDS. Ex India. Not established.	DAC	539
		1972	REPUBLIC OF SOUTH AFRICA. Ex Brazil via Australia. Not established.	PPRI	80,81,88
		1972	UGANDA. Ex Brazil via Australia. Not established.	IIBC	102

* See 'Introduction' for explanation of headings.

List A *continued*

Weed and its origin*	Agent and taxonomic references*	Released*	Status and degree of control*	Research organisation*	General references*
(VERBENACEAE continued)					
		1970	**ZAMBIA.** Ex Brazil via Australia. Not established.	CSIRO	100,240
	Teleonemia harleyi Froeschner (Hemiptera: Tingidae)	1969	**AUSTRALIA.** Ex Trinidad. Establishment confirmed at one site only in south eastern Queensland and has little effect.	CSIRO	249,579
	Teleonemia prolixa Stål (Hemiptera: Tingidae)	1974	**AUSTRALIA.** Ex Brazil. No establishment.	CSIRO	698
	Teleonemia scrupulosa Stål (has been referred to as *Teleonemia vanduzei* Drake) (Hemiptera: Tingidae)	1936	**AUSTRALIA.** Ex Mexico via Fiji. Populations often limited by unfavourable climate and resistant taxa of lantana. Released on Norfolk Island in 1937 (not established) and in 1948 where it established and is partially successful in retarding growth.	CSIRO QDL FCN	248,249, 706 339
		1969	Ex Brazil, Paraguay and Mexico. Effects increased following introduction of diversity from 28 separate South American colonies. Caused extensive defoliation and provided partial control. However populations appear to be declining.	CSIRO	252,686, 700
		1948	**CAROLINE ISLANDS.** Ex Mexico via Hawaii. Released on Pohnpei and established. Taken to Palau in 1960 and Yap in 1962. Established on Palau but not on Yap. Spread to Truk and thriving there.		167,176, 544,591
		1928	**FIJI.** Ex Mexico via Hawaii. Well established. Prevented flower production and seed-set over considerable areas. Adversely affected by wet weather. Predaceous lygaeid, *Germalus pacificus* Kirk, held it in check.	DAF	209,544, 600,608

* See 'Introduction' for explanation of headings.

List A continued

Weed and its origin*	Agent and taxonomic references*	Released*	Status and degree of control*	Research organisation*	General references*
(VERBENACEAE continued)					
		1971	**GHANA.** Ex Brazil via India. Not established.	IIBC	101,240
		1972	Ex Mexico and Trinidad via Hawaii, Kenya and Uganda. Established but no marked control.	IIBC	106,240, 584
		1902	**HAWAII, U.S.A.** Ex Mexico. Established.	HDOA	376,512
		1952	Ex Cuba, Florida, Brazil, British Honduras, Trinidad. Established. Causes considerable damage and provides partial to substantial control in dry areas (under 1270 mm annual rainfall). Summer defoliation by this insect complements winter defoliation by other introduced species.	HDOA	212,220, 290,377, 686,690
		1941	**INDIA.** Ex Mexico via Fiji via Australia. Not released but escaped from laboratory and became established. Spread was assisted between 1972 and 1976 but is of limited control value.	FRI	213,455, 544
		1940	**INDONESIA.** Ex Mexico via Fiji via Australia. Not released, escaped from laboratory. Spread throughout Java, Lesser Sunda Island and Sulawesi. Released in Timor in 1954. Well established but ineffective.	DAI	346,544
		1953	**KENYA.** Ex Mexico via Hawaii. Established but no marked control.	DAK	131b,236, 237
		1961	**MADAGASCAR.** Caused tip die-back and may have kept weed in check.		44
		1963	**MARIANA ISLANDS.** Ex Mexico via Hawaii. Released on Saipan, established but effects unknown. Released on Guam 1969 and 1971 and provides good control. Present on Aguijan and Tinian.	UOG	167,453, 458

* See 'Introduction' for explanation of headings.

List A continued

Weed and its origin*	Agent and taxonomic references*	Released*	Status and degree of control*	Research organisation*	General references*
(VERBENACEAE continued)					
		1935	**NEW CALEDONIA.** Ex Mexico via Hawaii via Fiji. Limits spread in conjunction with *Ophiomyia lantanae.*		243,390, 544
		1973	**PAPUA NEW GUINEA.** Ex Mexico via Fiji via Australia. Established but effective at one site only.	PNGDAL	498,499, 719
		1961	**REPUBLIC OF SOUTH AFRICA.** Ex Mexico via Hawaii. Widely established on pink flowering plant forms. Causes patchy defoliation in most years. In Natal coastal areas, in conjunction with other agents, retarded growth and vigour and caused decline of the weed.	PPRI	80,81,82, 85,472, 495
		1971	Ex numerous American localities via Australia. An attempt to improve the genetic pool.	PPRI	83
		1984	Ex Mauritius. Small number released in attempt to improve genetic pool.	PPRI	83
		1989	Ex Paraguay, and Florida U.S.A., in an attempt to increase genetic diversity.	PPRI	472
		1959	**TANZANIA.** Ex Mexico via Hawaii via Kenya. Established but no marked control.		236,237
		1937	**TONGA ISLANDS.** Ex Mexico via Hawaii via Fiji. Established but of little control value.		390,544
		1960	**UGANDA.** Ex Mexico via Hawaii via Kenya. Established.	IIBC	131b,236,
		1962	Ex Trinidad. Caused severe defoliation around Serere Research Station (in the centre of the country), after redistribution in 1983 from Kawanda release site, enabling thickets to be burned and cleared. Some of the surplus population fed on *Sesamum indicum*, but could not breed on it. Elsewhere control was minimal.	IIBC	131b,237

* See 'Introduction' for explanation of headings.

List A continued

(VERBENACEAE continued)

Weed and its origin*	Agent and taxonomic references*	Released*	Status and degree of control*	Research organisation*	General references*
	Thecla bazochii (Godart), 686 [previously referred to as *Strymon bazochii* (Godart) and *Thecla agra* (Hewitson)], 555, 721 (Lepidoptera: Lycaenidae)	1935	**VANUATU.** Ex Mexico via Hawaii via Fiji. Established on Efate, Anatom, Espiritu Santo and Malakula. Not effective.		92,390, 544,686
		1936	**WESTERN SAMOA.** Ex Mexico via Hawaii via Fiji. Not established.		544
		1940	Ex Mexico via Hawaii via Fiji. Established.		544,686
		1962	**ZAMBIA.** Ex Mexico via Hawaii via Kenya Not established.	MAZ	237
		1969	Ex Trinidad. Established and caused severe defoliation in some areas.	IIBC	99,100,240
		1958	**ZANZIBAR.** Ex Mexico via Hawaii via Kenya. Established.		236
		1961	**ZIMBABWE.** Ex Mexico via Hawaii via Kenya. Temporarily established but died out by 1965 without achieving control.	MAR	237
		1914	**AUSTRALIA.** Ex Mexico via Hawaii. No establishment.	QDAS	249,706
	Thecla sp. (*echion* group) 686 [previously referred to as *Thmolus* sp. (*echion* group) and *Strymon echion*], 555,721 (Lepidoptera: Lycaenidae)	1921	**FIJI.** Ex Mexico via Hawaii. Established but not abundant.	DAF	349,600-602
		1902	**HAWAII, U.S.A.** Ex Mexico. Established but of minor importance.	HDOA	212,512, 639,686
		1921	**FIJI.** Ex Mexico via Hawaii. No establishment.	DAF	349,600, 602
		1902	**HAWAII, U.S.A.** Ex Mexico. Established but of minor importance. Also feeds on flowers of the weed *Clidema hirta* but provides no control.	HDOA	91,212, 512,639, 686

* See 'Introduction' for explanation of headings.

List A continued

(VERBENACEAE continued)

Weed and its origin*	Agent and taxonomic references*	Released*	Status and degree of control*	Research organisation*	General references*
	Uroplata girardi Pic (Coleoptera: Chrysomelidae)	1966	**AUSTRALIA.** Ex Brazil via Hawaii. Readily established over much of the range of lantana but limited at high altitudes and in cooler climates. Provides control in open situations where it prevents regrowth and seedling regeneration after large old plants are killed with herbicide.	CSIRO QDL FCN	248,249, 700
			Released on Norfolk Island in 1971 where it established but exerted no control.	CSIRO	339
		1974	Ex Argentina. Indistinguishable from material previously released and now common.	CSIRO	250
		1963	**CAROLINE ISLANDS.** Ex Brazil via Hawaii. Released and established on Pohnpei. Taken to Palau in 1974. Established but effects unknown. Present on Truk.	UOG	167,591
		1969	**COOK ISLAND.** Ex Brazil via Hawaii via Australia via Fiji. Established.		544
		1976	Ex Brazil via Hawaii via Australia via India. Locally established.		686
		1969	**FIJI.** Ex Brazil via Hawaii. Rapidly established and is widespread. Causes severe damage especially in shady situations.	KRS	343
		1971	**GHANA.** Ex Brazil via Hawaii via Australia. Established and providing limited control.	IIBC	101-107, 584
		1961	**HAWAII, U.S.A.** Ex Brazil. Causes considerable damage and provides partial to substantial control. Well adapted to Hawaiian conditions.	HDOA	141,143, 212,686
		1972	**INDIA.** Ex Brazil via Hawaii via Australia. Established in North India but not effective.	FRI	455,597

* See 'Introduction' for explanation of headings.

List A continued

(VERBENACEAE continued)

Weed and its origin*	Agent and taxonomic references*	Released*	Status and degree of control*	Research organisation*	General references*
		1963	**MARIANA ISLANDS.** Ex Brazil via Hawaii. Released on Saipan but effect unknown.	UOG	167,458
		1967	Ex Brazil via Hawaii. Released on Guam and established. Provides partial to substantial control. Recently distributed to Tinian. Under evaluation.		167,453, 458
		1967	**MAURITIUS.** Ex Trinidad. Believed not established but found during 1984.	IIBC	237
		1977	**NEW CALEDONIA.** Ex Brazil via Hawaii via Australia. Established and spreading. Causing significant damage.	RSTO	243
		1972	**PAPUA NEW GUINEA.** Ex Brazil via Hawaii via Australia. Established. Effects unknown.	PNGDAL	579,686
		1985	**PHILIPPINES.** Ex Brazil via Hawaii via Fiji. Recovered in Mindanao.	IIBC PCA	95
		1974	**REPUBLIC OF SOUTH AFRICA.** Ex Argentina, Brazil, Paraguay via Hawaii via Australia.	PPRI	81,85,88
		1981	Ex Argentina, Brazil, Paraguay via Hawaii via Australia. Established in the Natal coastal area and Transvaal lowveld. Numbers still increasing and with other agents causes growth retardation and loss of vigour of a pink flowering form of the weed.	PPRI	81,85,88
		1984	Ex Trinidad via Mauritius. Small number released.	PPRI	83,88
		1984	Ex South America via Australia. From a southern area of South America in an attempt to increase the genetic pool and tolerance to temperate climatic conditions.	PPRI	83,88
		1967	**TANZANIA.** Ex Brazil via Trinidad. Not established.	IIBC	97

* See 'Introduction' for explanation of headings.

List A continued

(VERBENACEAE continued)

Weed and its origin*	Agent and taxonomic references*	Released*	Status and degree of control*	Research organisation*	General references*
		1969	**TONGA ISLANDS.** Ex Brazil via Hawaii via Australia via Fiji. Established on Tongatapu and causing heavy damage but lantana remains a problem.		92,544, 686
		1969	**TRINIDAD.** Ex Brazil via Hawaii. Established but sites were destroyed. Current status unknown.	IIBC	91,99
		1963	**UGANDA.** Ex Brazil via Trinidad. Established, but no marked control.	IIBC	97,99, 100
		1983	**VANUATU.** Ex Brazil via Hawaii via Fiji. Established on Efate. Since been released on Santo, Tanna and Malekula. Damage obvious but no control.	IIBC	92,694
		1975	**WESTERN SAMOA.** Ex Brazil via Hawaii via Fiji. Established.		686
		1969	**ZAMBIA.** Ex Brazil via Trinidad. Probably failed to survive the dry season following release.	IIBC	99,100
		1970	Ex Brazil via Trinidad. Established, but no marked control.	IIBC	100
	Uroplata lantanae Buzzi & Winder (Coleoptera: Chrysomelidae)	1977	**AUSTRALIA.** Ex Brazil. Not established.	CSIRO	707,708
		1984	**REPUBLIC OF SOUTH AFRICA.** Ex Brazil via Australia. Small number released. Not established.	PPRI	88
	Uroplata sp. near *bilineata* Chapuis (Coleoptera: Chrysomelidae)	1976	**AUSTRALIA.** Ex Central America. Established at three sites in northern Queensland. Not effective.	QDL FCN	175,698

* See 'Introduction' for explanation of headings.

List A continued

Weed and its origin*	Agent and taxonomic references*	Released*	Status and degree of control*	Research organisation*	General references*
(VERBENACEAE continued)					
		1976	**FIJI.** Ex Central America via Australia. Not established.	KRS	384
		1978	**REPUBLIC OF SOUTH AFRICA.** Ex Costa Rica via Australia. Not established.	PPRI	81,88
ZYGOPHYLLACEAE					
Tribulus cistoides Linnaeus tropical and sub-tropical southern Africa, 536 (puncture vine, nohu)	*Microlarinus lareynii* (Jacquelin du Val) (Coleoptera: Curculionidae)	1968	**ST. KITTS.** Ex Italy via U.S.A. Recovered in 1969 and 1970 but not subsequently.	IIBC	26,27,91
		1962	**HAWAII, U.S.A.** Ex Italy via California, U.S.A. Substantial to complete control in conjunction with *Microlarinus lypriformis.*	HDOA	143-145, 212,397
	Microlarinus lypriformis (Wollaston) (Coleoptera: Curculionidae)	1966	**ST. KITTS.** Ex Italy via California, U.S.A. via Hawaii. Well established and providing excellent control.	IIBC	26,27,91
		1963	**HAWAII, U.S.A.** Ex Italy via California, U.S.A. Substantial to complete control in conjunction with *Microlarinus lareynii.*	HDOA	143,144, 145,212
		1967	**PAPUA NEW GUINEA.** Ex Italy via U.S.A. via Hawaii. Established and controlling plant at release point and spreading.	PNGDAL	498,499, 719
		1968	**NEVIS.** Extremely successful. Released on small infestation at airport and provided excellent control. Subsequent enlargement of airport destroyed the weed.	IIBC	91

* See 'Introduction' for explanation of headings.

List A continued

Weed and its origin*	Agent and taxonomic references*	Released*	Status and degree of control*	Research organisation*	General references*
(ZYGOPHYLLACEAE continued)					
Tribulus terrestris Linnaeus northern Africa, Mediterranean, 536 (puncture vine)	*Microlarinus lareynii* (Jacquelin du Val) (Coleoptera: Curculionidae)	1986	**CANADA.** Ex Europe via Colorado, U.S.A. Not established in British Columbia.	CDA	267
		1962	**HAWAII, U.S.A.** Ex Italy via California, U.S.A. Substantial to complete control in conjunction with *Microlarinus lypriformis*.	HDOA	142,145, 212,397
		1961	**UNITED STATES OF AMERICA.** Ex Italy. Established in AZ, CA, NV, OK, TX, UT, KS and FL. Released but not established in AL and MS. Greatest effect on weed in warmer areas of southwest U.S.A. "Cold adapted" strains were distributed to more northern areas but failed to establish in WA, ID, MT and WY. Weevils die back in hard winters and must migrate back into areas such as KS.	USDA (7,12) State (4,5, 6,9,13,15, 21)	12,24, 307,353, 398,399, 528,599, 621
	Microlarinus lypriformis (Wollaston) (Coleoptera: Curculionidae)	1986	**CANADA.** Ex Europe via Colorado, U.S.A. Not established in British Columbia.	CDA	267
		1963	**HAWAII, U.S.A.** Ex Italy via California, U.S.A. Substantial to complete control in conjunction with *Microlarinus lareynii*.	HDOA	143,145, 212
		1961	**UNITED STATES OF AMERICA.** Ex Italy. Established in AZ, CA, FL, KS, NV, NM, OK, OR, TX and UT. Released but not established in AL or MS. Impact on weed greatest in warmer areas of southwestern U.S.A. "Cold adapted" strains were distributed to more northern areas but failed to establish in ID, MT, WA and WY.	USDA (7,12) State (4,5, 6,9,13,15, 21)	12,24, 307,353, 398,399, 528,599, 621

* See 'Introduction' for explanation of headings.

List B: Exotic vertebrates released and their target weeds

Weed and its origin*	Agent and taxonomic references*	Released*	Status and degree of control*	Research organisation* references*	General references*
VARIOUS AQUATIC WEEDS AND ALGAE including; *Agonogeton distachyus*, *Alternanthera philoxeroides* (Martius) Grisebach, *Azolla* species, *Bacopa* species, *Brasenia schreberi* J.F. Gmelin, *Cabomba* species, *Callitriche* species, *Ceratophyllum dermensum* L., *Chara* species, *Cladophora* species, *Egeria densa* Planche, *Eleocharia* species, *Elodea canadensis* Michaux, *Enhydrias angustipetala* Ridley, *Eremochlea ophiuroides* Hacket, *Fimbristylis* species, *Fontinalis* species, *Fuirena scirpoidea* Michaux	*Aristichthys nobilis* (Richardson) (Pisces: Cyprinidae) (big head)	1964	**BULGARIA.** Ex China via U.S.S.R. Mainly used for food production but also for weed control.		381
		after 1962	**CZECHOSLOVAKIA.** Ex eastern Asia. Mainly cultured for food.		381
		prior 1970	**FRANCE.** Released in canals to control excessive weed growth.		305
		after 1962	**HUNGARY.** Ex China probably via U.S.S.R. Field stocking.		381
		1959	**RUMANIA.** Ex China. Used in polyculture for food production and weed control.		381
		-	**TAIWAN.** Ex China. Used in polyculture to control zooplankton and for food.		55
		after 1948	**UNION OF SOVIET SOCIALIST REPUBLICS.** Ex China. Successfully utilised in association with other species to control weeds.		5
	Ctenopharyngodon idella (Cuvier & Valenciennes) (Pisces: Cyprinidae) (grass carp, white amur)	1978	**ARGENTINA.** Ex China U.S.A. Released to control weeds.	INTA	115
Glyceria species, *Hydrilla verticillata* (Linnaeus f) Royle, *Isachne globosa* (Thunberg) Kuntze, *Lagarosiphon major* (Ridley) C.E. Moss, *Lemna* species, *Lyngbya* species, *Myriophyllum* species, *Najas* species, *Nitella* species, *Nymphaea* species,		appr. 1970	**AUSTRIA.** Ex China via U.S.S.R. and Hungary and Romania. Extensively used in lakes and ponds in the lowlands. Stocking rates depend on presence of predator fish.	BWA	238,432, 692,727, 729
		appr. 1975	**BELGIUM.** Under evaluation.	MEF	729
		1964	**BULGARIA.** Ex U.S.S.R. Field stockings mainly for food but also for weed control.		381,629, 729
		1961	**CZECHOSLOVAKIA.** Ex U.S.S.R. Mainly used in polyculture fish production ponds for weed control and meat production.	FRIC	381,432, 629,729

* See 'Introduction' for explanation of headings.

List B continued

Weed and its origin*	Agent and taxonomic references*	Released*	Status and degree of control*	Research organisation*	General references*
	(VARIOUS AQUATIC WEEDS AND ALGAE continued)				
Ottelia species, *Paspalum* species, *Phalaris* species, *Phragmites* species, *Pithophora* species, *Polygonum* species,		1976	**EGYPT.** Ex China via U.S.A. Effective and cheap means of controlling aquatic weeds in canals.	MIE	178,350, 673
		1975	**ETHIOPIA.** Ex China via Japan. Status unknown.		598
Potamogeton species, *Ranunculus* species, *Sagittaria* species,		1968	**FIJI.** Ex China via Malaysia. Rearing and releasing is continuing. Effectiveness not reported.		598,629
Schoenoplectus lacustris (Linnaeus) Palla, *Sirogonium* species,		prior 1970	**FRANCE.** Released in canals to control excessive weed growth.		238,305, 629,727
Spirodella species, *Spirogyra* species, *Trapa natans* Linnaeus,		1965	**FEDERAL REPUBLIC OF GERMANY.** Ex U.S.S.R. Released in German Democratic Republic. Excellent results in the field.	IBF	313,598, 727
Typha species, *Utricularia* species, *Vallisneria* species, *Wolffia* species,		1964	**GREAT BRITIAN.** Ex China via Hungary. Successful control in confined waters and drains.	MAFF WRO	195,238, 559,629-631
algae - blue green - filamentous - green,		prior 1958	**HONG KONG.** Ex China. Status unknown.		598
diatoms **phytoplankton**		1963	**HUNGARY.** Ex China and U.S.S.R. Field stocking to control weeds in rice fields.		381,629, 727,729
		1959	**INDIA.** Ex China via Hong Kong and Japan. Widely established and successful in fish ponds and tanks.	CIFRI	77,526, 544
		1972	**ITALY.** Ex U.S.S.R. via Yugoslavia. Regularly imported for consumption. Released in ponds near mouth of the Po River giving complete control of weeds.		238

* See 'Introduction' for explanation of headings.

List B continued

Weed and its origin*	Agent and taxonomic references*	Released*	Status and degree of control*	Research organisation*	General references*
(VARIOUS AQUATIC WEEDS AND ALGAE continued)					
		1878 1935	**JAPAN.** Ex China for culture. Importation of large numbers. Widely used to control weeds in ponds, lakes, reservoirs and paddy fields. Reproduction occurs in Japan.		598,629, 665
		1960	**MEXICO.** Ex Taiwan and China. Natural reproduction occurs in Mexico.		598,637
		1976	**NETHERLANDS.** Ex China via Taiwan and Hungary. Yearly experimental field stockings of 300 ha. Excellent to moderate results.	CAR	238,727-730,673
		1984	**NEW ZEALAND.** Ex Malaysia in 1966, 1967 and 1969. Ex Hong Kong in 1971. Very effective in enclosed waters. Unintentionally released but unlikely to breed. Weed management using sterile triploid carp now underway.	MANZ	71,293, 435,578, 648
		1964	**PAKISTAN.** Under evaluation for weed control in reservoirs.		598
		1978	**PANAMA.** Ex China via U.S.A. Under evaluation.		128,129
		1966	**PHILIPPINES.** Origin and status not known.		598,629
		1946	**POLAND.** Ex China via U.S.S.R. Stocking to control weeds in power plant cooling ponds has been successful and replaced other control methods.	IFI	381,432, 629
		1982	**REPUBLIC OF SOUTH AFRICA.** Ex China via Hungary via West Germany. Successful control of *Potamogeton pectinatus* L. in an artificial lake where augmentative releases are made.	DNC RAU	589,590

* See 'Introduction' for explanation of headings.

List B continued

Weed and its origin*	Agent and taxonomic references*	Released*	Status and degree of control*	Research organisation*	General references*
(VARIOUS AQUATIC WEEDS AND ALGAE continued)					
		1959	**ROMANIA.** Ex China. Used in polyculture and weed control.		381,598, 629,729
		1973	**SUDAN.** Used for culture and weed control.		598
		1970	**SWEDEN.** Ex China via Poland via U.S.S.R. Under evaluation.	WPRC	3,598, 629,729
		1964	**SWITZERLAND.** Unsuccessful introduction into a reservior in the Upper Rhine Valley.		238
		1974	Introduced to Upper Rhine. Status unknown.		238
		–	**TAIWAN.** Ex China. Used in polyculture to control weeds and algae and for food.		55
		1950's	**THAILAND.** Ex China via Hong Kong. Used mainly as protein source. Weed control is secondary.		469
		1949	**UNION OF SOVIET SOCIALIST REPUBLICS.** Native to eastern U.S.S.R. and China. Distributed to European and Central Asian areas. Excellent results.	MSU	5,381, 432,598, 674
		1968	**UNITED ARAB EMIRATES.** Ex China via Hong Kong.		598
		1963	**UNITED STATES OF AMERICA.** Ex China. First introduced into AR and AL. Demonstrated to be cost efficient in controlling weeds including *Hydrilla verticillata*. To minimise ecological disruption, attempts have been made to develop sterile variants by: hybridisation of *Ctenopharyngodon idella* x *Aristichthys nobilis*, but the hybrid consumed less vegetation; surgically altering grass carp, but vegetation intake was reduced and sterility not guaranteed; inducing sterile triploids by applying temperature shock or, more recently, high hydrostatic pressure	State (16, 17)	6,114

* See 'Introduction' for explanation of headings.

List B continued

Weed and its origin*	Agent and taxonomic references*	Released*	Status and degree of control*	Research organisation*	General references*

(VARIOUS AQUATIC WEEDS AND ALGAE continued)

Weed and its origin*	Agent and taxonomic references*	Released*	Status and degree of control*	Research organisation*	General references*
			to fertilized diploid eggs. Diploid and/or sterile-triploid grass carp were permitted and released in AL, AR, CO, HI, IA, KS, MO, MS, OK and TN. Only sterile-triploid grass carp were permitted and released in AZ, CA, FL, GA, ID, IL, KY, MA, NC, NE, NM, NV, NY, OH, OR, SD, SC, TX, UT, VA, WV and WY. High pressure-induced sterile-triploid grass carp reduced *Hydrilla verticillata* biomass in irrigation canals by more than 90% in southern CA.		
		1964	**FEDERAL REPUBLIC OF GERMANY.** Ex China and U.S.S.R. via Hungary. Used routinely for localised weed problems. Feasibility studies are underway for larger water bodies and reservoirs.	PO BWRA	40,432, 550,598, 727
		1971	**YUGOSLAVIA.** Successful control but upset aquatic ecosystem.		238
	Hypophthalmichthys molitrix (Cuvier & Valenciennes) (Pisces: Cyprinidae) (silver carp)	appr. 1970	**AUSTRIA.** Field stockings give variable results in controlling algal blooms.	BWA	238,727
		1964	**BULGARIA.** Ex China via U.S.S.R. Mainly used for food production but also for weed control.		381
		after 1962	**CZECHOSLOVAKIA.** Ex China via U.S.S.R. Field stocking for food and weed control.		381
		prior 1970	**FRANCE.** Released in canals to control excessive weed growth.		305
		after 1962	**HUNGARY.** Ex China probably via U.S.S.R. Field stocking.		381
		1959	**INDIA.** Established but not very effective.	CIFRI	526

* See 'Introduction' for explanation of headings.

List B continued

(VARIOUS AQUATIC WEEDS AND ALGAE continued)

Weed and its origin*	Agent and taxonomic references*	Released*	Status and degree of control*	Research organisation*	General references*
		after 1969	NEW ZEALAND. Ex Malaysia. Three releases in enclosed hyper-euthrophic waters with limited success. Weed management using sterile triploid carp now underway.	MANZ	576
		1959	RUMANIA. Ex China. Used in polyculture for food production and weed control.		381
			SWITZERLAND. Released into Greater Moossee to control phytoplankton. Not assessed.		238
		-	TAIWAN. Ex China. Used in polyculture to control plankton algae.		55
		after 1948	UNION OF SOVIET SOCIALIST REPUBLICS. Ex eastern Asia. Successfully utilised in association with other herbivorous fish species.		5
		1968	FEDERAL REPUBLIC OF GERMANY. Satisfactory results providing oxygen levels are sufficiently high and stocking rates adequate.		238
	Oreochromis aureus (Steinbachner)(previously referred to as *Sartherodon aureus*) (Pisces: Cichlidae)	1961	UNITED STATES OF AMERICA. Ex Africa. Established but has detrimental effects on the aquatic systems.		527
	Oreochromis mossambicus (Peters) (Pisces: Cichlidae)	1951	HAWAII, U.S.A. Ex Africa via Singapore. Established on all islands. Introduced for weed control in irrigation systems, live bait for tuna fishing, food fish and sport fish.	BAF	50,542
		1953	INDIA. Ex Africa. Well established but of limited value in controlling soft-leaved weeds and filamentous algae.	CIFRI	526,581

* See 'Introduction' for explanation of headings.

List B continued

(VARIOUS AQUATIC WEEDS AND ALGAE continued)

Weed and its origin*	Agent and taxonomic references*	Released*	Status and degree of control*	Research organisation* references*	General references*
		-	**INDONESIA.** Helped control filamentous algae.		544
		1956	**MARIANA ISLANDS.** Successfully controlled *Potamogeton crispus* and possibly *Utricularia* species.		458,544
		1965	**THAILAND.** Ex East Africa via Japan. Used mainly as a protein source. Weed control is secondary.		469
		1916	**UNION OF SOVIET SOCIALIST REPUBLICS.** Ex Africa. Successfully controlling weeds in power plant cooling ponds.	MSU	674
	Oreochromis niloticus (Linnaeus) (formerly *Tilapia nilotica*) (Pisces: Cichlidae)	-	**THAILAND.** Ex East Africa via Japan. Protein source. Weed control is secondary.		469
	Osphronemus goramy Lacepedes (Pisces: Osphronemidae) (giant gourami)	appr. 1800	**INDIA.** Ex Java. Stocked in Botanic Gardens at Calcutta but perished by 1941.	CBG	331,526
		1865	Ex Mauritius. Breeding occurred in Government House ponds at Madras but condition of stock not satisfactory.	GM	331
		1916	Ex Java and Mauritius. Well established in Madras State and successfully transplanted to other areas.		331
	Puntius javanicus (Bleeker) (Pisces: Cyprinidae)	-	**INDONESIA.** In conjunction with *Ctenopharyngodon idella* effectively controls *Enhydrias augustipetala* and *Chara* species.		544
		-	**MALAYSIA.** Used to control weeds in fish culture ponds.		544
	Tilapia macrochir (Boulenger) (Pisces: Cichlidae)	1958	**HAWAII, U.S.A.** Ex Zaire. Established on Oahu and Maui. Provides some control.	BAF	50,542

* See 'Introduction' for explanation of headings.

List B *continued*

Weed and its origin*	Agent and taxonomic references*	Released*	Status and degree of control*	Research organisation*	General references*
(VARIOUS AQUATIC WEEDS AND ALGAE continued)					
	Tilapia melanopleura Dumeril (Pisces: Cichlidae)	1957	**HAWAII, U.S.A.** Ex Zaire. Established on Kauai. Introduced to control weeds too coarse for *Oreochromis mossambicus*, such as water hyacinth.	BAF	50,542
		-	**INDONESIA.** Not as effective as *Tilapia zillii* in controlling *Fimbristylis* species.		544,598
		1965	**THAILAND.** Ex East Africa via Japan. Used mainly as a protein source. Weed control is secondary.		469
	Tilapia zillii (Gervais) (Pisces: Cichlidae)	1957	**HAWAII, U.S.A.** Ex Africa via Antigua. Established on Hawaii, Maui and Oahu. Successfully controlled weeds in reservoirs.	BAF	50,542
			INDONESIA. More effective than *Tilapia melanopleura* in controlling *Fimbristylis* species.		544
		1956	**MARIANA ISLANDS.** Ex Hawaii. Released on Guam. Not established.		458
		-	**UNITED STATES OF AMERICA.** Ex Africa. Unsuitable for control because of high mortality and low feeding activity.		527

* See 'Introduction' for explanation of headings.

List C: Native organisms utilised and their target weeds

Weed and its origin*	Agent and taxonomic references*	Status and degree of control*	Research organisation*	General references*
AMARANTHACEAE				
Amaranthus retroflexus Linnaeus (pigweed)	*Disonycha glabrata* (Fabricius) (Coleoptera: Chrysomelidae)	**UNITED STATES OF AMERICA.** Releases of adult beetles from MS were made in the Red River Valley, ND in 1979 and 1980 but failed to overwinter.	State (27)	21
Amaranthus spinosus Linnaeus tropical America (spiny amaranth)	*Hypolixus truncatulus* (Fabricius) (Coleoptera: Curculionidae)	**THAILAND.** Augmentative releases of this insect have resulted in a satisfactory degree of control and replaced the use of herbicides.	NBCRC	466,469
ARACEAE				
Pistia stratiotes Linnaeus cosmopolitan tropical, sub-tropical (water lettuce)	*Epipsammia pectinicornis* (Hampson) (previously referred to as *Namangana pectinicornis* (Hampson) and incorrectly referred to as *Episamia pectinicornis* Hampson) (Lepidoptera: Noctuidae)	**THAILAND.** Augmentative releases have resulted in successful natural control. Used to replace herbicides in controlling occasional infestations.	NBCRC	632,469
ASCLEPIADACEAE				
Morrenia odorata Lindle Argentina (milkweed vine, strangler vine)	*Phytophthora palmivora* (Butler) Butler [previously incorrectly referred to as *Phytophthora citrophthora* (R.E. & E.H. Smith) Leonian] (fungus: Peronosporales)	**UNITED STATES OF AMERICA.** Formulation registered in 1981 and marketed as DeVine to control the weed in citrus orchards. Excellent control of seedlings and large plants through effects of the disease on roots.		73,74, 198,554, 649,651

* See 'Introduction' for explanation of headings.

List C continued

Weed and its origin*	Agent and taxonomic references*	Status and degree of control*	Research organisation*	General references*
ASTERACEAE				
Acropilon repens (Linnaeus) de Candolle (= *Centaurea repens* Linnaeus) eastern Europe, central and western Asia (Russian knapweed)	*Aceria acroptiloni* Shevtchencko & Kovalev (Acarina: Eriophyidae)	**UNION OF SOVIET SOCIALIST REPUBLICS.** Ex central Asia. Abundance in cultivation is maintained by means of preservation of this species on special plots (two hectares) among crops in Uzbekistan. Successful control of seed production of Russian knapweed is observed in different crops.	ZIAS	372
	Subanguina picridis Kirjanova & Ivanova (previously referred to as *Paranguina picridis* Kirjanova & Ivanova) (Nematoda: Tylenchidae)	**UNION OF SOVIET SOCIALIST REPUBLICS.** Ex central Asia. Application of a suspension of nematode larvae and water in autumn and spring proved to be particularly successful in perennial grass crops, e.g. alfalfa, in Uzbekistan. Mass rearing of nematodes and gall collection were performed on special plots (two hectares) in crops.	ZIAS	372
Baccharis halimifolia Linnaeus North America (groundsel baccharis, consumption weed)	*Rhopalomyia californica* Felt (Diptera: Cecidomyiidae)	**UNITED STATES OF AMERICA.** Ex CA and released in TX in 1985. Not established.	USDA (9) State (22)	41
Baccharis neglecta Britton south-west United States and Mexico (baccharis, jara dulce)	*Rhopalomyia californica* Felt (Diptera: Cecidomyiidae)	**UNITED STATES OF AMERICA.** Ex CA and released in TX in 1985. Not established.	USDA (9) State (22)	41
CACTACEAE				
Opuntia ficus-indica (Linnaeus) Miller (= *Opuntia megacantha* (Salm-Dyck) Central America	*Fusarium oxysporum* Schlecktendahl ex Fries (fungus: Hyphomycetes)	**HAWAII, U.S.A.** Field inoculations utilized between 1943 and 1949 gave good control but were discontinued when introduction of insect agents began.	BAF	205,312, 704

* See 'Introduction' for explanation of headings.

List C continued

(CACTACEAE continued)

Weed and its origin*	Agent and taxonomic references*	Status and degree of control*	Research organisation*	General references*
Opuntia littoralis (Engelmann) Cockerell southwest coast U.S.A. including Santa Cruz Island (prickly pear)	*Chelinidea tabulata* (Burmeister) (Hemiptera: Coreidae)	**UNITED STATES OF AMERICA.** Ex TX 1945. Found established in 1961 prior to making the second release on Santa Cruz Island. Ex TX 1961. Established but of minor inportance on Santa Cruz Island.	State (5)	220,223
	Chelinidea vittiger Uhler (Hemiptera: Coreidae)	**UNITED STATES OF AMERICA.** Ex TX 1945. Not established on Santa Cruz Island. Ex southern CA 1961. Stocks obtained from *Opuntia vaseyi*. Establishment on Santa Cruz Island is tenuous due to competition by *Dactylopius opuntiae*.	State (5)	151,220, 223
	Dactylopius confusus (Cockerell) (Hemiptera: Dactylopiidae)	**UNITED STATES OF AMERICA.** Ex AZ 1942. Not established on Santa Cruz Island.	State (5)	220,223
	Dactylopius opuntiae (Cockerell) (Hemiptera: Dactylopiidae)	**UNITED STATES OF AMERICA.** Ex CA 1940. Not established on Santa Cruz Island.	State (5)	220,223
	Dactylopius tomentosus (Lamarck) (Hemiptera: Dactylopiidae)	**UNITED STATES OF AMERICA.** Ex CA 1940. Released on Santa Cruz Island. Not established.	State (5)	223
	Melitara prodenialis Walker (Lepidoptera: Pyralidae)	**UNITED STATES OF AMERICA.** Ex TX 1945. Released on Santa Cruz Island. Not established. Ex TX 1962. Released on Santa Cruz Island. Not established.	State (5)	220,223
	Olycella juctolineella (Hulst) (Lepidoptera: Pyralidae)	**UNITED STATES OF AMERICA.** Ex TX 1961. Released on Santa Cruz Island. Not established.	State (5)	220,223

* See 'Introduction' for explanation of headings.

List C continued

Weed and its origin*	Agent and taxonomic references*	Status and degree of control*	Research organisation*	General references*
(CACTACEAE continued)				
Opuntia oricola Philbrick southwest coast U.S.A. including Santa Cruz Island (prickly pear)	*Chelinidea tabulata* (Burmeister) (Hemiptera: Coreidae)	**UNITED STATES OF AMERICA.** Ex TX 1945. Found established in 1961 prior to making the second release on Santa Cruz Island. Ex TX 1961. Established, but of minor importance on Santa Cruz Island.	State (5)	220,223
	Chelinidea vittiger Uhler (Hemiptera: Coreidae)	**UNITED STATES OF AMERICA.** Ex TX 1945. Not established on Santa Cruz Island. Ex southern CA 1961. Stocks obtained from *Opuntia vaseyi*. Establishment on Santa Cruz Island is tenuous due to competition by *Dactylopius opuntiae*.	State (5)	151,220, 223
	Dactylopius confusus (Cockerell) (Hemiptera: Dactylopiidae)	**UNITED STATES OF AMERICA.** Ex AZ 1942. Not established on Santa Cruz Island.	State (5)	220,223
	Dactylopius opuntiae (Cockerell) (Hemiptera: Dactylopiidae)	**UNITED STATES OF AMERICA.** Ex CA 1940. Not established on Santa Cruz Island.	State (5)	220,223
	Dactylopius tomentosus (Lamarck) (Hemiptera: Dactylopiidae)	**UNITED STATES OF AMERICA.** Ex CA 1940. Released on Santa Cruz Island. Not established.	State (5)	223
	Melitara prodenialis Walker (Lepidoptera: Pyralidae)	**UNITED STATES OF AMERICA.** Ex TX 1945. Released on Santa Cruz Island. Not established. Ex TX 1962 and released on Santa Cruz Island. Not established.	State (5)	220,223
	Olycella junctolineella (Hulst) (Lepidoptera: Pyralidae)	**UNITED STATES OF AMERICA.** Ex TX 1961. Released on Santa Cruz Island. Not established.	State (5)	220,223

* See 'Introduction' for explanation of headings.

List C continued

Weed and its origin*	Agent and taxonomic references*	Status and degree of control*	Research organisation*	General references*
CAESALPINIACEAE				
Cassia obtusifolia Linnaeus (sicklepod)	*Alternaria cassiae* Jurair & Khan (fungus: Hyphomycetes)	**UNITED STATES OF AMERICA.** Excellent control was obtained in widespread field trials. A micoherbicide, CASST, is pending registration.	USDA (5)	73,76,94, 679,680
CONVOLVULACEAE				
Convolvulus arvensis Linnaeus Eurasia, northern Africa (European bindweed, field bindweed)	*Chelymorpha cassidea* (Fabricius) (Coleoptera: Chrysomelidae)	**CANADA.** Native organism collected in 1979 in Saskatchewan and released in Alberta in an attempt to extend its range. Not established.	CDA	408
	Chirida guttata (Olivier) (Coleoptera: Chrysomelidae)	**CANADA.** Native organism collected in 1979 in Saskatchewan and released in Alberta in an attempt to extend its range. Not established.	CDA	408
	Metriona purpurata (Boheman) (Coleoptera: Chrysomelidae)	**CANADA.** Native organism collected in 1979 in Saskatchewan and released in Alberta in an attempt to extend its range. Not established.	CDA	408
Convolvulus sepium Linnaeus North America (hedge bindweed)	*Chirida guttata* (Olivier) (Coleoptera: Chrysomelidae)	**CANADA.** Native organism collected in 1971 in Ontario and released in British Columbia. Not established.	UBC	408
	Metriona bicolor (Fabricius) (Coleoptera: Chrysomelidae)	**CANADA.** Native organism collected in 1971 in Ontario. Released and established in British Columbia. In 1985 found 14 km from release site.	CDA	267,408
CUSCUTACEAE				
Cuscuta australis R. Brown (dodder)	*Colletotrichum gloeosporioides* f. sp. *cuscutae* (Penzig) Penzig & Saccardo (fungus: Coelomycetes)	**PEOPLE'S REPUBLIC OF CHINA.** Micoherbicide formulated with trade name LUBAO 1 used to control weed in soybean fields. Degradation of fungus strain occurred in 1970's followed by decrease in use of the formulation. New formulation, LUBAO 1 S22, is now in use.	CAAS	73,683

* See 'Introduction' for explanation of headings.

List C continued

Weed and its origin*	Agent and taxonomic references*	Status and degree of control*	Research organisation*	General references*
(CUSCUTACEAE continued)				
Cuscuta chinensis Lamarck (dodder)	*Colletotrichum gloeosporioides* f. sp. *cuscutae* (Penzig) Penzig & Saccardo (fungus: Coelomycetes)	**PEOPLE'S REPUBLIC OF CHINA.** Micoherbicide formulated with trade name LUBAO 1 used to control weeds in soybean fields. Degradation of fungus strain occurred in 1970's followed by decrease in use of the formulation. New formulation, LUBAO 1 S22, is now in use.	CAAS	73,683
Cuscuta europaea Linnaeus (dodder)	*Melanagromyza cuscutae* Héring (Diptera: Agromyzidae)	**UNION OF SOVIET SOCIALIST REPUBLICS.** Natural populations augmented in Kazakhstan by spring releases of adults emerging from plant material kept indoors during winter.		218
Cuscuta lehmanniana Bunge (dodder)	*Melanagromyza cuscutae* Héring (Diptera: Agromyzidae)	**UNION OF SOVIET SOCIALIST REPUBLICS.** Natural populations augmented in Kazakhstan by spring releases of adults emerging from plant material kept indoors during winter.		218
Cuscuta lupuliformis Krock (dodder)	*Melanagromyza cuscutae* Héring (Diptera: Agromyzidae)	**UNION OF SOVIET SOCIALIST REPUBLICS.** Natural populations augmented in Kazakhstan by spring releases of adults emerging from plant material kept indoors during winter.		218
Cuscuta maritima Makino (dodder)	*Colletotrichum gloeosporioides* f. sp. *cuscutae* (Penzig) Penzig & Saccardo (fungus: Coelomycetes)	**PEOPLE'S REPUBLIC OF CHINA.** Micoherbicide formulated with trade name LUBAO 1 used to control weed in soybean fields. Degradation of fungus strain occurred in 1970's followed by decrease in use of the formulation. New formulation, LUBAO 1 S22, is now in use.	CAAS	73,683
Cuscuta spp. (dodders)	*Phytomyza orobanchia* Kaltenbach (Diptera: Agromyzidae)	**UNION OF SOVIET SOCIALIST REPUBLICS.** Large scale experiments in the 1950s. Results not reported but effects may have been limited by parasitism.		360,370

* See 'Introduction' for explanation of headings.

List C continued

Weed and its origin*	Agent and taxonomic references*	Status and degree of control*	Research organisation*	General references*
CYPERACEAE				
Cyperus rotundus Linnaeus India (nut grass, purple nutsedge)	*Bactra verutana* Zeller (Lepidoptera: Tortricidae)	**UNITED STATES OF AMERICA.** 1972. Within release plots there was a 30 to 68% reduction of aboveground growth 4 to 7 weeks after last release, depending on number of larvae per release and the number of releases. Seed cotton crop yield following control of *Cyperus rotundus* with *Bactra verutana* was equivalent to yield from crops not infected with the weed.	USDA (5)	202
	Chaetococcus australis (Froggatt) (previously referred to as *Antonina australis* Green) (Hemiptera: Pseudococcidae)	**AUSTRALIA.** May cause severe damage locally but overall control is slight. Dispersed by farmers between 1901 and 1910.		204,314, 634,664, 706
EBENACEAE				
Diospyros virginiana Linnaeus North America (persimmon)	*Acremonium diospyri* (Crandall) W. Gams (= *Cephalosporium diospyri* Crandall) (fungus: Hyphomycetes)	**UNITED STATES OF AMERICA.** Very effective when cut stumps are inoculated with a spore suspension of this pathogen. Using this method only unwanted trees are killed. In practical use.	State (2)	73,651, 704
FABACEAE				
Aeschynomene virginica (Linnaeus) Britton, Stern & Poggenburg Central and North America (northern jointvetch)	*Colletotrichum gloeosporioides* (Penzig) Penzig & Saccardo f. sp. *aeschynomene* (fungus: Coelomycetes)	**UNITED STATES OF AMERICA.** Formulation registered in 1982 and marketed as COLLEGO. Effective control of the weed in rice and soybean crops by girdling the hollow stems. Is active over a wide range of environmental conditions.	State (3)	73,130, 198,613, 650,651
HALORAGACEAE				
Myriophyllum spicatum Linnaeus Eurasia (Eurasian watermilfoil)	*Phytobius leucogaster* (Marsham) [previously referred to as *Litodactylus leucogaster* (Marsham)] (Coleoptera: Curculionidae)	**UNITED STATES OF AMERICA.** Transferred to FL from CA in 1979. Establishment not confirmed.	USDA (3)	57

* See 'Introduction' for explanation of headings.

List C continued

Weed and its origin*	Agent and taxonomic references*	Status and degree of control*	Research organisation*	General references*
MALVACEAE				
Abutilon theophrasti Medikus China (velvet leaf)	*Colletotrichum coccodes* (Wallroth) Hughes (fungus: Coelomycetes)	**UNITED STATES OF AMERICA.** Under large scale field tests with fair prospects for commercial/practical use.		73,715, 716
Malva pusilla (= *M. rotundifolia* Linnaeus) (round-leaf mallow)	*Colletotrichum gloeosporioides* (Penzig) Penzig & Saccardo f. sp. *malvae* (fungus: Coelomycetes)	**CANADA.** Mycoherbicide BioMal is currently being developed.		73,448
ONAGRACEAE				
Ludwigia adscendens (Linnaeus) Hara Indo-Australian (water primrose)	*Altica foveicollis* Jacoby (Coleoptera: Chrysomelidae)	**THAILAND.** Caused considerable damage with satisfactory degree of control.	NBCRC	469
OROBANCHACEAE				
Orobanche crenata Forskal (broomrape)	*Phytomyza orobanchia* Kaltenbach (Diptera: Agromyzidae)	**SYRIA.** Achieving 79% damage in coastal areas. Less effective inland but with mass rearing may prove a very effective agent.	ICARDA	392
Orobanche cumana Walter Eurasia (broomrape)	*Phytomyza orobanchia* Kaltenbach (Diptera: Agromyzidae)	**YUGOSLAVIA.** Can achieve considerable control by destroying up to 96% of seeds.	PPIB	389,615
Orobanche ramosa Linnaeus Eurasia (broomrape)	*Fusarium oxysporum* var. *orthoceras* Schlechtendahl ex Fries (fungus: Hyphomycetes)	**UNION OF SOVIET SOCIALIST REPUBLICS.** Can destroy up to 70% of seed. Effectiveness depends on soil temperature and humidity. Presumed under practical use.		73,218
	Phytomyza orobanchia Kaltenbach (Diptera: Agromyzidae)	**UNION OF SOVIET SOCIALIST REPUBLICS.** Good control achieved resulting in significantly increased crop production.	AUPPI	186,218, 360,370, 615

* See 'Introduction' for explanation of headings.

List C continued

Weed and its origin*	Agent and taxonomic references*	Status and degree of control*	Research organisation*	General references*
(OROBANCHACEAE continued)		YUGOSLAVIA. Can achieve considerable control by destroying up to 96% of seeds.	PPIB	389,615
POLYGONACEAE				
Rumex obtusifolius Linnaeus Europe, west and north Asia, North America, northern Africa (broadleaf dock)	*Gastrophysa atrocyanea* Motschulsky (Coleoptera: Chrysomelidae)	JAPAN. Released in the Noto Peninsula. Quickly established, increased their population and spread rapidly. Populations of the beetle reached satisfactory levels within four years of release.	MAF PIJ	437,460, 461
PONTEDERIACEAE				
Eichhornia crassipes (Martius) Solms-laubach South America (water hyacinth)	*Bellura densa* (Walker) [previously referred to as *Arzama densa* (Walker)] (Lepidoptera: Noctuidae)	UNITED STATES OF AMERICA. Field releases of laboratory-reared first instar larvae and eggs had little impact. Field releases of larvae dipped in 2,4-D provided total supression in small plots in LA. Larvae reported naturally from taro *Calocasia esculenta* L., in FL.	USAE USDA (5) State (23)	17,244, 676,677
	Cercospora rodmanii Conway (fungus: Hyphomycetes)	UNITED STATES OF AMERICA. Undergone testing for commercial development. Plant reaction is variable and must be judged from site to site.	USDA (4)	72,73,75, 113,199,
	Neochetina bruchi Hustache (Coleoptera: Curculionidae)	ARGENTINA. Transferred in 1974 from Rio Panama Delta region to near La Rioja Province in arid central west. After six years water surface cover was reduced from 50% to 4-8%.	USDAA	162
SOLANACEAE				
Solanum elaeagnifolium Cavanilles North America (silverleaf nightshade)	*Nothanguina phyllobia* Thorne (Nematoda: Neotylenchidae)	UNITED STATES OF AMERICA. When large numbers of infective larvae are introduced to the plant they spread rapidly and cause reduced top growth. Activity of the nematodes depends on moist conditions.	USDA (6)	496,558

* See 'Introduction' for explanation of headings.

List D: Previously used or potential agents found in exotic ranges where their deliberate release has not been recorded

Weed and its origin*	Agent and taxonomic references*	Observation date*	Status and degree of control*	Research organisation*	General references*
ASTERACEAE					
Ageratina adenophora (Sprengel) R. King & H. Robinson (= *Eupatorium adenophorum* Sprengel), 351 Central America (crofton weed)	*Cercospora eupatorii* Peck (fungus: Hyphomycetes)	1954	**AUSTRALIA.** Accidental introduction from U.S.A. via Hawaii. Probably carried by *Proccidochares utilis* when it was released (see List A). Impact unknown.		292
		1958	**NEW ZEALAND.** Accidental introduction probably ex U.S.A. via Hawaii via Australia with *Proccidochares utilis* (see List A). Impact unknown.	DSIR	292
	Proccidochares utilis Stone (Diptera: Tephritidae)	pre 1984	**PEOPLE'S REPUBLIC OF CHINA.** Found in Nepalese/ Chinese border (see List A).	KIEC	289,720
Ambrosia artemisiifolia Linnaeus North America (annual ragweed)	*Albugo tragopogonis* Persoon ex S.F. Gray (fungus: Peronosporales)	1965	**UNION OF SOVIET SOCIALIST REPUBLICS.** Accidental introduction. Endemic to Canada. 90% reduction of plant weight and 95 to 100% reduction in seed production when spores were applied to field populations of the weed.		281,678
Carduus acanthoides Linnaeus Eurasia, North Africa, western Asia (plumeless thistle)	*Cassida rubiginosa* Müller (Coleoptera: Chrysomelidae)	prior 1902	**CANADA.** Accidental introduction of European origin with minimal effect.		685
		–	**UNITED STATES OF AMERICA.** Accidental introduction of European origin. Established in MD, VA and throughout northeastern U.S.A. No significant control.	USDA (1) State (1)	291,685
Carduus nutans Linnaeus Europe, Asia (nodding thistle, musk thistle)	*Cassida rubiginosa* Müller (Coleoptera: Chrysomelidae)	prior 1902	**CANADA.** Accidental introduction of European origin with minimal effect. Not main host.		64,685

* See 'Introduction' for explanation of headings.

List D continued

Weed and its origin*	Agent and taxonomic references*	Observation date*	Status and degree of control*	Research organisation*	General references*
(ASTERACEAE continued)					
Carduus thoermeri Weinmann (previously referred to as *Carduus nutans* Linnaeus) Europe, Asia (nodding thistle, musk thistle)	*Cassida rubiginosa* Müller (Coleoptera: Chrysomelidae)	-	**UNITED STATES OF AMERICA.** Accidental introduction of European origin. Established in MD, VA and throughout northeastern U.S.A. No significant control.	USDA (1) State (1)	291,685
Centaurea cyanus Linnaeus Europe (cornflower, bachelor button)	*Urophora quadrifasciata* (Meigen) (Diptera: Tephritidae)	prior 1979	**UNITED STATES OF AMERICA.** Ex U.S.S.R. via natural dispersal from established colonies in Canada. Attacks more than 30% of capitula in WA.	State (9)	529
Centaurea diffusa Lamarck southern Europe, Asia Minor (diffuse knapweed)	*Urophora quadrifasciata* (Meigen) (Diptera: Tephritidae)	prior 1979	**UNITED STATES OF AMERICA.** Ex U.S.S.R. via natural dispersal from established colonies in Canada. Established in ID, OR, MT and WA. Attacks more than 90% of capitula in WA.	State (6, 7,9,15)	114,528, 620,621
Centaurea jacea x nigra Europe (meadow knapweed)	*Urophora quadrifasciata* (Meigen) (Diptera: Tephritidae)	prior 1979	**UNITED STATES OF AMERICA.** Ex U.S.S.R. via natural dispersal from established colonies in Canada. Established in OR and WA.	State (9,15)	114,529
Centaurea maculosa Lamarck southern Europe (spotted knapweed)	*Urophora quadrifasciata* (Meigen) (Diptera: Tephritidae)	prior 1979	**UNITED STATES OF AMERICA.** Ex U.S.S.R. via natural dispersal from established colonies in Canada. Established in ID, MT, OR and WA. Attacks more than 90% of capitula in WA.	State (6, 7,9,15)	114,410, 528,620, 621
Centaurea virgata Lamarck ssp. *squarrosa* Gugler Eurasia (squarrose knapweed)	*Urophora quadrifasciata* (Meigen) (Diptera: Tephritidae)	prior 1979	**UNITED STATES OF AMERICA.** Ex U.S.S.R. via natural dispersal from established colonies in Canada. Moved into this weed in OR from populations of *Centaurea diffusa* and *C. maculosa*. At one site in OR, 79% of weed capitula were galled by the fly, which reduced seed production by 68%.	State (9)	560

* See 'Introduction' for explanation of headings.

List D *continued*

(ASTERACEAE continued)

Weed and its origin*	Agent and taxonomic references*	Observation date*	Status and degree of control*	Research organisation*	General references*
Chromolaena odorata (Linnaeus) R. King & H. Robinson (= *Eupatorium odoratum* Linnaeus) 352 Caribbean, Central and South America (Siam weed)	*Pareuchaetes pseudoinsulata* Rego Barros (previously referred to as *Ammalo insulata* Walker) (Lepidoptera: Arctiidae)	-	**BRUNEI.** Natural spread from Malaysia (Sabah).		91,92
		-	**PHILIPPINES.** Natural spread probably from Malaysia (Sabah) or accidental introduction.		92
Cirsium arvense (Linnaeus) Scopoli Europe, northern Africa (Canada thistle, creeping thistle, Californian thistle)	*Cassida rubiginosa* Müller (Coleoptera: Chrysomelidae)	prior 1902	**CANADA.** Ex Europe in eastern Canada. Causes local defoliation but no control is achieved. High larval parasitism.	CDA	361,685
		-	**UNITED STATES OF AMERICA.** Accidental introduction of Eurasian origin. Established in MD, VA and throughout northeastern U.S.A. No significant control.	USDA (1) State (1)	291,363, 685
	Puccinia punctiformis (Strauss) Roehling (fungus: Uredinales)	prior 1918	**AUSTRALIA.** Accidental introduction. Negligible effect	DCE	52
		-	**NEW ZEALAND.** Accidental introduction of European origin. Reduces vigour and retards development when the spread of spores is assisted.		96
Cirsium vulgare (Savi) Tenore Eurasia, northern Africa (bull thistle, spear thistle)	*Cassida rubiginosa* Müller (Coleoptera: Chrysomelidae)	prior 1902	**CANADA.** Ex Europe in eastern Canada. Not the main host and effects insignificant. No control.		267,685
		-	**UNITED STATES OF AMERICA.** Accidental introduction of European origin. Established in MD, VA and throughout northeastern U.S.A. No significant control.	USDA (1) State (1)	291,685

* See 'Introduction' for explanation of headings.

List D continued

Weed and its origin*	Agent and taxonomic references*	Observation date*	Status and degree of control*	Research organisation*	General references*
(ASTERACEAE continued)					
Elephantopus mollis Humbolt, Bonplaud & Kunth (= *Elephantopus scaber* Linnaeus) Central America, West Indies (elephant's foot, tobacco weed, tavoko ni veikau)	*Tetreuaresta obscuriventris* Loew (Diptera: Tephritidae)	-	**NUIE.** Accidental introduction of South American origin.		686
		1958	**TONGA.** Accidental or unrecorded introduction, probably from Fiji. Found on Tongatapu.		91,92
		-	**VANUATU.** Accidental or unrecorded introduction, probably from Fiji. Found on Efate, Malakula and Anatom.		91,92
Matricaria perforata Merat	*Apion hookeri* Kirby (Coleoptera: Curculionidae)	prior 1990	**CANADA.** Ex Europe. 20% of capitula attacked in Nova Scotia. Possible release in western Canada in 1992.		267
Xanthium spinosum Linnaeus cosmopolitan (Bathurst burr)	*Euaresta bullans* (Wiedemann) (previously referred to as *Camaromyia bullans*) (Diptera: Tephritidae)	1928	**AUSTRALIA.** Accidental introduction of South American origin. Not generally effective but may destroy local weed stands.		706
		-	**REPUBLIC OF SOUTH AFRICA.** Accidental introduction of South American origin. Infests up to 20% of burrs.		237
Xanthium strumarium Linnaeus (=*Xanthium pungens* Wallroth) cosmopolitan (noogoora burr, cockleburr)	*Puccinia xanthii* Schweinitz (fungus: Uredinales)	1974	**AUSTRALIA.** Accidental introduction of North American origin. Rapidly established and spread throughout all of eastern Australia. Progressive reduction in seed bank has resulted in excellent control in wetter areas. Weed no longer a problem in most of Queensland. No control in the drier Northern Territory.		79,340

* See 'Introduction' for explanation of headings.

List D continued

Weed and its origin*	Agent and taxonomic references*	Observation date*	Status and degree of control*	Research organisation*	General references*
CACTACEAE					
Opuntia dillenii (Ker-Gawler) Haworth Florida and West Indies (prickly pear)	*Cactoblastis cactorum* (Bergroth) (Lepidoptera: Pyralidae)	1963	**U.S. VIRGIN ISLANDS.** Probably spread naturally from releases made on Nevis, Antigua and Monserrat in 1957 to 1960. Also recorded on *Opuntia antillana*, *Consolea (Opuntia) rubescens* and *Consolea (Opuntia) moniliformis*.		607,666
		1966	**PUERTO RICO.** Probably spread naturally from releases made on Nevis, Antigua and Monserrat in 1957 to 1960. Also recorded on *Opuntia antillana*, *Consolea (Opuntia) rubescens* and *Consolea (Opuntia) moniliformis*.		666
Opuntia ficus-indica (Linnaeus) Miller (= *Opuntia megacantha* Salm-Dyck) Central and North America (Indian fig)	*Cactoblastis cactorum* (Bergroth) (Lepidoptera: Pyralidae)	1963	**U.S. VIRGIN ISLANDS.** Probably spread naturally from releases made on Nevis, Antigua and Monserrat in 1957 to 1960.		666
		1966	**PUERTO RICO.** Probably spread naturally from releases made on Nevis, Antigua and Monserrat in 1957 to 1960.		666
Opuntia inermis de Candolle Mexico (common pest pear, common prickly pear)	*Tetranychus opuntiae* Banks (Acarina: Tetranychidae)	1922 or 1923	**AUSTRALIA.** Introduced accidentally with other organisms. It spread rapidly to the field from cages and began providing good control of the pear in conjunction with *Dactylopius opuntiae* in some situations. Following the control of pear by *Cactoblastis cactorum* the mite declined to a scattered distribution.	CPPB	169,170, 173,284, 706
Opuntia repens Bello Americas north of Guatemala	*Cactoblastis cactorum* (Bergroth) (Lepidoptera: Pyralidae)	1963	**U.S. VIRGIN ISLANDS.** Probably spread naturally from releases made on Nevis, Antigua and Monserrat in 1957 to 1960.		666
		1966	**PUERTO RICO.** Probably spread naturally from releases made on Nevis, Antigua and Monserrat in 1957 to 1960.		666

* See 'Introduction' for explanation of headings.

List D continued

(CACTACEAE continued)

Weed and its origin*	Agent and taxonomic references*	Observation date*	Status and degree of control*	Research organisation*	General references*
Opuntia triacantha (Willdenow) Sweet, 670,671 Caribbean Islands	Cactoblastis cactorum (Bergroth) (Lepidoptera: Pyralidae)	1963	U.S. VIRGIN ISLANDS. Probably spread naturally from releases made on Nevis, Antigua and Monserrat in 1957 to 1960.		666
		1966	PUERTO RICO. Probably spread naturally from releases made on Nevis, Antigua and Monserrat in 1957 to 1960.		666
Opuntia vulgaris Miller Argentina, Brazil, Paraguay, Uruguay (drooping prickly pear, Barbary fig)	Dactylopius ceylonicus (Green) (Hemiptera: Dactylopiidae)	1795	INDIA. Ex Brazil. Introduced for commercial purposes in the mistaken belief that it was Dactylopius coccus Costa. Established on Opuntia vulgaris and provided control of the weed. Subsequently the insect was spread to southern India and Sri Lanka (see List A) as the first attempt at deliberate biological control of a weed. Complete control was achieved in India.		220,544, 662
	Dactylopius opuntiae (Cockerell) (Hemiptera: Dactylopiidae)	-	KENYA. Accidental introduction probably from U.S.A. via South Africa via Tanzania in 1958 when Dactylopius ceylonicus was introduced.		150
Opuntia spp. (prickly pear)	Cactoblastis cactorum (Bergroth) (Lepidoptera: Pyralidae)	after 1957	ST. KITTS. Natural spread from Nevis by 1964.	IIBC	27,91, 607
		1963	U.S. VIRGIN ISLAND. Probably from Nevis. Established.		607
		1989	UNITED STATES OF AMERICA. Found on Opuntia sp. in Florida. Concern is that this moth will become a pest of native Opuntia sp.	FDA State (3)	246
	Dactylopius sp. (Hemiptera: Dactylopiidae)	early 1900's	REUNION. Probably ex Mauritius. Successfully controlled Opuntia speices.		237

* See 'Introduction' for explanation of headings.

List D continued

Weed and its origin*	Agent and taxonomic references*	Observation date*	Status and degree of control*	Research organisation*	General references*
CLUSIACEAE					
Hypericum perforatum Linnaeus Asia, Europe, northern Africa (St John's wort, klamath weed)	*Chrysolina hyperici* (Forster) [previously referred to as *Chrysomela hyperici* (Forster)] (Coleoptera: Chrysomelidae)	1965	**HAWAII, U.S.A.** Ex England via California, U.S.A. Discovered in 1970. Believed to have been introduced accidentally with *C. quadrigemina*. Present status unknown.	HDOA	136,138, 212
CYPERACEAE					
Cyperus rotundus Linnaeus India (nut grass, purple nutsedge)	*Bactra venosana* (Zeller) (previously referred to as *Bactra truculenta* Meyrick) (Lepidoptera: Tortricidae)	-	**NEW CALEDONIA.** Accidental introduction.		686
FABACEAE					
Cytisus scoparius (Linnaeus) Link central and southern Europe (Scotch broom)	*Leucoptera spartifoliella* Hübner (Lepidoptera: Lyonetiidae)	1950	**NEW ZEALAND.** Accidental introduction of European origin. Widely established and very numerous in some areas. Kills broom twigs, and sometimes complete branches.	DSIR	583
		prior 1960	**UNITED STATES OF AMERICA.** Accidental introduction of European origin. Established in CA, OR and WA. Deliberate introduction ex France in 1960 (see List A). Pupae heavily parasitised by Hymenoptera in OR. Impact negligible.	USDA (7) State (9,15)	10,200, 681
Sesbania punicea (Cavanille) Bentham Argentina, Brazil, Uruguay	*Trichapion lativentre* (Béguin-Billecocq) (Coleoptera: Apionidae)	prior 1980	**REPUBLIC OF SOUTH AFRICA.** Accidental introduction. First noticed near Durban. Populations increased and spread widely. Redistributed to new areas since 1983. Prevents seed production and stunts growth of plants (see List A).	PPRI	296,298, 299,300, 440

* See 'Introduction' for explanation of headings.

List D continued

Weed and its origin*	Agent and taxonomic references*	Observation date*	Status and degree of control*	Research organisation* references*	General references*
HYDROCHARITACEAE					
Hydrilla verticillata (Linnaeus f) Royle, Asia, Australia, Africa (hydrilla)	*Parapoynx diminutalis* Snellen (Lepidoptera: Pyralidae)	prior 1975	**UNITED STATES OF AMERICA**. Accidental introduction of Asian origin. Well established and range expanding in FL. Noticeable damage to the weed at some sites but no substantial control.	USDA (4) State (3)	20,57,60, 155
		prior 1980	**PANAMA**. Accidental introduction or natural spread from U.S.A. Status unknown.	USDA (3,4) State (3)	19,57,60
MELASTOMATACEAE					
Clidema hirta (Linneaus) D. Don tropical Central and south America (Koster's curse)	*Liothrips urichi* Karny (Thysanoptera: Phlaeothripidae)	-	**SAMOA**. Accidental or unrecorded introduction. Status unknown.		686
MIMOSACEAE					
Mimosa pigra (Linnaeus) tropical America (giant sensitive plant, mimosa)	*Acanthoscelides puniceus* Johnson (Coleoptera: Bruchidae)	1989	**MALAYSIA**. Found in Kota Bharu, Kelantan near the Thai border. Spread from southern Thailand.	NBCRC	469
		1987	**UNION OF MYANMAR (Burma)**. Found in the western part of the country adjacent to Thailand. Spread from southern Thailand.	NBCRC	469
	Acanthoscelides quadridentatus (Schaeffer) (Coleoptera: Bruchidae)	1989	**MALAYSIA**. Found in Kota Bharu, Kelantan near the Thai border. Spread from southern Thailand.	NBCRC	469
		1987	**UNION OF MYANMAR (Burma)**. Found in the western part of the country adjacent to Thailand. Spread from Thailand.	NBCRC	469
		prior 1986	**UNITED STATES OF AMERICA**. Found at one site in Florida. Natural spread from Central America.	USDA (4)	69

* See 'Introduction' for explanation of headings.

List D continued

Weed and its origin*	Agent and taxonomic references*	Observation date*	Status and degree of control*	Research organisation*	General references*
MYRTACEAE					
Leptospermum scoparium J.R. Forster & Forster F. Australasia (manuka)	*Eriococcus orariensis* Hoy (Hemiptera: Eriococcidae)	1940	**NEW ZEALAND.** Accidental introduction from Australia giving complete control in dry areas. The weed is native to New Zealand.		303
PONTEDERIACEAE					
Eichhornia crassipes (Martius) Solms-Laubach South America (water hyacinth)	*Alternaria eichhorniae* Nagaraj & Ponappa (fungus: Hyphomycetes)	prior 1990	**REPUBLIC OF SOUTH AFRICA.** In 1990 found in the South West Cape, causing significant leaf damage. Being redistributed.	PPRI	429
	Cercospora piaropi Tharp (fungus: Hyphomycetes)	prior 1987	**REPUBLIC OF SOUTH AFRICA.** Found established in the eastern Transvaal, and causing appreciable damage to leaves. Since distributed to other localities.	PPRI	472
	Neochetina eichhorniae Warner (Coleoptera: Curculionidae)	-	**MEXICO.** Specimen collected in 1974. Culture sent from U.S.A. in 1976 but no record of release. Observed in the field in 1977 and again during the 1980s.		30,250, 481
		1977	**CUBA.** Accidental introduction.		30
		1969	**JAMAICA.** Status unknown.		25,30
	Orthogalumna terebrantis Wallwork (previously referred to as *Leptogalumna* sp.) (Acarina: Galumnidae)	prior 1991	**MALAWI.** Spread from releases in Zambia. Appears to have a depressing effect on growth in some areas.		250
		1977	**MEXICO.** Accidental introduction.		30
		1990	**REPUBLIC OF SOUTH AFRICA.** Found established and locally abundant in eastern Transvaal.		30,472

* See 'Introduction' for explanation of headings.

List D continued

Weed and its origin*	Agent and taxonomic references*	Observation date*	Status and degree of control*	Research organisation*	General references*
(PONTEDERIACEAE continued)					
		prior 1900	**UNITED STATES OF AMERICA.** Accidental introduction of South American origin. Widespread and sporadic but provides no substantial control. In combination with the fungus *Acremonium zonatum* can have locally severe but temporary impact.	USDA (4)	153
ROSACEAE					
Rubus fruticosus Linnaeus, aggregate Asia, Europe (blackberry)	*Phragmidium violaceum* (Schultz) Winter (fungus: Uredinales)	1983	**AUSTRALIA.** Thought to be illegally introduced. Attacks *Rubus selmeri, Rubus laciniatus, Rubus polyanthemus, Rubus ulmifolius, Rubus ulmifolius* hybrids, *Rubus procerus, Rubus vestitus.* Not pathogenic to *Rubus rosaceus* and *Rubus cissburiensis.* Extremely common in Victoria, present in New South Wales, Western Australia and Tasmania.	DCE	53,405
SALVINIACEAE					
Salvinia minima Baker (= *Salvinia rotundifolia* Willdenow), 152 North, Central and South America	*Cyrtobagous salviniae* Calder & Sands (Coleoptera: Curculionidae)	prior 1962	**UNITED STATES OF AMERICA.** Accidental introduction of South American origin. Now widespread in FL. Noticeable damage at some sites but overall impact unknown.	USDA (3)	57,59, 61,354
(water fern, salvinia)	*Samea multiplicalis* (Guenée) (Lepidoptera: Pyralidae)		**UNITED STATES OF AMERICA.** Accidental introduction or natural spread of South American origin. Established in FL.	USDA (3)	245
Salvinia molesta D.S. Mitchell Brazil (water fern, salvinia, Kariba weed)	*Cyrtobagous salviniae* Calder & Sands (Coleoptera: Curculionidae)	1984	**BOTSWANA.** Released in Namibia in 1983 and spread naturally to Botswana. Very successful control. Manual distribution has been carried out since 1984 (see List A).	DWAN	193,215
	Cyrtobagous singularis Hustache (Coleoptera: Curculionidae)	1984 1976	**NAMIBIA.** Released in Botswana in 1971 and and spread naturally to Namibia.		409,885

* See 'Introduction' for explanation of headings.

List D continued

Weed and its origin*	Agent and taxonomic references*	Observation date*	Status and degree of control*	Research organisation*	General references*
(SALVINIACEAE continued)					
		1984	**ZIMBABWE.** Released in Zambia in 1971 and spread naturally to Zimbabwe.		409
SCROPHULARIACEAE					
Linaria dalmatica (Linnaeus) Miller [also referred to as *Linaria genistifolia* (Linnaeus) Miller ssp. *dalmatica* (Linnaeus) Marie & Petitmengin] Europe (Dalmation toadflax)	*Brachypterolus pulicarius* Linnaeus (Coleoptera: Nitidulidae)	1953	**CANADA.** Accidental introduction of European origin. In combination with *Gymnaetron antirrhini* it reduces seed production.	CDA	257,263, 270
		prior 1919	**UNITED STATES OF AMERICA.** Accidental introduction of European origin. Established in ID and WA. Minimal impact.	State (6)	410,612
	Gymnaetron antirrhini (Paykull) (Coleoptera: Curculionidae)	prior 1911	**CANADA.** Accidental introduction of European origin. Occurs in small numbers on the narrow leaf form of the weed.	CDA	257,263, 270,612
Linaria vulgaris Miller Europe (common toadflax, butter-and-eggs)	*Brachypterolus pulicarius* Linnaeus (Coleoptera: Nitidulidae)	prior 1919	**CANADA.** Ex Europe. With *Gymnaetron antirrhini* reduces seed by 80-90% and since 1953 controlled the weed on most of the Prairies.	CDA	131a,257, 263,270, 514
		prior 1919	**UNITED STATES OF AMERICA.** Accidental introduction of European origin. Established in ID, MT, NY and OR.	CDA	479,612
	Gymnaetron antirrhini (Paykull) (Coleoptera: Curculionidae)	prior 1917	**CANADA.** Accidental introduction of European origin. Distributed from Ontario to Alberta and Saskatchewan in 1957 and established. In combination with *Brachypterolus pulicarius*, provides some control. Released in New Brunswick during 1990.	CDA	131a,257, 267,263, 270,514, 612
		prior 1909	**UNITED STATES OF AMERICA.** Accidental introduction of European origin. Established in northeastern and northwestern U.S.A. Caused 85-90% seed destruction in WA.	State (9)	479,612

* See 'Introduction' for explanation of headings.

List D continued

Weed and its origin*	Agent and taxonomic references*	Observation date*	Status and degree of control*	Research organisation*	General references*
VERBENACEAE					
Lantana camara Linnaeus tropical America (lantana)	*Calcomyza lantanae* Frick (previous referred to as *Phytobia lantanae*) (Diptera: Agromyzidae)	after 1977	**INDONESIA.** Natural spread probably from Australia. Found on Java and Sulawesi.		250,493
		after 1977	**MALAYSIA.** Natural spread probably from Australia through Papua New Guinea. Causes defoliation.		493
		after 1977	**PAPUA NEW GUINEA.** Natural spread probably from Australia.		493
		1983	**PHILIPPINES.** Accidental introduction. Found on Luzon and Mindanao.		95
		after 1977	**SINGAPORE.** Natural spread probably from Australia through Papua New Guinea.		493
		after 1974	**THAILAND.** Probably natural spread from Australia through Papua New Guinea, Indonesia, Singapore and Malaysia. No substantial control.	NBCRC	250,469
	Epinotia lantana (Busck) (Lepidoptera: Tortricidae)	-	**INDIA.** Accidental or unrecorded introduction. Insect is of Mexican origin.		455
		after 1949	**MARIANA ISLANDS.** Spread probably from Caroline Islands (Pohnpei), to Guam, Saipan, and Tinian. With *Lantanophaga pusillidactyla* causes 70-80% decline in berry production.		167,453
	Hypena strigata (Fabricius) (Lepidoptera: Noctuidae)	1967	**MAURITIUS.** Probably from Africa. In conjunction with *Teleonemia scrupulosa* causes significant damage in drier periods.		604
	Lantanophaga pusillidactyla (Walker) (previously referred to as *Platyptilia pusillidactyla*) (Lepidoptera: Pterophoridae)	-	**AUSTRALIA.** Established but of minor importance.		249
		1933	**HONG KONG.** Accidental introduction of Mexican origin. Deliberately released in 1933 (see List A).		220

* See 'Introduction' for explanation of headings.

List D continued

Weed and its origin*	Agent and taxonomic references*	Observation date*	Status and degree of control*	Research organisation* references*	General references*
(VERBENACEAE continued)					
		1919	**INDIA.** Accidental introduction. Not effective.		455
		after 1949	**MARIANA ISLANDS.** Spread probably from Caroline Is. (Pohnpei), to Guam, Saipan and Tinian. With *Epinotia lantana* causes 70-80% decline in berry production.		167,453
	Leptobyrsa decora Drake (Hemiptera: Tingidae)	1969	**TONGA ISLANDS.** Origin and status unknown.		686
	Ophiomyia lantanae Froggatt (Diptera: Agromyzidae)	prior 1976	**ARGENTINA.** Status unknown.		672
		-	**GHANA.** Accidental introduction of Central American origin. Status unknown.	IIBC	584
		prior 1921	**INDIA.** Thought not to have established from a deliberate release in 1921 (see List A) but to have been accidentally introduced and established earlier. Not effective.		633
		1958	**KENYA.** Accidental introduction of Central American origin. Deliberately released in 1958 (see List A).		236,237
		after 1977	**MALAYSIA.** Accidental introduction. Widespread but not providing effective control.		493,615
		1968	**MADAGASCAR.** Accidental introduction of Central American origin. Casual observation only.		237
		1973	**PAPUA NEW GUINEA.** Status unknown.		242
		1983	**PHILIPPINES.** Accidental introduction. Found on Luzon.		95

* See 'Introduction' for explanation of headings.

List D continued

Weed and its origin*	Agent and taxonomic references*	Observation date*	Status and degree of control*	Research organisation* references*	General references*
(VERBENACEAE continued)					
		prior 1961	**REPUBLIC OF SOUTH AFRICA.** Present prior to deliberate release in 1961 (see List A). Widely established but not effective.	PPRI	495
		-	**SINGAPORE.** Status unknown.		492,615
		prior 1932	**SRI LANKA.** Status unknown.		615,633
		prior 1960	**UGANDA.** Accidental introduction of Central American origin. Not effective.		615
		prior 1934	**UNION OF MYANMAR (Burma).** Status unknown.		615,633
		1983	**VANUATU.** Accidental introduction. Found on Espiritu Santo and Malakula.		92
		prior 1960	**ZANZIBAR.** Accidental introduction of Central American origin. Not effective.		615
		-	**ZIMBABWE.** Accidental introduction of Central American origin. Not effective.		237
	Orthezia insignis Browne (Hemiptera: Ortheziidae)	1902	**HAWAII, U.S.A.** Accidental introduction. Not effective.		512
		1915	**INDIA.** Accidental or unrecorded introduction. Status unknown.		455
	Teleonemia scrupulosa Stål (has been referred to as *Teleonemia vanduzei*) (Hemiptera: Tingidae)	1940	**INDONESIA.** Ex Mexico via Fiji via Australia. Not released, escaped from laboratory. Spread throughout Java, Lesser Sunda Island and Sulawesi. Released in Timor in 1954 (see List A). Well established but ineffective.	DAI	346,544

* See 'Introduction' for explanation of headings.

List D continued

Weed and its origin*	Agent and taxonomic references*	Observation date*	Status and degree of control*	Research organisation* references*	General references*
(VERBENACEAE continued)					
		-	**MALAYSIA** (Sabah). Naturally spread probably from Indonesia.		346,544
		1952	**MAURITIUS.** Origin uncertain, no record of release. Caused extensive damage and prevented spread of the weed until 1964.	MAM	237
		1983	**PHILIPPINES.** Accidental introduction probably from Malaysia. Established on Luzon and Mindanao.		95
ZYGOPHYLLACEAE					
Tribulus cistoides Linnaeus tropical and sub-tropical southern Africa, 536 (puncture vine)	*Microlarinus lypriformis* (Wollaston) (Coleoptera: Curculionidae)	-	**BAHAMAS.** Ex Europe. Natural spread from U.S.A. or other Caribbean islands.		91,33
		prior 1984	**CURACAO.** Ex Europe. Natural spread from U.S.A. or other Caribbean islands.		33
		prior 1979	**JAMAICA.** Ex Europe. Natural spread from U.S.A. or other Caribbean islands.		91,33
		prior 1979	**MEXICO.** Ex Europe. Natural spread probably from U.S.A.		91
		prior 1987	**PUERTO RICO.** Ex Europe to California. Natural spread from U.S.A. or other Caribbean islands.		33
		prior 1971	**UNITED STATES OF AMERICA.** Accidental introduction from Europe. Causing some damage but is attacked by native parasites.		33,617
		prior 1984	**VENEZUELA.** Ex Europe. Natural spread probably from the Caribbean.		33

* See 'Introduction' for explanation of headings.

REFERENCES

1. Ablin, M. (personal communication 1991) Tropical Weeds Research Centre, Queensland Department of Lands, Natal Downs Road, Charters Towers, Queensland 4820, Australia.

2. Adair, R.J.; Scott, J.K. (1989) The life-history and host specificity of *Comostolopsis germana* Prout (Lepidoptera: Geometridae), a biological control agent of *Chrysanthemoides monilifera* (Compositae). *Bulletin of Entomological Research* **79**, 649-657.

3. Ahling, B.; Jernelov, A. (1971) Weed control with grass carp in Lake Osbyjon. *Mimeograph, Swedish Water and Air Pollution Research Laboratory,* 15 pp.

4. Alexander, W.B. (1925) Natural enemies of prickly pear and their introduction into Australia. *Bulletin, Commonwealth of Australia, Institute of Science and Industry* **29**, 50 pp.

5. Aliyev, D.S. (1976) The role of phytophagous fishes in the reconstruction of commercial fish fauna and the biological improvement of water. *Journal of Ichthyology* **16**, 216-229.

6. Anderson, L.W. (personal communication 1991) United States Department of Agriculture, Agricultural Research Service, Aquatic Weeds Control Research, Botany Department, University of California, Davis, California 95616, United States of America.

7. Andres, L.A. (personal communication 1991) United States Department of Agriculture, Biological Control of Weeds Laboratory, 800 Buchanan Street, Albany, California 94710, United States of America.

8. Andres, L.A.; Hawkes, R.B.; Rizza, A. (1967) Apion seed weevil introduced for biological control of Scotch Broom. *California Agriculture* **21**, 13.

9. Andres, L.A.; Davis, C.J. (1973) The biological control of weeds with insects in the United States. *Proceedings of the 2nd International Symposium on Biological Control of Weeds,* 11-28.

10. Andres, L.A.; Coombs, E. (1992) Scotch Broom, *Cytisus scoparius* (L.) Link (Leguminosae). In; Nechols, J.R.; Andres, L.A.; Beardsley, J.W.; Goeden, R.D.; Jackson, C.G. *(Eds) Biological Control in the U.S. Western Region: Accomplishments and Benefits of Regional Research Project W-84 (1964-1989).* Berkeley; University of California, Division of Agriculture and Natural Resources, in press.

11. Andres, L.A.; Coombs, E.; McCaffrey, J.P. (1992) Mediterranean Sage, *Salvia aethiopis* L. (Labiatae). In; Nechols, J.R.; Andres, L.A.; Beardsley, J.W.; Goeden, R.D.; Jackson, C.G. *(Eds) Biological Control in the U.S. Western Region: Accomplishments and Benefits of Regional Research Project W-84 (1964-1989).* Berkeley; University of California, Division of Agriculture and Natural Resources, in press.

12. Andres, L.A.; Goeden, R.D. (1992) Puncturevine, *Tribulus terrestris* L. (Zygophyllaceae). In; Nechols, J.R.; Andres, L.A.; Beardsley, J.W.; Goeden, R.D.; Jackson, C.G. *(Eds) Biological Control in the U.S. Western Region: Accomplishments and Benefits of Regional Research Project W-84 (1964-1989).* Berkeley; University of California, Division of Agriculture and Natural Resources, in press.

13. Andres, L.A.; Rees, N.E. (1992) Musk thistle, *Carduus nutans* L. (Asteraceae). In; Nechols, J.R.; Andres, L.A.; Beardsley, J.W.; Goeden, R.D.; Jackson, C.G. *(Eds) Biological Control in the U.S. Western Region: Accomplishments and Benefits of Regional Research Project W-84 (1964-1989).* Berkeley; University of California, Division of Agriculture and Natural Resources, in press.

14. Annecke, D.P.; Karny, M.; Burger, W.A. (1969) Improved biological control of the prickly pear, *Opuntia megacantha* Salm-Dyck, in South Africa through the use of an insecticide. *Phytophylactica* **1**, 9-13.

15. Annecke, D.P.; Neser, S. (1977) On the biological control of some Cape pest plants. *Proceedings of the 2nd National Weeds Conference, South Africa,* 303-319.

16. Annecke, D.P.; Moran, V.C. (1978) Critical reviews of biological pest control in South Africa. 2. The prickly pear, *Opuntia ficus-indica* (L.) Miller. *Journal of the Entomological Society of South Africa* **41**, 161-188.

17. Baer, R.G.; Quimby, P.C. jr. (1984) Rearing, storing and efficacy studies on *Arzama densa* for release programs against waterhyacinth. *Technical Report, United States Army Corps of Engineers, Aquatic Plant Control Research Program* **A-84-4**, 33 pp.

18.   Baker, C.R.B.; Blackman, R.L.; Claridge, M.F. (1972) Studies on *Haltica carduorum* Guérin (Coleoptera: Chrysomelidae) an alien beetle released in Britain as a contribution to the biological control of the creeping thistle, *Cirsium arvense* (L.) Scop. *Journal of Applied Ecology* 9, 819-830.

19.   Balciunas, J.K. (personal communication 1984) Aquatic Plant Management Laboratory, 3205 College Avenue, Fort Lauderdale, Florida 33314, United States of America.

20.   Balciunas, J.K.; Habeck, D.H. (1981) Recent range extension of hydrilla-damaging moth, *Parapoynx diminutalis* (Lepidoptera: Pyralidae). *Florida Entomolologist* **64**, 195-196.

21.   Balsbaugh, E.U. jr.; Frye, R.D.; Scholl, C.G.; Anderson, A.W. (1981) Insects for weed control: status in North Dakota. *Farm Research* **40**, 3-7.

22.   Barreto, R.W.; Evans, H.C. (1988) Taxonomy of a fungus introduced into Hawaii for biological control of *Ageratina riparia* (Eupatorieae; Compositae), with observations on related weed pathogens. *Transactions of the British Mycological Society* **91**, 81-97.

23.   Batra, S.W.T. (1983) Establishment of *Hyles euphorbiae* (L.) (Lepidoptera: Sphingidae) in the United States for control of the weedy spurges *Euphorbia esula* L. and *E. cyparissias* L. *New York Entomological Society* **91**, 304-311.

24.   Bell, K.O. (personal communication 1991) Kansas State Board of Agriculture, Topeka, Kansas, United States of America.

25.   Bennett, F.D. (1970) Recent investigations on the biological control of some tropical and sub-tropical weeds. *Proceedings of the 10th British Weed Control Conference*, 660-668.

26.   Bennett, F.D. (1970) Insects attacking water hyacinth in the West Indies, British Honduras and the U.S.A. *Hyacinth Control Journal* **8**, 10-13.

27.   Bennett, F.D. (1971) Some recent successes in the field of biological control in the West Indies. *Review Peru Entomology* **14**, 369-373.

28.   Bennett, F.D. (1974) Biological control of aquatic weeds. *Proceedings of the Summer Institute of Biological Control, University of Mississippi*, 224-237.

29.   Bennett, F.D. (1975) Insects and plant pathogens for the control of *Salvinia* and *Pistia*. *Proceedings of a Symposium on Water Quality Management Through Biological Control, University of Florida*, 28-35.

30.   Bennett, F.D. (1979) Records of natural enemies of water hyacinth *Eichhornia crassipes* and of puncture vine *Tribulus cistoides* from Mexico. *VII Reunion Nacional de Control Biologica, Veracruz*, 137-141.

31.   Bennett, F.D. (personal communication 1979) Department of Entomology and Nematology, 3103 McCarthy Hall, University of Florida, Gainesville 32611, Florida, United States of America.

32.   Bennett, F.D. (1984) Biological control of aquatic weeds. *Proceedings of the International Conference on Water Hyacinth, Hyderabad*, 14-40.

33.   Bennett, F.D. (1989) *Microlarinus lypriformis* (Coleoptera: Curculionidae) in Curacao, Venezuela, and Puerto Rico: new distribution records. *The Coleopterists Bulletin* **43**, 390-391.

34.   Beshir, M.O. (1983) Water hyacinth in Sudan - early results. *Biocontrol News and Information* **4**, 1.

35.   Beshir, M.O. (1984) The establishment and distribution of natural enemies of water hyacinth released in Sudan. *Tropical Pest Management* **30**, 320-323.

36.   Beshir, M.O.; Bennett, F.D. (1985) Biological control of water hyacinth on the White Nile, Sudan. *Proceedings of the 6th International Symposium on Biological Control of Weeds*, 491-496.

37.   Bess, H.A.; Haramoto, F.H. (1958) Biological control of Pamakani, *Eupatorium adenophorum*, in Hawaii by a Tephritid gall fly, *Procecidochares utilis*. I. The life history of the fly and its effectiveness in the control of the weed. *Proceedings of the 10th International Congress of Entomology* **4**, 543-548.

38.   Bess, H.A.; Haramoto, F.H. (1972) Biological control of Pamakani, *Eupatorium adenophorum*, in Hawaii by a Tephritid gall fly, *Procecidochares utilis*. 3. Status of the weed, fly and parasites of the fly in 1966-71 vs. 1950-57. *Proceedings of the Hawaiian Entomological Society* **21**, 165-178.

39.   Bezark, L. (personal communication 1990) California Department of Food and Agriculture, Biological Control Program, 1220 N Street, Sacramento, California 95814, United States of America.

40.   Bohl, M. (1979) Oekologische Aspekte beim Aussatz von Grasfishen (*Ctenopharyngodon idella* Val.) in Binnengewassern. *Arbeiten des Deutschen Fischerei Verbandes* **25**, 71-88.

41.   Boldt, P.E. (personal communication 1991) United States Department of Agriculture, Agricultural Research Service, Grasslands Research Laboratory, 808 Blackland Road, Temple, Texas 76502, United States of America.

42.   Boldt, P.E.; Deloach, C.J. (1985) Evaluating *Rhinocyllus conicus* (Coleoptera : Curculionidae) on *Silybum marianum* (Compositae) in Texas. *Proceedings of the 6th International Symposium on Biological Control of Weeds*, 417-422.

43.   Bornemissza, G.F. (1966) An attempt to control ragwort in Australia with the cinnabar moth, *Callimorpha jacobaeae* L. (Arctiidae: Lepidoptera). *Australian Journal of Zoology* **14**, 201-243.

44.   Breniere, J. (1965) La lutte biologique a Madagascar. *Congres de la Protection des Cultures Tropicales. Compte Rendus des Travaux, Marseilles*, 845-850. (Reference provided by D.J. Greathead; not seen by the editor).

45.   Briese, D.T. (1985) A survey to evaluate the long-term relationship between *Chrysolina quadrigemina* and its host-weed, St. John's wort, in southeastern Australia. *Proceedings of the 6th International Symposium on Biological Control of Weeds*, 691-708.

46.   Briese, D.T. (1986) Factors affecting the establishment and survival of *Anaitis efformata* (Lepidoptera: Geometridae) introduced into Australia for the biological control of St. John's wort, *Hypericum perforatum*. II. Field trials. *Journal of Applied Ecology* **23**, 821-839.

47.   Briese, D.T (1988) Bionomics of *Aphis chloris* Koch (Hemiptera: Aphididae) for biological control of St John's wort in Australia. *Ecological Entomology* **13**, 365-374.

48.   Briese, D.T. (1989) Host-specificity and virus-vector potential of *Aphis chloris* [Hemiptera: Aphididae], a biological control agent for St John's wort in Australia. *Entomophaga* **34**, 247-264.

49.   Briese, D.T. (personal communication 1991) Commonwealth Scientific and Industrial Research Organisation, Division of Entomology, P.O. Box 1700, Canberra 2601, Australia.

50.   Brock, V.E. (1960) The introduction of aquatic animals into Hawaiian waters. *International Revue der Gesamten Hydrobiologie* **45**, 463-480.

51.   Bruchart, W.L. (personal communication 1991) United States of America Department of Agriculture, Agricultural Research Service, Fredrick, Maryland 21701, United States of America.

52.   Bruzzese, E. (personal communication 1990) Keith Turnbull Research Institute, P.O. Box 48, Frankston, Victoria 3199, Australia.

53.   Bruzzese, E.; Field, R.P. (1985) Occurrence and spread of *Phragmidium violaceum* on blackberry (*Rubus fruticosus*) in Victoria, Australia. *Proceedings of the 6th International Symposium on Biological Control of Weeds*, 609-612.

54.   Buchanan, G. (personal communication 1986) Department of Agriculture, P.O. Box 460, Irymple, Victoria 3498, Australia.

55.   Buck, H.D. (1977) The integration of aquaculture with agriculture. *Fisheries* **2**, 11-16.

56.   Buckingham, G.R. (1988) Reunion in Florida - hydrilla, a weevil, and a fly. *Aquatics* **10**, 19-25.

57.   Buckingham, G.R. (personal communication 1991) United States Department of Agriculture, Agricultural Research Service, Biological Control Laboratory, P.O. Box 1269, Gainesville, Florida 32602, United States of America.

58.   Buckingham, G.R.; Boucias, D.; Theriot, R.F. (1983) Reintroduction of the alligatorweed flea beetle (*Agasicles hygrophila* Selman and Vogt) into the United States from Argentina. *Journal of Aquatic Plant Management* **21**, 101-102.

59.   Buckingham, G.R.; Haag, K.H.; Habeck, D.H. (1986) Native insect enemies of aquatic macrophytes - beetles. *Aquatics* **8**, 28-34.

60.   Buckingham, G.R.; Bennett, C.A. (1989) Laboratory host range of *Parapoynx diminutalis* (Lepidoptera: Pyralidae), an Asian aquatic moth adventive in Florida and Panama on *Hydrilla verticillata* (Hydrocharitaceae). *Environmental Entomology* **18**, 526-530.

61.   Calder, A.A.; Sands, D.P.A. (1985) A new Brazilian *Cyrtobagous* Hustache (Coleoptera: Curculionidae) introduced into Australia to control salvinia. *Journal of the Australian Entomological Society* **24**, 57-64.

62.   Campbell, C.L.; McCaffrey, J.P. (1991) Population trends, seasonal phenology and impact of *Chrysolina quadrigemina*, *C. hyperici* (Coleoptera: Chyrsomelidae) and *Agrilus hyperici* (Coleoptera: Buprestidae) associated with *Hypericum perforatum* in northern Idaho. *Environmental Entomology* **20**, 303-315.

63.   Cartwright, B.; Kok, L.T. (1985) Growth responses of the musk and plumeless thistles (*Carduus nutans* and *C. acanthoides*) to damage by *Trichosirocalus horridus* (Coleoptera: Curculionidae). *Weed Science* **33**, 57-62.

64.   Cartwright, B.; Kok, L.T. (1990) Feeding by *Cassida rubiginosa* (Coleoptera: Chrysomelidae) and the effects of defoliation on growth of musk thistles. *Journal of Entomological Science* **25**, 538-547.

65.   Casañas-Arango, A.; Trujillo, E.E.; de Hernandez, A.M.; Taniguchi, G. (1990) Field biology of *Cyanotricha necyria* Felder (Lep., Dioptidae), a pest of *Passiflora* spp., in southern Colombia's and Ecuador's Andean region. *Journal of Applied Entomology* **109**, 93-97.

66.   Center, T.D. (personal communication 1991) United States Department of Agriculture, Agricultural Reserach Service, Aquatic Weed Control Research, 3205 College Avenue, Ft. Lauderdale, Florida 33314, United States of America.

67.   Center, T.D.; Durden, W.C. (1986) Variation in waterhyacinth/weevil interactions resulting from temporal differences in weed control efforts. *Journal of Aquatic Plant Management* **24**, 28-38.

68.   Center, T.D.; Cofrancesco, A.F.; Balciunas, J.K. (1989) Biological control of wetland and aquatic weeds in the southeastern United States. *Proceedings 7th International Symposium on Biological Control of Weeds*, 239-262.

69.   Center, T.D.; Kipker, R.L. (1991) First record in Florida of *Acanthoscelides quadridentatus* (Coleoptera: Bruchidae), a potential biological control agent of *Mimosa pigra*. *Florida Entomologist* **74**, 59-61.

70.   Chacko, M.J.; Narasimham, A.U. (1988) Biocontrol attempts against *Chromolaena odorata* in India - a review. *Proceedings of the First International Workshop on Biological Control of Chromolaena odorata*, 65-74.

71.   Chapman, V.J.; Coffey, B.J. (1971) Experiments with grass carp in controlling exotic macrophages in New Zealand. *Hydrobiologia* **12**, 313-323.

72.   Charudattan, R. (1990) Chapter 9. Biological Control of Aquatic Weeds. (c) Biological control of aquatic weeds by means of fungi. In; Pieterse, A.H.; Murphy, K.J. *(Eds) Aquatic Weeds. The Ecology and Management of Nuisance Aquatic Vegetation*. Oxford University Press, Oxford, pp. 186-201.

73.   Charudattan, R. (1991) Chapter 2. The Mycoherbicide Approach with Plant Pathogens. In; TeBeest, D.O. *(Ed) Microbial Control of Weeds*, Chapman and Hall, New York, pp. 24-57.

74.   Charudattan, R. (personal communication 1991) Plant Pathology Department, University of Florida, 1453 Fifield Hall, 513 IFAS, Gainesville, Florida 32611-0513, United States of America.

75.   Charudattan, R.; Linda, S.B.; Kluepfel, M.; Osman, Y.A. (1985) Biological efficacy of *Cercosporum rodmani* on waterhyacinth. *Phytopathology* **75**, 1263-1269.

76.   Charudattan, R.; Walker, H.L.; Boyette, C.D.; Ridings, W.H.; TeBeest, D.O.; Van Dyke, C.G.; Worsham, A.D. (1986) Evaluation of *Alternaria cassiae* as a mycoherbicide for sicklepod *(Cassia obtusifolia)* in regional field tests. *Bulletin, South Cooperative Series, Agricultural Experiment Station, Auburn University, Alabama* **317**, 19 pp.

77.   Chaudhuri, H.; Murty, D.S.; Dey, R.K.; Reddy, P.V.G.K. (1976) Role of Chinese grass carp *Ctenopharyngodon idella* (Val.) in biological control of noxious aquatic weeds in India: a review. In; Varshney, C.K.; Rzoska, J. *(Eds) Aquatic Weeds in South East Asia*. The Hague; W. Junk, pp. 315-322.

78.   Chikwenhere, G.P.; Forno, I.W. (1991) Introduction of *Neohydronomus affinis* for biological control of *Pistia stratiotes* in Zimbabwe. *Journal of Aquatic Plant management* **29**, 53-55.

79.   Chippendale, J. (personal communication 1991) Department of Lands, Alan Fletcher Research Station, Sherwood, Queensland 4075, Australia.

146

80.   Cilliers, C.J. (1977) On the biological control of *Lantana camara* in South Africa. *Proceedings of the 2nd National Weeds Conference South Africa,* 341-344.

81.   Cilliers, C.J. (1983) The weed, *Lantana camara* L., and the insect natural enemies imported for its biological control into South Africa. *Journal of the Entomological Society of South Africa* **46**, 131-138.

82.   Cilliers, C.J. (1987) An evaluation of three insect natural enemies for the biological control of the weed *Lantana camara* L. *Journal of the Entomological Society of South Africa* **50**, 15-34.

83.   Cilliers, C.J. (personal communication 1987) Department of Agriculture and Water Supply, Plant Protection Research Institute, Private Bag X134, Pretoria 0001, Republic of South Africa.

84.   Cilliers, C.J. (1987) First attempt at and early results on the biological control of *Pistia stratiotes* L. in South Africa. *Koedoe* **30**, 35-40.

85.   Cilliers, C.J. (1987) Notes on the biology of the insect natural enemies of *Lantana camara* L. (Verbenaceae) and their seasonal history in South Africa. *Journal of the Entomological Society of South Africa* **50**, 1-13.

86.   Cilliers, C.J. (1991) Biological control of water fern, *Salvinia molesta* (Salviniaceae), in South Africa. *Agriculture, Ecosystems and Environment* **37**, 219-224.

87.   Cilliers, C.J. (1991) Biological control of water hyacinth, *Eichhornia crassipes* (Pontederiaceae), in South Africa. *Agriculture, Ecosystems and Environment* **37**, 207-217.

88.   Cilliers, C.J.; Neser, S. (1991) Biological control of *Lantana camara* (Verbenaceae) in South Africa. *Agriculture, Ecosystems and Environment* **37,** 57-75.

89.   Claridge, M.F.; Blackman, R.L.; Baker, C.R.B. (1970) *Haltica carduorum* Guérin introduced into Britain as a potential control agent for creeping thistle *Cirsium arvense* (L.) Scop. *Entomologist (London)* **103**, 210-212.

90.   Cock, M.J.W. (1984) Possibilities for biological control of *Chromolaena odorata*. *Tropical Pest Management* **30**, 7-13.

91.   Cock, M.J.W. (Ed) (1985) A review of biological control of pests in the Commonwealth Caribbean and Bermuda up to 1982. *Technical Communication, Commonwealth Institute of Biological Control* **9**, 218 pp.

92.   Cock, M.J.W. (personal communication 1986) Commonwealth Institute of Biological Control, Imperial College, Silwood Park, Ascot Berks SL5 7PY, United Kingdom.

93.   Cock, M.J.W.; Holloway, J.D. (1982) The history of, and prospects for, the biological control of *Chromolaena odorata* (Compositae) by *Pareuchaetes pseudoinsulata* Rego Barros and allies (Lepidoptera: Arctiidae). *Bulletin of Entomological Research* **72**, 193-205.

94.   Cock, M.J.W.; Evans, H.C. (1984) Possibilities for biological control of *Cassia tora* and *C. obtusifolia*. *Tropical Pest Management* **30**, 339-350.

95.   Cock, M.J.W.; Godfray, H.C.J. (1985) Biological control of *Lantana camara* L. in the Philippines. *Journal of Plant Protection in the Tropics* **2**, 61-63.

96.   Cockayne, A.H. (1915) Californian thistle rust (*Puccinia suaveolens*) as a check on the spread of Californian thistle (Cnicus arvensis). *Journal of Agriculture, New Zealand* **11**, 300-302.

97.   Commonwealth Institute of Biological Control. Annual Report for 1967.

98.   Commonwealth Institute of Biological Control. Annual Report for 1968.

99.   Commonwealth Institute of Biological Control. Annual Report for 1969.

100. Commonwealth Institute of Biological Control. Annual Report for 1970.

101. Commonwealth Institute of Biological Control. Annual Report for 1971.

102. Commonwealth Institute of Biological Control. Annual Report for 1972.

103. Commonwealth Institute of Biological Control. Annual Report for 1973.

104. Commonwealth Institute of Biological Control. Annual Report for 1974.

105. Commonwealth Institute of Biological Control. Annual Report for 1975.

106. Commonwealth Institute of Biological Control. Annual Report for 1976.

107. Commonwealth Institute of Biological Control. Annual Report for 1977-1978.

108. Commonwealth Institute of Biological Control. Annual Report for 1978-1979.

109. Commonwealth Institute of Biological Control. Annual Report for 1980-1981.

110. Commonwealth Institute of Biological Control. Annual Report for 1981-1982.

111. Commonwealth Institute of Biological Control. Annual Report for 1982-1983.

112. Commonwealth Institute of Entomology and The British Museum of Natural History. (1986) Insect names collated by staff of the CIE and BMNH, United Kingdom.

113. Conway, K.E.; Freeman, T.E.; Charudattan, R. (1978) Development of *Cercospora rodmanii* as a biological control for *Eichhornia crassipes*. *Proceedings of the 5th International Symposium on Aquatic Weeds*, 225-230.

114. Coombs, E.M. (personal communication 1990) Oregon Department of Agriculture, Salem, Oregon 97310, United States of America.

115. Cordo, H.A. (personal communication 1991) Biological Control of Weeds Laboratory, United States Department of Agriculture, Agricultural Research Service, Bolivar 1559, Hurlingham, Buenos Aires, Argentina.

116. Coulson, J.R. (1977) Biological control of alligatorweed, 1959-1972. A review and evaluation. *Technical Bulletin, United States Department of Agriculture* **1547**, 98 pp.

117. Coulson, J.R. (1981) The Soviet-American environmental agreement and exchange of beneficial organisms, 1972-1979. *Proceedings of the Joint American-Soviet Conference on Use of Beneficial Organisms in the Control of Crop Pests, Washington*, 1-11.

118. Cowley, J.M. (1983) Life cycle of *Apion ulicis* (Coleoptera: Apionidae), and gorse seed attack around Auckland, New Zealand. *New Zealand Journal of Zoology* **10**, 83-86.

119. Crouzel, I.S. de; Cordo, H.A.; Saini, E.D. (1983) Sobre el control biologico del "Yuyo Esqueleto" *Chondrilla juncea* L. en la Republica Argentina. *Malezas: Revista de la Asociacion Argentina para el Control de Malezas (ASAM)* **11**, 216-232.

120. Cullen, J.M. (1974) Seasonal and regional variation in the success of organisms imported to combat skeleton weed *Chondrilla juncea* L. in Australia. *Proceedings of the 3rd International Symposium on Biological Control of Weeds*, 111-117.

121. Cullen, J.M. (1978) Evaluating the success of the programme for the biological control of *Chondrilla juncea* L. *Proceedings of the 4th International Symposium on Biological Control of Weeds*, 117-121.

122. Cullen, J.M. (1980) Considerations in rearing *Bradyrrhoa gilveolella* for control of *Chondrilla juncea* in Australia. *Proceedings of the 5th International Symposium on Biological Control Weeds*, 233-239.

123. Cullen, J.M. (personal communication 1991) Commonwealth Scientific and Industrial Research Organisation, Division of Entomology, P.O. Box 1700, Canberra 2601, Australia.

124. Cullen, J.M.; Kable, P.F.; Catt, M. (1973) Epidemic spread of a rust imported for biological control. *Nature (London)* **244**, 462-464.

125. Cullen, J.M.; Moore, A.D. (1981) Preliminary observations on *Longitarsus jacobaeae* introduced for the control of ragwort in Australia. *Proceedings of the 5th International Symposium on Biological Control of Weeds*, 499-505.

126. Cullen, J.M.; Groves, R.H.; Alex, J.F. (1982) The influence of *Aceria chondrillae* on the growth and reproduction capacity of *Chondrilla juncae*. *Journal of Applied Ecology* **19**, 529-537.

127. Currie, G.A.; Fyfe, R.V. (1938) The fate of certain European insects introduced into Australia for the control of weeds. *Journal of the Council for Scientific and Industrial Research* **11**, 289-301.

128. Custer, P.E. (1978) Panel discussion. Hydrilla research and control. *Miscellaneous Paper, United States Army Engineer Waterways Experimental Station A-78-1*, 106-111.

129. Custer, P.E.; Halverson, F.D.; Malone, J.M.; Von Chong, C.; Theriot, R.F. (1979) The white amur as a biological control agent of aquatic weeds in the Panama Canal. *Miscellaneous Paper, United States Army Engineers Waterways Experimental Station A-79-1*, 22 pp.

130. Daniel, J.T.; Templeton, G.E.; Smith, R.J. jr.; Fox, W.T. (1973) Biological control of northern jointvetch in rice with an endemic fungal disease. *Weed Science* **21**, 303-307.

148

131a.   Darwent, A.L.; Lobay, W.; Yarish, W.; Harris, P. (1975) Distribution and importance in northwestern Alberta of toadflax and its insect enemies. *Canadian Journal of Plant Science* **55**, 157-162.

131b.   Davies, J.C.; Greathead, D.J. (1967) Occurrence of *Teleonemia scrupulosa* on *Sesamum indicum* Linn. in Uganda. *Nature (London)* **213**, 102-103.

132.   Davis, C.J. (1959) Recent introductions for biological control in Hawaii IV. *Proceedings of the Hawaiian Entomological Society* **17**, 62-66.

133.   Davis, C.J. (1960) Recent introductions for biological control in Hawaii V. *Proceedings of the Hawaiian Entomological Society* **17**, 244-248.

134.   Davis, C.J. (1961) Recent introductions for biological control in Hawaii VI. *Proceedings of the Hawaiian Entomological Society* **17**, 389-393.

135.   Davis, C.J. (1970) Recent introductions for biological control in Hawaii XV. *Proceedings of the Hawaiian Entomological Society* **20**, 521-525.

136.   Davis, C.J. (1971) Recent introductions for biological control in Hawaii XVI. *Proceedings of the Hawaiian Entomological Society* **21**, 59-62.

137.   Davis, C.J. (1972) Recent introductions for biological control in Hawaii XVII. *Proceedings of the Hawaiian Entomological Society* **21**, 187-190.

138.   Davis, C.J. (1976) Notes and exhibitions. *Proceedings of the Hawaiian Entomological Society* **22**, 177.

139.   Davis, C.J.; Krauss, N.L.H. (1961) Recent developments in biological control of weed pests in Hawaii. *Abstracts, 10th Pacific Science Congress of the Pacific Science Association*, 204-205.

140.   Davis, C.J.; Krauss, N.L.H. (1962) Recent developments in the biological control of weed pests in Hawaii. *Proceedings of the Hawaiian Entomological Society* **18**, 65-67.

141.   Davis, C.J.; Krauss, N.L.H. (1962) Recent introductions for biological control in Hawaii VII. *Proceedings of the Hawaiian Entomological Society* **18**, 125-129.

142.   Davis, C.J.; Krauss, N.L.H. (1963) Recent introductions for biological control in Hawaii VIII. *Proceedings of the Hawaiian Entomological Society* **18**, 245-249.

143.   Davis, C.J.; Krauss, N.L.H. (1964) Recent introductions for biological control in Hawaii IX. *Proceedings of the Hawaiian Entomological Society* **18**, 391-397.

144.   Davis, C.J.; Krauss, N.L.H. (1965) Recent introductions for biological control in Hawaii X. *Proceedings of the Hawaiian Entomological Society* **19**, 87-90.

145.   Davis, C.J.; Krauss, N.L.H. (1966) Recent introductions for biological control in Hawaii XI. *Proceedings of the Hawaiian Entomological Society* **19**, 201-207.

*

147.   Davis, C.J.; Krauss, N.L.H. (1967) Recent introductions for biological control in Hawaii XII. *Proceedings of the Hawaiian Entomological Society* **19**, 375-380.

148.   Davis, C.J.; Chong, M. (1969) Recent introductions for biological control in Hawaii XIV. *Proceedings of the Hawaiian Entomological Society* **20**, 317-322.

149.   Davis, C.J.; Yoshioka, E.; Kageler, D. (1991) Biocontrol of *Lantana camara*, *Opuntia* spp., and *Ageratina riparia* in Hawaii: a review and update. In; Smith, C.; Tunison, T.; Stone, C.P. *(Eds) Alien Plant Invasions in Native Ecosystems of Hawaii*. University of Hawaii Press, in press.

150.   De Lotto, G. (1974) On the status and identity of the cochineal insects (Homoptera: Coccoidea: Dactylopiidae). *Journal of the Entomological Society of South Africa* **37**, 167-193.

151.   De Vol, J.E.; Goeden, R.D. (1973) Biology of *Chelinidea vittiger* with notes on its host-plant relationships and values in biological weed control. *Environmental Entomology* **2**, 231-240.

152.   De La Sota, E.R. (1976) Sinopsis de las especies Argentinas del genero *Salvinia* Adanson (Salviniaceae- Pteridophyta). *Boletin de la Sociedad Argentina de Botanica* **17**, 47-50.

153.   Delfosse, E.S. (1978) Effect on waterhyacinth of *Neochetina eichhorniae* (Col.: Curculionidae) combined with *Orthogalumna terebrantis* (Acari: Galumnidae). *Entomophaga* **23**, 379-387.

154.   Delfosse, E.S. (personal communication 1986) Commonwealth Scientific and Industrial Research Organisation, Division of Entomology, P.O. Box 1700, Canberra 2601, Australia. Current address: National Biological Control Institute, USDA APHIS, 6505 Belcrest Road, Hyattsville, Maryland 20782, United States of America.

* Reference 146 has been deleted

155.   Delfosse, E.S.; Perkins, B.D.; Stewart, K.K. (1976) A new U.S. record for *Parapoynx diminutalis* (Lepidoptera: Pyralidae), a possible biological control agent for *Hydrilla verticillata*. *Florida Entomologist* **59**, 19-20.

156.   Delfosse, E.S.; Cullen, J.M. (1981) New activities in biological control of weeds in Australia. I. Common heliotrope, *Heliotropium europaeum*. *Proceedings of the 5th International Symposium on Biological Control of Weeds*, 545-561.

157.   Delfosse, E.S.; Cullen, J.M. (1981) New activities in biological control of weeds in Australia. II. *Echium plantagineum:* curse or salvation? *Proceedings of the 5th International Symposium on Biological Control of Weeds*, 563-574.

158.   Delfosse, E.S.; Cullen, J.M. (1981) New activities in biological control of weeds in Australia. III. St. John's wort: *Hypericum perforatum*. *Proceedings of the 5th International Symposium on Biological Control of Weeds*, 575-581.

159.   Delfosse, E.S.; Cullen, J.M. (1982) Biological control of weeds of Mediterranean origin: a progress report. *Australian Weeds*, **March 1982**, 25-30.

160.   Delfosse, E.S.; Lewis, R.C.; Smith, C.S. (1987) Effect of drought and grasshoppers on establishment of *Dialectica scalariella* (Zeller) (Lepidoptera: Gracillariidae), a potential biological control agent for *Echium plantagineum* L. *Journal of the Australian Entomological Society* **26**, 279-280.

161.   DeLoach C.J. (personal communication 1991) United States Department of Agriculture, Agricultural Research Service, Grasslands Research Laboratory, 808 Blackland Road, Temple, Texas 76502, United States of America.

162.   Deloach, C.J.; Cordo, H.A. (1983) Control of waterhyacinth by *Neochetina bruchi* (Coleoptera: Curculionidae: Bagoini) in Argentina. *Environmental Entomology* **12**, 19-23.

163.   Dennill, G.B. (1985) The effect of the gall wasp *Trichilogaster acaciaelongifoliae* (Hymenoptera: Pteromalidae) on reproductive potential and vegetative growth of the weed *Acacia longifolia*. *Agricultural Ecosystems and Environment* **14**, 53-61.

164.   Dennill, G.B. (1990) The contribution of a successful biocontrol project to the theory of agent selection in weed biocontrol - the gall wasp *Trichilogaster acaciaelongifoliae* and the weed *Acacia longifolia*. *Agriculture, Ecosystems and Environment* **31**, 147-154.

165.   Dennill, G.B.; Gordon, A.J.; Neser, S. (1987) Difficulties with the release and establishment of the moth *Carposina autologa* on the weed *Hakea sericea* in South Africa. *Journal of the Entomological Society of South Africa* **50**, 463-468.

166.   Dennill, G.B.; Donnelly, D. (1991) Biological control of *Acacia longifolia* and related weed species (Fabaceae) in South Africa. *Agriculture, Ecosystems and Environment* **37**, 115-136.

167.   Denton, G.R.W.; Muniappan, R.; Marutani, M. (1991) Status and natural enemies of the weed, *Lantana camara*, in Micronesia. *Tropical Pest Management*, **37**, in press.

168.   Dharmadhikari, P.R.; Perera, P.A.C.R.; Hassen, T.M.F. (1977) The introduction of *Ammalo insulata* for the control of *Eupatorium odoratum* in Sri Lanka. *Technical Bulletin, Commonwealth Institute of Biological Control* **18,** 129-135.

169.   Dodd, A.P. (1927) The biological control of prickly pear in Australia. *Bulletin, Australian Commonwealth Council of Scientific and Industrial Research* **34**, 44 pp.

170.   Dodd, A.P. (1929) The Progress of Biological Control of Prickly pear in Australia. *Brisbane; Commonwealth Prickly Pear Board,* 44 pp.

171.   Dodd, A.P. (1933) The present position and future prospects in relation to the biological control of prickly pear. *Journal of the Council of Scientific and Industrial Research* **6**, 8-13.

172.   Dodd, A.P. (1936) The control and eradication of prickly pear in Australia. *Bulletin of Entomological Research* **27**, 503-517.

173.   Dodd, A.P. (1940) The Biological Campaign against Prickly Pear. *Brisbane; Commonwealth Prickly Pear Board,* 177 pp.

174.   Dodd, A.P. (1961) Biological control of *Eupatorium adenophorum* in Queensland. *Australian Journal of Science* **23**, 356-365.

175.   Donnelly, G. (personal communication 1991) Alan Fletcher Research Station, Department of Lands, 27 Magazine Street, Sherwood, Queensland 4075, Australia.

176.   Drake, C.J. (1956) Hemiptera: Tingidae. *Insects of Micronesia* **7**, 101-116.

177.   Dray, F.A. jr.; Center, T.D.; Habeck, D.H.; Thompson, C.R.; Cofrancesco, A.F.; Balciunas, J.K. (1990) Release and establishment in the southeastern United States of *Neohydronomus affinis* (Coleoptera: Curculionidae), an herbivore of waterlettuce. *Environmental Entomology* **19**, 799-802.

178.   Dubbers, F.A.A.; Ghoneim, S.; Siemelink, M.E.; El Gharably, Z.; Pieterse, A.H.; Blom, J.E. (1981) Aquatic weed control in irrigation and drainage canals in Egypt by means of grass carp *(Ctenopharyngodon idella)*. *Proceedings of the 5th International Symposium on Biological Control of Weeds,* 261-271.

179.   Dunn, P. (personal communication 1986) United States Department of Agriculture, Agricultural Research Service, Biological Control of Weeds Laboratory, Europe, American Embassy, AGR, APO New York, N.Y.09794-0007, United States of America.

180.   Dunn, P.H.; Rosenthal, S.S.; Campobasso, G.; Tait, S.M. (1989) Host specificity of *Pterolonche inspersa* [Lep.: Pterolonchidae] and its potential as a biological control agent for *Centaurea diffusa,* diffuse knapweed, and *C. maculosa,* spotted knapweed. *Entomophaga* **34**, 435-446.

181.   Dymock, J.J. (1987) Population changes of the seedfly, *Pegohylemyia jacobaeae* (Diptera: Anthomyiidae) introduced for biologial control of ragwort. *New Zealand Journal of Zoology* **14**, 337-342.

182.   Edwards, D.; Thomas, P.L. (1977) The *Salvinia molesta* problem in the northern Botswana and eastern Caprivi area. *Proceedings of the 2nd National Weeds Conference South Africa,* 221-237.

183.   Enrique, A.E.; Cordo, H.A.; de Crouzel, I.S.; Gimenez Tanzi, M.R. (1983) Importacion de *Rhinocyllus conicus* Froelich y *Trichosirocallus horridus* Panzer para el control biologico de los "Cardos" en la Argentina. *Malezas: Revista de la Asociacion Argentina para el Control de Malezas (ASAM)* **11**, 232-241.

184.   Evans, J.W. (1942) The gorse weevil. *Tasmanian Journal of Agriculture* **13**, 15-18.

185.   Evans, E.W. (personal communication 1991) Department of Biology, Utah State University, Logan, Utah 84322-5305, United States of America

186.   Fadeev, Y.N. (1981) Prospects for development of biological methods of plant protection in the U.S.S.R. *Proceedings of the Joint American-Soviet Conference on Use of Beneficial Organisms in the Control of Crop Pests, Washington,* 12-13.

187.   Field, R.P. (personal communication 1986) Department of Conservation, Forests and Soils, P.O. Box 48, Frankston, Victoria 3199, Australia.

188.   Field, R.P. (1989) Progress towards biological control of ragwort in Australia. *Proceedings of the 7th International Symposium on Biological Control of Weeds,* 315-322.

189.   Flanagan, G.J. (personal communication 1986) Department of Primary Production, Northern Regional Office, P.O. Box 51, Berrimah, Northern Territory 5788, Australia.

190.   Fornasari, L.; Turner, C.E.; Andres, L.A. (1991) *Eustenopus villosus* (Coleoptera: Curculionidae) for biological control of yellow starthistle (Asteraceae: Cardueae) in North America. *Environmental Entomology* **20**, 1187-1194.

191.   Forno, I.W. (1985) How quickly can insects control *Salvinia* in the tropics. *Proceedings of the 10th Asian-Pacific Weed Science Society,* 271-276.

192.   Forno, I.W. (1987) Biological control of the floating fern *Salvinia molesta* in north-eastern Australia: plant herbivore interactions. *Bulletin of Entomological Research* **77**, 9-17.

193.   Forno, I.W. (personal communication 1991) Commonwealth Scientific and Indusrial Research Organisation, Division of Entomology, Private Bag 3, Indooroopilly, Queensland 4068, Australia.

194.   Forno, I.W.; Miller, I.L.; Napompeth, B.; Thamasara, S. (1991) Management of *Mimosa pigra* in Southeast Asia and Australia. *Proceedings of the 3rd International Conference on Plant Protection in the Tropics,* in press.

195.   Fowler, M.C. (1985) The present status of grass carp *(Ctenopharyngodon idella)* for the control of aquatic weeds in England and Wales. *Proceedings of the 6th International Symposium on Biological Control of Weeds,* 537-542.

196.   Frappa, C. (1932) Sur *Dactylopius tomentosus* Lam. et son acclimatement a Madagascar. *Revue de Pathologie Vegetale et D'Entomologie Agricole de France* **19**, 48-55.

197.   Fraser, B.; Emberson, R. (1987) Rediscovery of *Chrysolina quadrigemina* (Suffrian) (Coleoptera: Chrysomelidae) in New Zealand. *New Zealand Entomologist* **9**, 57-59.

198.   Freeman, T.E.; Charudattan, R.; Conway, K.E. (1978) Status of the use of plant pathogens in the biological control of weeds. *Proceedings of the 4th International Symposium on Biological Control of Weeds,* 201-206.

199.   Freeman, T.E.; Charudattan, R. (1984) *Cercospora rodmanii* Conway a biological agent for waterhyacinth. *Technical Bulletin, University of Florida, Gainesville* **842**, 18 pp.

200.   Frick, K.E. (1964) *Leucoptera spartifoliella*, an introduced enemy of Scotch Broom in the Western United States. *Journal of Economic Entomology* **57**, 589-591.

201.   Frick, K.E. (1969) Tansy Ragwort control, aided by the establishment of seedfly from Paris. *California Agriculture* **23**, 10-11.

202.   Frick, K.E.; Chandler, J.M. (1978) Augmenting the moth *(Bactra verutana)* in field plots for early-season suppression of purple nutsedge *(Cyperus rotundus). Weed Science* **26**, 703-710.

203.   Friend, D. (personal communication 1991) Plant Protection Branch, Department of Primary Industries, Hobart, Tasmania 7000, Australia.

204.   Froggatt, W.W. (1904) The nut grass coccid *(Antonia australis,* Green). *Agricultural Gazette of New South Wales* **15**, 407-410.

205.   Fullaway, D.T. (1954) Biological control of cactus in Hawaii. *Journal of Economic Entomology* **47**, 696-700.

206.   Fullaway, D.T. (1958) Importations of natural enemies of the weed, *Emex spinosa* Campd. *Proceedings of the Hawaiian Entomological Society* **16**, 359-360.

207.   Funasaki, G.Y. (personal communication 1986) Department of Agriculture, 1428 So. King Street, Honolulu, Hawaii 96814-2512, United States of America.

208.   Furness, G. (personal communication 1986) Department of Agriculture, Loxton, South Australia 5333, Australia.

209.   Fyfe, R.V. (1935) The lantana bug in Fiji. *Agricultural Journal of Fiji* **8**, 35-36.

210.   Fyfe, R.V. (1936) The biological control of *Clidemia hirta* in Fiji. *Journal of the Australian Institute of Agricultural Science* **2**, 8-9.

211.   Gagne, R.J. (1990) Gall midge complex (Diptera: Cecidomyiidae) in bud galls of palearctic *Euphorbia* (Euphorbiaceae). *Annals of the Entomological Society of America* **83**, 335-345.

212.   Gardner, D.E.; Davis, C.J. (1982) The prospects for biological control of nonnative plants in Hawaiian National Parks. *Technical Report, University of Hawaii at Manoa* **45**, 55 pp.

213.   Gardner, J.C.M. (1944) A note on the imported lantana bug *(Teleonemia scrupulosa* Stål). *Indian Forester* **70**, 139-140.

214.   Gassman, A. (personal communication 1990) CAB International Institute of Biological Control, Europoean Station, 1 Chemin des Grillons, CH-2800 Delémont, Switzerland.

215.   Giliomee, J. (1986) The biological control of Kariba weed in the East Caprivi. *African Wildlife* **40**, 189-195.

216.   Gillett, J.D.; Harley, K.L.S.; Kassulke, R.C.; Miranda, H.J. (1991) Natural enemies of *Sida acuta* and *S. rhombifolia* (Malvaceae) in Mexico and their potential for biological control of these weeds in Australia. *Environmental Entomology* **20**, 882-888.

217.   Gilstrap, F.E.; Goeden, R.D. (1974) Biology of *Tarachidia candefacta*, a Nearctic noctuid introduced into the USSR for ragweed control. *Annals of the Entomological Society of America* **67**, 265-270.

218.   Girling, D.J.; Greathead, D.J.; Mohyuddin, A.I.; Sankaran, T. (1979) The potential for biological control in the suppression of parasitic weeds. *Biocontrol News and Information (Sample issue),* 7-16.

219.   Given, B.B.; Woods, G.F. (1964) Gall midge to assist in controlling St. John's Wort. *New Zealand Journal of Agriculture* **108**, 61-63.

220.   Goeden, R.D. (1978) Biological contol of weeds. In; Clausen, C.P. *(Ed) Introduced parasites and predators of arthropod pests and weeds. Agriculture Handbook, United States Department of Agriculture* **480**, 357-545.

221. Goeden, R.D. (1988) A capsule of biological control of weeds. *Biocontrol News and Information* **9**, 55-61.

222. Goeden, R.D. (1992) Milk thistle, *Silybum marianum* (L.) Gaertner (Asteraceae). In; Nechols, J.R.; Andres, L.A.; Beardsley, J.W.; Goeden, R.D.; Jackson, C.G. *(Eds) Biological Control in the U.S. Western Region: Accomplishments and Benefits of Regional Research Project W-84 (1964-1989).* Berkeley; University of California, Division of Agriculture and Natural Resources, in press.

223. Goeden, R.D.; Fleschner, C.A.; Ricker, D.W. (1967) Biological control of prickly pear cacti on Santa Cruz Island, California. *Hilgardia* **38**, 579-606.

224. Goeden, R.D.; Kovalev, O.V.; Ricker, D.W. (1974) Arthropods exported from California to the USSR for ragweed control. *Weed Science* **22**, 156-158.

225. Goeden, R.D.; Ricker, D.W. (1978) Establishment of *Rhinocyllus conicus* (Col.: Curculionidae) on Italian thistle in southern California. *Environmental Entomology* **7**, 787-789.

226. Goeden, R.D.; Ricker, D.W. (1979) Field analyses of *Coleophora parthenica* (Lep.: Coleophoridae) as an imported natural enemy of Russian thistle, *Salsola iberica*, in the Coachella Valley of southern California. *Environmental Entomology* **8**, 1099-1101.

227. Goeden, R.D.; Ricker, D.W. (1981) Santa Cruz Island - revisited. Sequential photography records. The causation, rates of progress, and lasting benefits of successful biological weed control. *Proceedings of the 5th International Symposium on Biological Control of Weeds,* 355-365.

228. Goeden, R.D.; Ricker, D.W. (1985) Seasonal asynchrony of Italian thistle, *Carduus pycnocephalus*, and the weevil, *Rhinocyllus conicus* (Coleoptera: Curculionidae), introduced for biological control in southern California. *Environmental Entomology* **14**, 433-436.

229. Goeden, R.D.; Ricker, D.W.; Hawkins, B.A. (1985) Ethological and genetic differences among three biotypes of *Rhinocyllus conicus* (Coleoptera: Curculionidae) introduced into North America for the biological control of asteraceous thistles. *Proceedings of the 6th International Symposium on Biological Control of Weeds,* 181-189.

230. Goeden, R.D.; Ricker, D.W.; Müller, H. (1987) Introduction, recovery, and limited establishment of *Coleophora klimeschiella* (Lepidoptera: Coleophoridae) on Russian thistles, *Salsola australis*, in southern California. *Environmental Entomology* **16**, 1027-1029.

231. Goeden, R.D.; Pemberton, R.W. (1992) Russian thistle, *Salsola australis* R. Brown (Chenopodiaceae). In; Nechols, J.R.; Andres, L.A.; Beardsley, J.W.; Goeden, R.D.; Jackson, C.G. *(Eds) Biological Control in the U.S. Western Region: Accomplishments and Benefits of Regional Research Project W-84 (1964-1989).* Berkeley; University of California, Division of Agriculture and Natural Resources, in press.

232. Gonzalez, R.H.; Rojas, S. (1966) Estudio anlitico del control biologico de plagas agricolas en Chile. *Agricultura Technica (Chile)* **26**, 133-147.

233. Gordon, A.J.; Kluge, R.L.; Neser, S. (1985) The effect of the gall midge, *Zeuxidiplosis giardi* (Diptera: Cecidomyiidae) on seedlings of St. John's wort, *Hypericum perforatum* (Clusiaceae). *Proceedings of the 6th International Symposium on Biological Control of Weeds,* 743-748.

234. Gordon, A.J.; Neser, S. (1986) The seasonal history of the gall midge *Zeuxidiplosis giardi* Kieffer (Diptera: Cecidomyiidae), an introduced natural enemy of St John's wort, *Hypericum perforatum* L. *Journal of the Entomological Society South Africa* **49**, 115-120.

235. Gordon, A.J.; Kluge, R.L. (1991) Biological control of St John's wort, *Hypericum perforatum* (Clusiaceae), in south Africa. *Agriculture, Ecosystems and Environment* **37**, 77-90.

236. Greathead, D.J. (1968) Biological control of *Lantana*. A review and discussion of recent developments in East Africa. *Pest Articles and News Summaries (PANS)* **14C**, 167-175.

237. Greathead, D.J. (1971) A review of biological control in the Ethiopian Region. *Technical Communication, Commonwealth Institute of Biological Control* **5**, 162 pp.

238. Greathead, D.J. (1976) A review of biological control in western and southern Europe. *Technical Communication, Commonwealth Institute of Biological Control* **7**, 75-78.

239. Greathead, D.J. (1984) The natural enemies of *Striga* spp. and the prospects for their utilisation as biological control agents. In; Ayensu, E.S.; Doggett, H.; Keynes, R.D.; Marton-Lefevre, J.; Musselman, L.J.; Parker, C.; Pickering, A. *(Eds) Striga. Biology and Control.* France; ICSU Press and IDRC, pp. 133-160.

240. Greathead, D.J. (personal communication 1991) CAB International Institute of Biological Control, Silwood Park, Buckhurst Road, Ascot, Berks, SL5 7TA, United Kingdom.

241. Greenwood, S. (personal communication 1988) CAB International Institute of Biological Control, Silwood Park, Buckhurst Road, Ascot, Berks, SL5 7TA, United Kingdom.

242. Greve, J.E. van S.; Ismay, J.W. (Eds) (1983) Crop insect survey of Papua New Guinea from July 1st 1969 to December 31st 1978. *Papua New Guinea Agricultural Journal* **32**, 1-120.

243. Gutierrez, J.; Forno, I.W. (1989) Introduction into New Caledonia of two hispine phytophages of lantana: *Octotoma scabripennis* and *Uroplata girardi* (Coleoptera, Chrysomelidae). *Acta Oecologica, Oecologia Applicata* **10**, 19-29.

244. Habeck, D.H. (1974) *Arzama densa* as a pest of dasheen. *Florida Entomologist* **57**, 409-410.

245. Habeck, D.H.; Haag, K.; Buckingham, G. (1986) Native insect enemies of aquatic macrophytes-moths. *Aquatics* **8**, 17-22.

246. Habeck, D.H.; Bennett, F.D. (1990) *Cactoblastis cactorum* Berg (Lepidoptera: Pyralidae), a Phycitine new to Florida. *Entomology Circular No. 333, FDA and Consumer Service, Division of Plant Industry* 4 pp.

247. Hancox, N.G.; Syrett, P.; Scott, R.R. (1986) Biological control of St. John's wort *(Hypericum perforatum)* in New Zealand: a review. *Plant Protection Quarterly* **1**, 152-155.

248. Harley, K.L.S. (1973) Biological control of Central and South American weeds in Australia. *Proceedings of the 2nd International Symposium on Biological Control of Weeds*, 4-8.

249. Harley, K.L.S. (1974) Biological control of *Lantana* in Australia. *Proceedings of the 3rd International Symposium on Biological Control of Weeds*, 23-29.

250. Harley, K.L.S. (personal communication 1991) Commonwealth Scientific and Industrial Research Organisation, Division of Entomology, Long Pocket Laboratories, Private Bag No. 3, Indooroopilly, Queensland 4068, Australia.

251. Harley, K.L.S.; Kunimoto, R.K. (1969) Assessment of the suitability of *Plagiohammus spinipennis* (Thoms.) (Col., Cerambycidae) as an agent for control of weeds of the genus *Lantana* (Verbenaceae). *II. Host specificity. Bulletin of Entomological Research* **58**, 787-792.

252. Harley, K.L.S.; Kassulke, R.C. (1971) Tingidae for biological control of *Lantana camara* (Verbenaceae). *Entomophaga* **16**, 389-410.

253. Harley, K.L.S.; Forno, I.W.; Kassulke, R.C.; Sands, D.P.A. (1984) Biological control of water lettuce. *Journal of Aquatic Plant Management* **22**, 101-102.

254. Harley, K.L.S.; Miller, I.L.; Napompeth, B.; Thamasara, S. (1985) An integrated approach to the management of *Mimosa pigra* L. in Australia and Thailand. *Proceedings of the 10th Asian-Pacific Weed Science Society Conference*, 209-215.

255. Harley, K.L.S.; Kassulke, R.C.; Sands, D.P.A.; Day, M.D. (1990) Biological control of water lettuce, *Pistia stratiotes* [Araceae] by *Neohydronomus affinis* [Coleoptera: Curculionidae]. *Entomophaga* **35**, 363-374.

256. Harman, H.M.; Syrett, P. (1989) Establishment and seasonality of two ragwort feeding insects at Hanmer, New Zealand. *Proceedings of the 42nd New Zealand Weed and Pest Control Conference*, 48-51.

257. Harris, P. (1961) Control of toadflax by *Brachypterolus pulicarius* (L.) (Coleoptera: Curculionidae) and *Gymnaetron antirrhini* (Payk.) (Coleoptera: Curculionidae) in Canada. *Canadian Entomologist* **93**, 977-981.

258. Harris, P. (1964) Host specificity of *Altica carduorum* Guer. (Coleoptera: Chrysomelidae). *Canadian Journal of Zoology* **42**, 857-862.

259. Harris, P. (1980) Effects of *Urophora affinis* Frfld. and *U. quadrifasciata* (Meig.) (Diptera: Tephritidae) on *Centaurea diffusa* Lam. and *C. maculosa* Lam. (Compositae). *Zeitschrift fur Angewandte Entomologie* **90**, 190-201.

260. Harris, P. (1980) Establishment of *Urophora affinis* Frfld. and *U. quadrifasciata* (Meig.) (Diptera: Tephritidae) in Canada for the biological control of diffuse and spotted knapweed. *Zeitschrift fur Angewandte Entomologie* **89**, 504-514.

154

261. Harris, P. (1984) *Carduus nutans* L., nodding thistle and *C. acanthoides* L., plumeless thistle (Compositae). In; Kelleher, J.S.; Hulme, M.A. *(Eds) Biological Control Programmes Against Insects And Weeds In Canada 1969-1980.* London; Commonwealth Agricultural Bureaux, pp. 115-126.

262. Harris, P. (1984) *Euphorbia esula-virgata* complex, leafy spurge and *E. cyparissias* L., cypress spurge (Euphorbiaceae). In; Kelleher, J.S.; Hulme, M.A. *(Eds) Biological Control Programmes Against Insects And Weeds In Canada 1969-1980.* London; Commonwealth Agricultural Bureaux, pp. 159-169.

263. Harris, P. (1984) *Linaria vulgaris* Miller, yellow toadflax and *L. dalmatica* (L.) Mill., broad-leaved toadflax (Scrophulariaceae). In; Kelleher, J.S.; Hulme, M.A. *(Eds) Biological Control Programmes Against Insects And Weeds In Canada 1969-1980.* London; Commonwealth Agricultural Bureaux, pp. 179-182.

264. Harris, P. (1984) *Salsola pestifer* A.Nels., Russian thistle (Chenopodiaceae). In; Kelleher, J.S.; Hulme, M.A. *(Eds) Biological Control Programmes Against Insects And Weeds In Canada 1969-1980.* London; Commonwealth Agricultural Bureaux, pp. 191-193.

265. Harris, P. (1986) Biological control of knapweed with *Urophora affinis* (Frfld.). *Canadex* **641.613**, 2 pp.

266. Harris, P. (1986) Biological control of knapweed with *Urophora quadrifasciata* MG. *Canadex* **641.613**, 2 pp.

267. Harris, P. (personal communication 1991) Agriculture Canada, Research Station, Box 440, Regina, Saskatchewan, S4P 3A2, Canada.

268. Harris, P.; Peschken, D.; Milroy, J. (1969) The status of biological control of the weed *Hypericum perforatum* in British Columbia. *Canadian Entomologist* **101**, 1-15.

269. Harris, P.; Alex, J. (1971) *Euphorbia esula* L., leafy spurge and *E. cyparissias* L., cypress spurge (Euphorbiaceae). *Technical Communication, Commonwealth Institute of Biological Control* **4**, 83-88.

270. Harris, P.; Carder, A.C. (1971) *Linaria vulgaris* Mill., yellow toadflax, and *L. dalmatica* (L.) Mill., broad-leaved toadflax (Scrophulariaceae). *Technical Communication, Commonwealth Institute of Biological Control* **4**, 94-97.

271. Harris, P.; Peschken, D.P. (1971) *Hypericum perforatum* L., St. John's wort (Hypericaceae). *Technical Communication, Commonwealth Institute of Biological Control* **4**, 89-94.

272. Harris, P.; Wilkinson, A.T.S.; Neary, M.E.; Thompson, L.W. (1971) *Senecio jacobaea* L., tansy ragwort (Compositae). *Technical Communication, Commonwealth Institute of Biological Control* **4**, 97-104.

273. Harris, P.; Zwolfer, H. (1971) *Carduus acanthoides* L. welted thistle, and *C. nutans* L., nodding thistle (Compositae). *Technical Communication, Commonwealth Institute of Biological Control* **4**, 76-79.

274. Harris, P.; Thompson, L.S.; Wilkinson, A.T.S.; Neary, M.E. (1978) Reproduction biology of tansy ragwort, climate and biological control by the cinnabar moth in Canada. *Proceedings of the 4th International Symposium on Biological Control of Weeds,* 163-173.

275. Harris, P.; Wilkinson, A.T.S.; Thompson, L.S.; Neary, M. (1978) Interaction between the cinnabar moth, *Tyria jacobaeae* L. (Lep.: Arctiidae) and ragwort *Senecio jacobaea* L. (Compositae) in Canada. *Proceedings of the 4th International Symposium on Biological Control of Weeds,* 174-180.

276. Harris, P.; Cranston, R. (1979) An economic evaluation of control methods for diffuse and spotted knapweed in western Canada. *Canadian of Journal Plant Science* **59**, 375-382.

277. Harris, P.; Maw, M. (1984) *Hypericum perforatum* L., St. John's wort (Hypericaceae). In; Kelleher, J.S.; Hulme M.A. *(Eds) Biological Control Programmes Against Insects And Weeds In Canada 1969-1980.* London; Commonwealth Agricultural Bureaux, pp. 171-177.

278. Harris, P.; Myers, J.H. (1984) *Centaurea diffusa* Lam. *C. maculosa* Lam. s. lat., diffuse and spotted knapweed (Compositae). In; Kelleher, J.S.; Hulme M.A. *(Eds) Biological Control Programmes Against Insects And Weeds In Canada 1969-1980.* London; Commonwealth Agricultural Bureaux, pp. 127-137.

279.   Harris, P.; Wilkinson, A.T.S. (1984) *Cirsium vulgare* (Savi) Ten., bull thistle (Compositae). In; Kelleher, J.S.; Hulme M.A. *(Eds) Biological Control Programmes Against Insects And Weeds In Canada 1969-1980.* London; Commonwealth Agricultural Bureaux, pp. 147-153.

280.   Harris, P.; Wilkinson, A.T.S.; Myers, J.H. (1984) *Senecio jacobaea* L., tansy ragwort (Compositae). In; Kelleher, J.S.; Hulme M.A. *(Eds) Biological Control Programmes Against Insects And Weeds In Canada 1969-1980.* London; Commonwealth Agricultural Bureaux, pp. 195-201.

281.   Hartmann, H.; Watson, A.K. (1980) Damage to common ragweed *(Ambrosia artemisiifolia)* caused by the white rust fungus *(Albugo tragopogonis)*. *Weed Science* **28**, 632-635.

282.   Hasan, S. (1988) Chapter 9. Biocontrol of weeds with Microbes. In; Mukerji, K.G.; Garg, K.L. *(Eds) Biocontrol of Plant Diseases Volume 1,* CRC Press; Boca Raton, Florida, pp. 129-151.

283.   Hasan, S. (personal communication 1991) Commonwealth Scientific and Industrial Research Organisation, Biological Control Unit, 335 Avenue Abbé Paul Parguel, 34090 Montpellier, France.

284.   Haseler, W.H. (1966) The status of insects introduced for the biological control of weeds in Queensland. *Journal of the Entomological Society of Queensland* **5**, 1-4.

285.   Hawkes, R.B. (1973) Natural mortality of cinnabar moth in California. *Annals of the Entomological Society of America* **66**, 137-146.

286.   Hawkes, R.B. (1981) Biological control of tansy ragwort in the State of Oregon, U.S.A. *Proceedings of the 5th International Symposium on Biological Control of Weeds,* 623-626.

287.   Hawkes, R.B.; Johnson, G.R. (1978) *Longitarsus jacobaeae* aids moth in biological control of tansy ragwort. *Proceedings of the 4th International Symposium on Biological Control of Weeds,* 193-196.

288.   Hawkes, R.B.; Mayfield, A. (1978) *Coleophora* spp. as biological control agents against Russian thistle. *Proceedings of the 4th International Symposium on Biological Control of Weeds,* 113-116.

289.   He, D.; Liu, L.; Jing, G.; Wei, Y. (1987) The safety testing of the Tephritid gallfly, *Procecidochares utilis* Stone. *Chinese Journal of Biological Control* **3**, 1-3. (In Chinese with English abstract).

290.   Higa, S.Y. (personal communication 1979) Department of Agriculture, 1428 So. King Street, Honolulu, Hawaii 96814, United States of America.

291.   Hight, S.D. (personal communication 1986) United States Department of Agriculture, Agricultural Research Service, Beltsville, Maryland 20705, United States of America.

292.   Hill, R.L. (1989) *Ageratina adenophora* (Sprengel) R. King & H. Robinson, Mexican devil weed (Asteraceae). In; Cameron, P.J.; Hill, R.L.; Bain, J.; Thomas, W.P. *Eds)* A review of biological control of invertebrate pests and weeds in New Zealand 1874 to 1987. *Technical communication, CAB International Institute of Biological Control* **10**, pp. 317-320.

293.   Hill, R.L. (personal communication 1991) Entomology Division, Department of Scientific and Industrial Research, Private Bag, Christchurch, New Zealand.

294.   Hill, R.L.; Gourlay, A.H.; Martin, L. (1991) Seasonal and geographic variation in the predation of gorse seed, *Ulex europaeus* L., by the seed weevil *Apion ulicis* Forst. *New Zealand Journal of Zoology* **18**, 37-43.

295.   Hill, R.L.; Grindell, J.M.; Winks, C.J.; Sheat, J.J.; Hayes, L.M. (1991) Establishment of gorse spider mite as a control agent for gorse. *Proceedings of the 44th New Zealand Weed and Pest Control Conference,* 31-34.

296.   Hoffman, J.H. (1988) An early assessment of *Trichapion lativentre* (Coleoptera: Apionidae) for biological control of the weed *Sesbania punicea* (Fabaceae) in South Africa. *Journal of the Entomological Society of Southern Africa* **51**, 265-273.

297.   Hoffmann, J.H.; Moran, V.C. (1988) The invasive weed, *Sesbania punicea* in South Africa and prospects for its biological control. *South African Journal of Science* **84**, 740-742.

298.   Hoffmann, J.H.; Moran, V.C. (1989) Novel graphs for depicting herbivore damage on plants: the biocontrol of *Sesbania punicea* (Fabaceae) by an introduced weevil. *Journal of Applied Ecology* **26**, 353-360.

156

299. Hoffmann, J.H.; Moran, V.C.; Underhill, L.G. (1990) Relationships between the history of colonization and abundance of *Trichapion lativentre* (Coleoptera: Apionidae) in the suppression of growth and reproduction of a weed, *Sesbania punicea* (Fabaceae). *Environmental Entomology* **19**, 1866-1871.

300. Hoffmann, J.H.; Moran, V.C. (1991) Biological control of *Sesbania punicea* (Fabaceae) South Africa. *Agriculture, Ecosystems and Environment* **37**, 157-174.

301. Holloway, B.A. (1983) Species of ragwort seedflies imported into New Zealand (Diptera: Anthomyiidae). *New Zealand Journal of Agricultural Research* **26**, 245-249.

302. Hosking, J.R. (1985) The role of insects in the long term control of *Opuntia aurantiaca*. *Proceedings of the 6th International Symposium on Biological Control of Weeds*, 761-769.

303. Hoy, J.M. (1949) Control of Manuka by blight. *New Zealand Journal of Agriculture* **79**, 321-324.

304. Hoy, J.M. (1960) Establishment of *Procecidochares utilis* Stone (Diptera: Trypetidae) on *Eupatorium adenophorum* Spreng. in New Zealand. *New Zealand Journal of Science* **3**, 200-208.

305. Huet, M. (1970) *Traite de Pisciculture*. 4th edition. Bruxelles; Editions Ch. de Wyngaert, 718 pp. [Cited by Vivier, P. (1970) *Bulletin Francais de Pisciculture* **238**, 31-33].

306. Huffaker, C.B.; Kennett, C.E. (1959) A ten-year study of vegetational changes associated with biological control of Klamath weed. *Journal of Range Management* **12**, 69-82.

307. Huffacker, C.B.; Hamai, J.; Nowierski, R.M. (1983) Biological control of puncturevine, *Tribulus terrestris* in California after twenty years of activity of introduced weevils. *Entomophaga* **28**, 387-400.

308. Igrc, J. (1987) The investigations of the beetles *Zygogramma suturalis* F. - as a potential agent for the biological control of the common ragweed. *Poljoprivredna znanstvena smotra* **76-77**, 31-56. (In Serbo-Croatian with English summary).

309. Igrc, J. (personal communication 1991) University of Zagreb, Institute for Plant Protection, 41000 Zagreb, Simunska 25, P.O. Box 281, Yugoslavia.

310. Ireson, J.E.; Friend, D.A.; Holloway, R.J.; Paterson, S.C. (1991) Biology of *Longitarsus flavicornis* (Stephens) (Coleoptera: Chrysomelidae) and its effectiveness in controlling ragwort *(Senecio jacobaea* L.) in Tasmania. *Journal of the Australian Entomological Society* **30**, 129-141.

311. Irving, N.S.; Bashir, M.O. (1982) Introduction of some natural enemies of water hyacinth to the White Nile, Sudan. *Tropical Pest Management* **28**, 20-26.

312. Isherwood, M.O. (personal communication 1991) Department of Agriculture, 1428 So. King Street, Honolulu, Hawaii 96814-2512, United States of America.

313. Jahnichen, H. (1978) Stand und Perspektive der biologischen Krautung durch Amurkarpfen *(Ctenopharyngodon idella* Val.) in der DDR. *Zeitschrift fur die Binnenfisch. DDR* **25**, 361-365. [Also *Weed Abstracts* (1979) **28**, 3567].

314. Jarvis, E. (1913) An insect enemy of nut grass. *Queensland Agricultural Journal* **31**, 390-392.

315. Jayanth, K.P. (1987) Biological control of the water fern *Salvinia molesta* infesting a lily pond in Bangalore (India) by *Cyrtobagous salviniae*. *Entomophaga* **32**, 163-165.

316. Jayanth, K.P. (1987) Biological control of Water Hyacinth in India. *Indian Institute of Horticultural Research Technical Bulletin No. 3*, 28 pp.

317. Jayanth, K.P. (1987) Introduction and establishment of *Zygogramma bicolorata* on *Parthenium hysterophorus* at Bangalore, India. *Current Science* **56**, 310-311.

318. Jayanth, K.P. (1987) Suppression of water hyacinth by the exotic insect *Neochetina eichhorniae* in Bangalore, India. *Current Science* **56**, 494-495.

319. Jayanth, K.P. (1988) Biological control of water hyacinth in India by release of the exotic weevil *Neochetina bruchi*. *Current Science* **17**, 968-970.

320. Jayanth, K.P. (1988) Successful biological control of water hyacinth *(Eichhornia crassipes)* by *Neochetina eichhorniae* (Coleoptera: Curculionidae) in Bangalore, India. *Tropical Pest Management* **34**, 263-266.

321. Jayanth, K.P. (personal communication 1991) Indian Institute of Horticultural Research, Hessaraghatta Lake Post, Bangalore-560089, India.

322. Jayanth, K.P.; Visalakshi, P.N.G. (1989) Establishment of the exotic mite *Orthogalumna terebrantis* Wallwork on water hyacinth in Bangalore, India. *Journal of Biological Control* **3**, 75-76.

323. Jessep, C.T. (1970) St.John's Wort in New Zealand. *Review, Tussock Grasslands and Mountain Lands Institute* **20**, 76-83.

324. Jessep, C.T. (1975) Introduction of a weevil for biological control of nodding thistle. *Proceedings of the 28th New Zealand Weed Pest Control Conference*, 205-206.

325. Jessep, C.T. (1980) Progress report on biological control of nodding thistle *(Carduus nutans)* in New Zealand. *Proceedings of the 5th International Symposium on Biological Control of Weeds*, 635-637.

326. Jessep. C.T. (1989) *Carduus nutans* L., nodding thistle (Asteraceae). In; Cameron, P.J.; Hill, R.L.; Bain, J.; Thomas, W.P. *(Eds)* A review of biological control of invertebrate pests and weeds in New Zealand 1874 to 1987. *Technical Communication, CAB International Institute of Biological Control* **10**, pp. 339-342.

327. Jessep, C.T. (1989) *Cirsium arvense* (L.) Scopoli, Californian thistle (Asteraceae). In; Cameron, P.J.; Hill, R.L.; Bain, J.; Thomas, W.P. *(Eds)* A review of biological control of invertebrate pests and weeds in New Zealand 1874 to 1987. *Technical communication, CAB International Institute of Biological Control* **10**, pp. 343-345.

328. Jessep, C.T. (1989) Introduction of the crown weevil *(Trichosirocalus horridus)* as an additional biocontrol agent against nodding thistle. *Proceedings of the 42nd New Zealand Weed and Pest Control Conference*, 52-54.

329. Jessep, C.T. (1990) Aspects of the biology of nodding thistle *(Carduus nutans* L.) in Canterbury, New Zealand. *New Zealand Journal of Agricultural Research* **33**, 173-183.

330. Jessep, C.T. (personal communication 1990) Department of Scientific and Industrial Research, Entomology Division, Lincoln Research Centre, Private Bag, Christchurch, New Zealand.

331. Jones, S.; Sarojini, K.K. (1951) History of transplantation and introduction of fishes in India. *Journal of the Bombay Natural History Society* **50**, 594-609.

332. Joseph, P.T. (personal communication 1972) Department of Agriculture, Plant Protection, Government of the Cook Islands, Rarotonga.

333. Joy, P.J. (personal communication 1991) Kerala Agricultural University, College of Horticulture, Vellanikkara, Trichur-680 654, South India.

334. Joy, P.J.; Varghese, K.C.; Abraham, C.C. (1981) Studies on biology and host range of *Paulina acuminata* De Geer (Orthoptera: Acrididae) and its efficacy for the control of *Salvinia molesta* Mitchell an aquatic floating weed in Kerala. *Proceedings of the 8th Asian-Pacific Weed Science Society Conference*, 201-206.

335. Joy, P.J.; Satheesan, N.V.; Lyla, K.R.; Joseph, D. (1985) Successful biological control of the floating weed *Salvinia molesta* Mitchell using the weevil *Cyrtobagous salviniae* Calder and Sands in Kerala (India). *Proceedings of the 10th Asian-Pacific Weed Science Society* **2**, 622-626.

336. Julien, M.H. (1981) A discussion of the limited establishment of *Perapion antiquum* and a review of the current status of biological control of *Emex* spp. in Australia. *Proceedings of the 5th International Symposium on Biological Control of Weeds*, 507-514.

337. Julien, M.H. (1981) Control of aquatic *Alternanthera philoxeroïdes* in Australia; another success for *Agasicles hygrophila. Proceedings of the 5th International Symposium on Biological Control of Weeds*, 583-588.

338. Julien, M.H. (1988) Weeds in wetlands; biological control may help. *Proceedings of the International Symposium on Wetlands, Newcastle*, 199-212.

339. Julien, M.H. (personal observations 1991) Commonwealth Scientific and Industrial Research Organisation, Division of Entomology, Long Pocket Laboratories, Private Bag No. 3, Indooroopilly, Queensland 4068, Australia.

340. Julien, M.H.; Broadbent, J.E.; Matthews, N.C. (1979) Effects of *Puccinia xanthii* on *Xanthium strumarium* (Compositae). *Entomophaga* **24**, 29-34.

341. Julien, M.H.; Chan, R.R. (1992) Biological control of alligator weed: unsuccessful attempts to control terrestrial growth using the flea beetle *Disonycha argentinensis* [Col.: Chrysomelidae]. *Entomophaga*, **37**, in press.

342. Jupp, P. (personal communication 1991) Commonwealth Scientific and Industrial Research Organisation, Division of Entomology, G.P.O. Box 1700, Canberra, Australian Capital Territory 2601, Australia.

343. Kamath, M.K. (1979) A review of biological control of insect pests and noxious weeds in Fiji (1969-1978). *Agricultural Journal of Fiji* **41**, 55-72.

344. Kamath, M.K. (personal communication 1980) Ministry of Agriculture and Fisheries, Koronivia Research Station, P.O. Box 77, Nausori, Fiji Islands.

345. Kapoor, V.C.; Malla, Y.K. (1978) The infestation of the gall fruit-fly, *Procecidochares utilus* (Stone) on crofton weed, *Eupatorium adenophorum* Sprengel in Kathmandu. *Indian Journal of Entomology* **40**, 337-339.

346. Kasno,; Aziz, K.A.; Soerjani, M. (1979) Prospects for biological control of weeds in Indonesia. *Proceedings of the 7th Asian-Pacific Weed Science Society Conference, Supplementary volume*, 35-38.

347. Kassulke, R.C.; Harley, K.L.S.; Maynard, G.V. (1990) Host specificity of *Acanthoscelides quadridentatus* and *A. puniceus* [Col.: Bruchidae] for biological control of *Mimosa pigra* (with preliminary data on their biology). *Entomophaga* **35**, 85-97.

348. Kelsey, J.M. (1955) Ragwort seed-fly establishment in New Zealand. *New Zealand Journal of Science and Technology*. Section **A 36**, 605-607.

349. Kermack, J. (1928) Action taken in regard to control of noxious weeds. *Agricultural Journal of Fiji* **1**, 9-10.

350. Khattab, A.F.; El-Gharably, Z. (1986) Management of aquatic weeds in irrigation systems with special reference to the problems in Egypt. *Proceedings of the 7th International Symposium on Aquatic Weeds*, 199-206.

351. King, R.M.; Robinson, H. (1970) Studies in the *Eupatorieae* (Compositae). XIX. New combinations in Ageratina. *Phytologia* **19**, 208-229.

352. King, R.M.; Robinson, H. (1970) Studies in the *Eupatorieae* (Compositae). XXIX. The genus *Chromolaena*. *Phytologia* **20**, 196-209.

353. Kirkland, R.L.; Goeden, R.D. (1978) An insecticidal-check study of the biological control of puncturevine *(Tribulus terrestris)* by imported weevils, *Microlarinus lareynii* and *M. lypriformis* (Col.: Curculionidae). *Environmental Entomology* **7**, 349-354.

354. Kissinger, D.G. (1966) *Cyrtobagous Hustache*, a genus of weevils new to the United States fauna (Coleoptera: Curculionidae: Bagoini). *The Coleopterist's Bulletin* **20**, 125-127.

355. Kluge, R.L. (1991) Biological control of crofton weed, *Ageratina adenophora* (Asteraceae), in South Africa. *Agriculture, Ecosystems and Environment* **37**, 187-191.

356. Kluge, R.L. (1991) Biological control of triffid weed, *Chromolaena odorata* (Asteraceae), in South Africa. *Agriculture, Ecosystems and Environment* **37**, 193-197.

357. Kluge, R.L. (personal communication 1991) Department of Agriculture and Water Supply, Plant Protection Research Institute, Private Bag X134, Pretoria, Republic of South Africa.

358. Kluge, R.L.; Siebert, M.W. (1985) *Erytenna consputa* Pascoe (Coleoptera: Curculionidae) as the main mortality factor of developing fruits of the weed *Hakea sericea* Schrader, in South Africa. *Journal of the Entomological Society of South Africa* **48**, 241-245.

359. Kluge, R.L.; Neser, S. (1991) Biological control of *Hakea sericea* (Proteaceae) in South Africa. *Agriculture, Ecosystems and Environment* **37**, 91-113.

360. Klyueva, M.P.; Pamukchi, G.V. (1978) Broomrape midge - the natural enemy of broomrape in Moldavia. *Izvestiya Akademii Nauk Moldavskoi SSR, Seriya Biologicheskikh i Khimicheskikh Nauk* **4**, 21-25. [*Weed Abstracts* (1980) **29**, 827].

361. Kok, L.T. (1978) Status of biological control of musk thistle in Virginia. In; Frick, K.E. *(Ed) Biological Control of Thistles in the Genus Carduus in the United States. A Progress Report. United States Department of Agriculture, Southern Weed Science Laboratory, Stoneville, Mississippi*, pp. 23-30.

362. Kok, L.T. (1981) Status of two European weevils introduced for the biological control of *Carduus* thistles in the USA. *Acta Phytopathologica Academiae Scientiarum Hungaricae* **16**, 139-142.

363.   Kok, L.T. (1989) Biological control of weeds in Virginia from 1969-1986. *Proceedings of the 7th International Symposium on Biological Control of Weeds,* 623-629.

364.   Kok, L.T. (personal communication 1991) Virginia Polytechnic Institute and State University, Blacksburg, Virginia 24061, United States of America.

365.   Kok, L.T.; Surles, W.W. (1975) Successful biocontrol of musk thistle by an introduced weevil, *Rhinocyllus conicus. Environmental Entomology* **4**, 1025-1027.

366.   Kok, L.T.; Trumble, J.T. (1979) Establishment of *Ceuthorhynchidius horridus* (Col.: Curculionidae), an imported thistle-feeding weevil, in Virginia. *Environmental Entomology* **8**, 221-223.

367.   Kok, L.T.; Pienkowski, R.L. (1985) Biological control of musk thistle by *Rhinocyllus conicus* (Coleoptera: Curculionidae) in Virginia from 1969 to 1980. *Proceedings of the 6th International Symposium on Biological Control of Weeds,* 433-438.

368.   Kok, L.T. (1986) Impact of *Trichosirocalus horridus* (Coleoptera: Curculionidae) on *Carduus* thistles in pastures. *Crop Protection* **5**, 214-217.

369.   Kovalev, O.V. (1971) Phytophages of ragweeds *(Ambrosia* L.) in North America and their application in biological control in USSR. *Zoologichesky Zhurnal* **50**, 199-209. (In Russian with English abstract).

370.   Kovalev, O.V. (1973) Modern outlooks of biological control of weed plants in the U.S.S.R. and the international phytophagous exchange. *Proceedings of the 2nd International Symposium on Biological Control of Weeds,* 166-172.

371.   Kovalev, O.V. (1981) The introduction and acclimatization of phytophagous insect pests of *Ambrosia* (Ambrosia L., Asteraceae) in the USSR. *Trudy Vsesoyuznogo Entomologicheskogo Obshchestva* **63**, 9-11. (In Russian with English abstract).

372.   Kovalov, O.V. (personal communication 1991) Zoological Institute of the USSR Academy of Sciences, Leningrad 199034, Union of the Soviet Socialist Republics.

373.   Kovalev, O.V.; Runeva, T.D. (1970) *Tarachidia candefacta* Hubn. (Lepidoptera, Noctuidae) - an efficient phytophagous insect in the biological control of weeds of the genus *Ambrosia* L. *Entomologocheskoe Obozreniye* **49**, 23-26. (In Russian with English abstract).

374.   Kovalev, O.V.; Reznik, S.Y.; Cherkashin, V.N. (1983) Specific features of methods of using *Zygogramma* Chevr. (Coloeptera, Chrysomelidae) in the biological control of ragweeds *(Ambrosia artemisiifolia* L., *Ambrosia psilostachya* DC.). *Entomologicheskoe Obozreniye* **62**, 402-408. (In Russian with English abstract).

375.   Kovalev, O.V.; Sivushkova, V.K.; Yakutina, M.A. (1989) Influence of the ambrosia leaf beetle on vegetation dynamics of stratified communities. *Proceedings of the Zoological Institute* **189**, 200-211. (In Russian with English abstract).

376.   Krauss, N.L.H. (1962) Biological control investigations on insect, snail and weed pests in tropical America 1961. *Proceedings of the Hawaiian Entomological Society* **18**, 131-133.

377.   Krauss, N.L.H. (1962) Biological control investigations on lantana. *Proceedings of the Hawaiian Entomological Society* **18**, 134-136.

378.   Krauss, N.L.H. (1963) Biological control investigations on christmas berry *(Schinus terebinthifolius)* and emex *(Emex* spp.). *Proceedings of the Hawaiian Entomological Society* **18**, 281-287.

379.   Krauss, N.L.H. (1965) Investigations on biological control of melastoma *(Melastoma melabathricum* L.). *Proceedings of the Hawaiian Entomological Society* **19**, 97-101.

380.   Krauss, N.L.H. (1966) Biological control investigations on some Hawaiian weeds. *Proceedings of the Hawaiian Entomological Society* **19**, 223-231.

381.   Krupauer, V. (1971) The use of herbivorous fishes for ameliorative purposes in Central and Eastern Europe. *Proceedings of the 3rd International Symposium on Aquatic Weeds,* 95-103.

382.   Lai, P.Y.; Funasaki, G.Y.; Higa, S. (1982) Introductions for biological control in Hawaii: 1979 and 1980. *Proceedings of the Hawaiian Entomological Society* **24**, 109-113.

383.   Lai, P.Y.; Funasaki, G.Y. (1985) Introductions for biological control in Hawaii 1981 and 1982. *Proceedings of the Hawaiian Entomological Society* **25**, 83-86.

384.   Lal, S.N. (personal communication 1990) Ministry of Primary Industries, Koronivia Research Station, P.O. Box 77, Nausori, Fiji.

385.   Laup, S. (1986) Biological control of water hyacinth: early observations. *Harvest* **12**, 35-40.

386.   Laup, S. (1986) Biological control of water lettuce: early observations. *Harvest* **12**, 41-43.

387.   Laup, S. (personal communication 1986) Department of Primary Industries, Wewak, Papua New Guinea.

388.   Lavigne, R. (personal communication 1991) Plant Science Department, University of Wyoming, Laramie, Wyoming 82071, United States of America.

389.   Lekic, M. (1970) The role of the dipteron *Phytomyza orobanchia* Kalt. (Agromyzidae) in reducing parasitic phanerogam populations of the *Orobanche* genus in Vojvodina. *Savremena Poljoprivreda* **18**, 627-637.

390.   Lever, R.J.A.W. (1938) Economic insects in some western Pacific Islands. *Agricultural Journal of Fiji* **4**, 11-12.

391.   Liebregts, W. (personal communication 1991) CSIRO Biological Control Project, P.O. Box 2293, Nuku'alofa, Tonga.

392.   Linke, K.-H.; Vorlaender, C.; Saxena, M.C. (1990) Occurrence and impact of *Phytomyza orobanchia* [Diptera: Agromyzidae] on *Orobanche crenata* [Orobanchaceae] in Syria. *Entomophaga* **35**, 633-639.

393.   Littlefield, J.L. (personal communication 1989) United States Department of Agriculture, Animal and Plant Health Inspection Service, Bozeman, Montana 59717, United States of America.

394.   Lonsdale, W.M. (personal communication 1986) Commonwealth Scientific and Industrial Research Organisation, Division of Entomology, Darwin Laboratories, PMB 44, Winnellie, Northern Territory 5788, Australia.

395.   Maceljski, M. (personal communication 1991) University of Zagreb, Faculty of Agricultural Sciences, Institute for Plant Protection, 41000 Zagreb, Simunska 25, P.O.B. 281, Yugoslavia.

396.   Macfarlane, B. (personal communication 1980) Ministry of Agriculture and Lands, P.O. Box G11, Honiara, Solomon Islands.

397.   Maddox, D.M. (1976) History of weevils on puncturevine in and near the United States. *Weed Science* **24**, 414-419.

398.   Maddox, D.M. (1981) Seed and stem weevils of puncturevine, a comparative study of impact, interaction, and insect strategy. *Proceedings of the 5th International Symposium on Biological Control of Weeds*, 447-467.

399.   Maddox, D.M.; Andres, L.A. (1979) Status of puncturevine weevils and their host plant in California. *California Agriculture* **22**, 7-9.

400.   Maddox, D.M.; Sobhian, R.; Joley, D.B.; Mayfield, A.; Supkoff, D. (1986) New biological control for yellow starthistle. *California Agriculture*, November-December, 4-6.

401.   Maddox, D.M.; Joley, D.B.; Mayfield, A.; Mackey, B.E. (1991) Impact of *Bangasternus orientalis* (Coleoptera: Curculionidae) on achene production of *Centaurea solstitialis* (Asterales: Asteraceae) at a low and high elevation site in California. *Environmental Entomology* **20**, 335-337.

402.   Markin, G.P.; Nagata, R.F.; Taniguchi, G. (1989) Biology and behaviour of the South American moth, *Cyanotricha necyria* (Felder and Rogenhofer) (Lepidoptera: Notodontidae), a potential biocontrol agent in Hawaii of the forest weed, *Passiflora mollissima* (HBK) Bailey. *Proceedings of the Hawaiian Entomological Society* **29**, 115-123

403.   Markin, G.P.; Yoshioka, E.R. (1989) Present status of biological control of the weed gorse (*Ulex europaeus* L.) in Hawaii. *Proceedings of the 7th International Symposium on Biological Control of Weeds*, 357-362.

404.   Markin, G.P.; Yoshioka, E.R.; Brown, R.E. (1992) Gorse, *Ulex europaeus* L. (Leguminosae). In; Nechols, J.R.; Andres, L.A.; Beardsley, J.W.; Goeden, R.D.; Jackson, C.G. *(Eds) Biological Control in the U.S. Western Region: Accomplishments and Benefits of Regional Research Project W-84 (1964-1989)*. Berkeley; University of California, Division of Agriculture and Natural Resources, in press.

405.   Marks, G.C.; Pascoe, I.G.; Bruzzese, E. (1984) First record of *Phragmidium violaceum* on blackberry in Victoria. *Australasian Plant Pathology* **13**, 12-13.

406.   Marshall, B.E.; Junor, F.J.R. (1981) The decline of *Salvinia molesta* on Lake Kariba. *Hydrobiologia* **83**, 477-484.

407.   Maw, M.G. (1984) *Biological control of weeds (1984). An update of Julien's world catalogue of agents and their target weeds.* Regina; Canada Agriculture, 45 pp.

408.   Maw, M.G. (1984) *Convolvulus arvensis* L., field bindweed (Convolvulaceae). In; Kelleher, J.S.; Hulme, M.A. *(Eds) Biological control Programmes Against Insects and Weeds In Canada 1969-1980.* London; Commonwealth Agricultural Bureaux, pp. 155-157.

409.   May, B.M.; Sands, D.P.A. (1986) Descriptions of larvae and biology of *Cyrtobagous* (Coloeptera: Curculionidae): agents for the biological control of salvinia. *Entomological Society of Washington* **88**, 303-312.

410.   McCaffrey, J.P. (personal communication 1986) Department of Plant, Soil and Entomological Sciences, University of Idaho, Moscow, Idaho 83843-4196, United States of America.

411.   McCaffrey, J.P.; Campbell, C.L. ; Andres, L.A. (1992) St. John's wort, *Hypericum perforatum* L. (Clusiaceae). In; Nechols, J.R.; Andres, L.A.; Beardsley, J.W.; Goeden, R.D.; Jackson, C.G. *(Eds) Biological Control in the U.S. Western Region: Accomplishments and Benefits of Regional Research Project W-84 (1964-1989).* Berkeley; University of California, Division of Agriculture and Natural Resources, in press.

412.   McClay, A.S. (1983) Biology and host-specificity of *Stobaera concinna* (Stål) (Homoptera: Delphacidae), a potential biocontrol agent for *Parthenium hysterophorus* L. (Compositae). *Folia Entomológica Mexicana* **56**, 21-30.

413.   McClay, A.S.; McFadyen, R.E.; Bradley, J.D. (1990) Biology of *Bucculatrix parthenica* Bradley sp. n. (Lepidoptera: Bucculatricidae) and its establishment in Australia as a biological control agent for *Parthenium hysterophorus* (Asteraceae). *Bulletin of Entomological Research* **80**, 427-432.

414.   McDermott, G.J.; Nowierski, R.M.; Story, J.M. (1990) First report of establishment of *Calophasia lunula* Hufn. (Lepidoptera: Noctuiidae) on Dalmatian toadflax, *Linaria genistifolia* ssp. *dalmatica* (L.) Maire and Petitmengin, in North America. *Canadian Entomologist* **122**, 767-768.

415.   McEvoy, P.B.; Cox, C.S.; James, R.R.; Rudd, N.T. (1989) Ecological mechanisms underlying successful biological weed control: field experiments with ragwort, *Senecio jacobaea*. *Proceedings of the 7th International Symposium on Biological Control of Weeds*, 55-66.

416.   McEvoy, P.; Cox, C.; Coombs, E. (1991) Successful biological control of ragwort, *Senecio jacobaea*, by introduced insects in Oregon. *Ecological Applications*, in press.

417.   McFadyen, R.E. (1980) A *Cactoblastis* (Lep.: Phycitidae) for the biological control of *Eriocereus martinii* (Cactaceae) in Australia. *Entomophaga* **25**, 37-42.

418.   McFadyen, R.E. (1985) The biological control programme against *Parthenium hysterophorus* in Queensland. *Proceedings of the 6th International Symposium on Biological Control of Weeds*, 789-796.

419.   McFadyen, R.E. (1989) Ragweed, parthenium and noogoora burr control in the post-*Epiblema* era. *Proceedings of the 5th Biennial Noxious Plants Conference* **1**, 5-8.

420.   McFadyen, R.E. (personal communication 1991) Department of Lands, Alan Fletcher Research Station, Sherwood, Queensland 4075, Australia.

421.   McFadyen, R.E.; McClay, A.S. (1981) Two new insects for the biological control of parthenium in Queensland. *Proceedings of the 6th Australian Weeds Conference*, 145-149.

422.   McFadyen, R.E.; Tomley, A.J. (1981) The successful biological control of Harrisia cactus *(Eriocereus martinii)* in Queensland. *Proceedings of the 6th Australian Weeds Conference*, 139-144.

423.   McFadyen, R.E.; Marohasy, J.J. (1990) A leaf feeding moth, *Euclasta whalleyi* [Lep.: Pyralidae], for the biological control of *Cryptostegia grandiflora* [Asclepiadaceae] in Queensland, Australia. *Entomophaga* **35**, 431-435.

424.   McFadyen, P.J. (1978) A review of the biocontrol of groundsel-bush *(Baccharis halimifolia* L.) in Queensland. *Proceedings of the 1st Conference of the Council of Australian Weed Science Societies*, 123-125.

425.   McFadyen, P.J. (1983) Host specificity and biology of *Megacyllene mellyi* (Coleoptera: Cerambycidae) introduced into Australia for the biological control of *Baccharis halimifolia* (Compositae). *Entomophaga* **28**, 65-72.

426.   McFadyen, P.J. (1985) Introduction of the gall fly, *Rhopalomyia californica* from the U.S.A. into Australia for the control of the weed *Baccharis halimifolia. Proceedings of the 6th International Symposium on Biological Control of Weeds*, 779-796.

427.   McFadyen, P.J. (personal communication 1986) Department of Lands, Alan Fletcher Research Station, Sherwood, Queensland 4075, Australia.

428.   McLaren, D.A. (personal communication 1991) Keith Turnbull Research Station, P.O. Box 48, Frankston, Victoria 3199, Australia

429.   McLennan, S. (personal communication 1991) Plant Protection Research Institute, Private Bag X5017, Stellenbosch 7600, Republic of South Africa.

430.   Michelsen, V. (1988) Taxonomy of the species of *Pegomya* (Diptera: Anthomyiidae) developing in the
*   shoots of spurges (*Euphorbia* spp.) *Entolomogica Scandinavica* **18**, 425-435.

432.   Miley, W.W.; Sutton, D.L.; Stanley, J.G. (1979) The role and impact of introduced grass carp (*Ctenopharyngodon idella* Val.) in the Union of Soviet Socialist Republics and several other European countries. *Proceedings of the Grass Carp Conference, Gainesville*, 177-183.

433.   Miller, D. (1948) Control of St. John's wort by imported beetle. *New Zealand Journal of Agriculture* **76**, 351-352.

434.   Miller, D. (1970) Biological control of weeds in New Zealand 1927-48. *Information Serial, New Zealand Department of Scientific and Industrial Research* 74.

435.   Mitchell, C.P. (1977) The use of grass carp for submerged weed control. *Proceedings of the 30th New Zealand Weed Pest Control Conference, 145-148. [Weed Abstracts (1978)* **27**, 1293].

436.   Mitchell, D.S.; Rose, D.J.W. (1979) Factors affecting fluctuations in extent of *Salvinia molesta* on Lake Kariba. *Pest Articles and Summaries (PANS)* **25**, 171-177.

437.   Miyazaki, M.; Naito, A. (1981) Biological Control of *Rumex obtusifolius* L. by *Gastrophysa atrocyanea* Mots. (Coleoptera: Chrysomelidae): Biology of the Insect. *Proceedings of the 1st Japan/USA Symposium on IPM, Tsukuba (Japan)*, 181-190.

438.   Moorhouse, J. (personal communication 1991) Commonwealth Scientific and Industrial Resarch Organisation, Division of Entomology, P.O. Box 1700, Canberra, Australian Capital Territory 2601, Australia.

439.   Moran, V.C.; Annecke, D.P. (1979) Critical reviews of biological control in South Africa. 3. The jointed cactus, *Opuntia aurantiaca* Lindley. *Journal of the Entomological Society of South Africa* **42**, 299-329.

440.   Moran, V.C.; Hoffmann, J.H. (1989) The effects of herbivory by a weevil species, acting alone and unrestrained by natural enemies, on growth and phenology of the weed *Sesbania punicea. Journal of Applied Ecology* **26**, 967-977.

441.   Moran, V.C.; Zimmermann, H.G. (1991) Biological control of cactus weeds of minor importance in South Africa. *Agriculture, Ecosystems and Environment* **37**, 37-55.

442.   Moran, V.C.; Zimmermann, H.G. (1991) Biological control of jointed cactus, *Opuntia aurantiaca* (Cactaceae), in South Africa. *Agriculture, Ecosystems and Environment* **37**, 5-27.

443.   Morris, M.J. (1987) Biology of the *Acacia* gall rust, *Uromycladium tepperianum. Plant Pathology* **36**, 100-106.

444.   Morris, M.J. (1989) Host specificity studies of a leaf spot fungus, *Phaeoramularia* sp., for the
*   biological control of crofton weed *(Ageratina adenophora)* in South Africa. *Phytophylactica* **21**, 281-283.

446.   Morris, M.J. (personal communication 1991) Plant Protection Research Institute, Private Bag X5017, Stellenbosch 7600, Republic of South Africa.

447.   Morris, M.J. (1991) The use of pathogens for biological weed control in South Africa. *Agriculture, Ecosystems and Environment* **37**, 239-.

448.   Mortensen, K. (1988) The potential of an endemic fungus, *Colletotrichum gloeosporioides*, for biological control of round-leaved mallow (*Malva pusilla*) and veletleaf (*Abutilon theophrasti*). *Weed Science* **36**, 473-478.

449.   Moutia, L.A.; Mamet, R. (1946) A review of twenty-five years of economic entomology in the Island of Mauritius. *Bulletin of Entomological Research* **36**, 439-472.

✱ References 431 and 445 have been deleted

450. Müller, H.; Schröder, D.; Gassmann, A. (1988) *Agapeta zoegana* (L.) (Lepidoptera: Cochylidae), a suitable prospect for biological control of spotted knapweed and diffuse knapweed, *Centaurea maculosa* Monnet de la Marck and *Centaurea diffusa* Monnet de la Marck (Compositae) in North American. *Canadian Entomologist* **120**, 109-124.

451. Müller, H.; Goeden, R.D. (1990) Parasitoids acquired by *Coleophora parthenica* [Lepidoptera: Coleophoridae], ten years after its introduction into southern California for the biological control of Russian thistle. *Entomophaga* **35**, 257-268.

452. Müller, H.; Nuessly, G.S.; Goeden, R.D. (1990) Natural enemies and host-plant asynchrony contributing to the failure of the introduced moth, *Coleophora parthenica* Meyrick (Lepidoptera: Coleophoridae), to control Russian thistle. *Agriculture, Ecosystems and Environment* **32**, 133-142.

453. Muniappan, R. (1988) Biological control of the weed, *Lantana camara* in Guam. *Journal of Plant Protection in the Tropics* **5**, 99-101.

454. Muniappan, R. (personal communication 1991) Agricultural Experiment Station, University of Guam, Mangilao, Guam 96923, United States of America.

455. Muniappan, R.; Viraktamath, C.A. (1986) Status of biological control of the weed, *Lantana camara* in India. *Tropical Pest Management* **32**, 40-42.

456. Muniappan, R.; Marutani, M.; Denton, G.R.W.; (1988) Introduction and establishment of *Pareuchaetes pseudoinsulata* Rego Barros (Arctiidae) against *Chromolaena odorata* in the Western Caroline Islands. *Journal of Biological Control* **2**, 141-142.

457. Myer, J.H. (1978) Biological control introductions as grandiose field experiments: adaptations of the cinnabar moth to new surroundings. *Proceedings of the 4th International Symposium on Biological Control of Weeds*, 181-188.

458. Nafus, D.; Schreiner, I. (1989) Biological control activities in the Mariana Islands from 1911 to 1988. *Micronesica* **22**, 65-106.

459. Nagata, R.F.; Markin, G.P. (1986) Status of insects introduced into Hawaii for the biological control of the wild blackberry *Rubus argutus* Link. *Proceedings of the 6th Conference in Natural Sciences, University of Hawaii, Manoa*, 53-64.

460. Naito, A. (personal communication 1987) National Agriculture Research Center, Ministry of Agriculture, Forestry and Fisheries, Yatabe, Tsukuba, 305 Japan.

461. Naito, A.; Miyazaki, M.; Kanda, K. (1979) Studies on the biological control of *Rumex obtusifolius* L., a grassland weed, by *Gastrophysa atrocyanea* Mots. (Coleoptera: Chrysomelidae). II. Dispersal of overwintered adult insects. *Applied Entomology and Zoology* **14**, 51-55.

462. Nakao, H.K. (1967) Releases of blackberry insects. *Proceedings of the Hawaiian Entomological Society* **19**, 339 and 376.

463. Nakao, H.K.; Funasaki, G.Y.; Davis, C.J. (1975) Introductions for biological control in Hawaii 1973. *Proceedings of the Hawaiian Entomological Society* **22**, 109-112.

464. Nakao, H.K.; Funasaki, G.Y. (1976) Introductions for biological control in Hawaii, 1974. *Proceedings of the Hawaiian Entomological Society* **22**, 329-331.

465. Nakao, H.K.; Funasaki, G.Y. (1979) Introductions for biological control in Hawaii: 1975 and 1976. *Proceedings of the Hawaiian Entomological Society* **13**, 125-128.

466. Napompeth, B. (1982) Biological research and development in Thailand. *Proceedings of the International Conference on Plant Protection in the Tropics*, 301-323.

467. Napompeth, B. (1984) Biological control of water hyacinth in Thailand. *Proceedings of the International Conference on Water Hyacinth, Hyderabad*, 811-822.

468. Napompeth, B. (1985) Biological methods of aquatic vegetation management in tropical Asia. *Ecology and Management Workshop, Aquatic Vegetation in the Tropics, University of Jakarta*, 16 pp.

469. Napompeth, B. (personal communication 1991) National Biological Control Research Centre, Karsetsart University, Bangkok 9, Thailand.

470. Napompeth, B.; Thi Hai, N.; Winotai, A. (1988) Attempts on biological control of Siam seed, *Chromolaena odorata* in Thailand. *Proceedings of the First International Workshop on Biological Control of* Chromolaena odorata, 57-62.

471.   Neser, S. (1985) A most promising bud-galling wasp, *Trichilogaster acaciaelongifoliae* (Pteromalidae), established against *Acacia longifolia* in South Africa. *Proceedings of the 6th International Symposium on Biological Control of Weeds*, 797-803.

472.   Neser, S. (personal communication 1991) Department of Agriculture and Water Supply, Plant Protection Research Institute, Private Bag X134, Pretoria, 0001, Republic of South Africa.

473.   Neser, S.; Annecke, D.P. (1973) Biological control of weeds in South Africa. *Entomology Memoir, Republic of South Africa Department of Agricultural Technical Services* **28**, 1-27.

474.   Neser, S.; Kluge, R.L. (1985) A seed-feeding insect showing promise in the control of a woody invasive plant: the weevil *Erytenna consputa* Pascoe on *Hakea sericea* (Proteaceae) in South Africa. *Proceedings of the 6th International Symposium on Biological Control of Weeds*, 805-809.

475.   Neser, S.; Zimmermann, H.G.; Erb, H.E.; Hoffmann, J.H. (1989) Progress and prospects for the biological control of two *Solanum* weeds in South Africa. *Proceedings of the 7th International Symposium on Biological Control of Weeds*, 371-381.

476.   Nieman, E. (1991) The introduction of *Mimorista pulchellalis* [Lepidoptera: Pyraustidae] into South Africa for the biological control of jointed cactus, *Opuntia aurantiaca*. 2. Field evaluation. *Entomophaga* **36**, 77-86.

477.   Norambuena, H.; Carrillo, R.; Neira, M. (1986) Introduccion, establecimento y potencial de *Apion ulicis* como antagonista de *Ulex europaeus* en el sur de Chile. *Entomophaga* **31**, 3-10.

478.   Nowierski, R.M. (personal communication, 1991) Department of Entomology, Montana State University, Bozeman, Montana 59717, United States of America.

479.   Nowierski, R.M. (1992) Dalmatian toadflax, *Linaria genistifolia* ssp. *dalmatica* (L.) Maine and Petitmengin (Scrophulariaceae). In; Nechols, J.R.; Andres, L.A.; Beardsley, J.W.; Goeden, R.D.; Jackson, C.G. *(Eds) Biological Control in the U.S. Western Region: Accomplishments and Benefits of Regional Research Project W-84 (1964-1989).* Berkeley; University of California, Division of Agriculture and Natural Resources, in press.

480.   Nowierski, R.M.; Story, J.M.; Lund, R.E. (1987) Two-level numerical sampling plans and optimal subsample size computations for *Urophora affinis* and *Urophora quadrifasciata* (Diptera: Tephritidae) on spotted knapweed. *Environmental Entomology* **16**, 933-937.

481.   O'Brien, C. (1976) A taxonomic revision of the new world subaquatic genus *Neochetina* (Coleoptera: Curculionidae: Bagoini). *Annals of the Entomological Society of America* **69**, 165-174.

482.   O'Connor, B.A. (1950) Biological control of insects and plants in Fiji. *Agricultural Journal of Fiji* **21**, 43-54.

483.   O'Connor, B.A. (1952) An introduced parasite of Noogoora burr. *Agricultural Journal of Fiji* **23**, 105-106.

484.   O'Connor, B.A. (1957) Entomological notes. *Agricultural Journal of Fiji* **28**, 79-87.

485.   O'Connor, B.A. (1960) A decade of biological control work in Fiji. *Agricultural Journal of Fiji* **30**, 44-54.

486.   Oehrens, E. (1977) Biological control of the blackberry through the introduction of rust, *Phragmidium violaceum*, in Chile. *FAO Plant Protection Bulletin* **25**, 26-28.

487.   Oehrens, E.B.; Gonzalez, S.M. (1974) Introduccion de *Phragmidium violaceum* (Schultz) Winter como factor de control biologico de zarza mora (*Rubus constrictus* Lef. et M. y R. *ulmifolius* Schott.). *Agro Sur* **2**, 30-33.

488.   Oehrens, E.; Gonzalez, S. (1975) Introduccion de *Uromyces galegae* (Opiz) Saccardo como factor de control biologico de alega *(Galega officinalis* L.). *Agro Sur* **3**, 87-91.

489.   Oehrens, E.; Gonzalez, S. (1977) Dispersion, ciclo biologico y danos causados por *Phragmidium violaceum* (Schultz) Winter en zarzamora (*Rubus constrictus* Lef. et M. y R. *ulmifolius* Schott.) en las zonas centro-sur y sur de Chile. *Agro Sur* **5**, 73-85.

490.   Olckers, T.; Zimmermann, H.G. (1991) Biological control of silverleaf nightshade, *Solanum elaeagnifolium*, and bugweed, *Solanum mauritianum*, (Solanaceae), in South Africa. *Agriculture, Ecosystems and Environment* **37**, 137-155.

491.   Ooi, P.A.C. (1981) *Eurytoma attiva* Burks (Hym., Eurytomidae) attacking *Cordia curassavica* (Jacq.) R. and S. in Kedah and Perlis, Malaysia. II. Incidence of *E. attiva*. *The Malaysian Agricultural Journal* **53**, 1-8.

492.   Ooi, P.A.C. (personal communication 1986) Commonwealth Institute of Biological Control, c/- Ebor Research, Bag No. 202, Batu Tiga, Selangor, Malaysia.

493.   Ooi, P.A.C. (1987) A fortuitous biological control of *Lantana* in Malaysia. *Tropical Pest Management* **33**, 234-235.

494.   Ooi, P.A.C.; Sim, C.H.; Tay, E.B. (1988) Status of the Arctiid moth introduced to control Siam weed in Sabah, Malaysia. *Planter, Kuala Lumpur* **64**, 298-304.

495.   Oosthuizen, M.J. (1964) The biological control of *Lantana camara* L. in Natal. *Journal of the Entomological Society of South Africa* **27**, 3-16.

496.   Orr, C.C.; Abernathy, J.R.; Hudspeth, E.B. (1975) *Nothanguina phyllobia,* a nematode parasite of silverleaf nightshade. *Plant Disease Reporter* **59**, 416-418.

497.   Panetta, F.D. (1990) Growth of *Emex australis* out-of-season: relevance to biological control of an annual weed. *Weed Research* **30**, 181-187.

498.   Papua New Guinea Department of Agriculture, Stock and Fisheries. (1969) Insect pest survey for the year ending 30th June, 1967. *Papua New Guinea Agricultural Journal* **21**, 49-75.

499.   Papua New Guinea Department of Agriculture, Stock and Fisheries. (1971) Insect pest survey for the year ending 30th June, 1968. *Papua New Guinea Agricultural Journal* **22**, 181-197.

500.   Parris, S.D. (1980) Aquatic plant control activity in the Panama Canal zone. *Miscellaneous Paper, United States Army Waterways Experimental Station A-80-3*, pp. 384-389.

501.   Parsons, W.T. (1957) St. John's wort in Victoria. History, distribution and control. *The Journal of Agriculture, Victoria* **55**, 781-788.

502.   Pawar, A.D.; Gupta, M. (1984) Importation of exotic phytophagous insects for the control of water hyacinth in India. *Plant Protection Bulletin* **36**, 79-82.

503.   Pecora, P.; Pemberton, R.W.; Stazi, M.; Johnson, G.R. (1991) Host specificity of *Spurgia esulae* Gagné (Diptera: Cecidomyiidae), a gall midge introduced into the United States for control of leafy spurge *(Euphorbia esula* L. "Complex"). *Environmental Entomology* **20**, 282-287.

504.   Pemberton, C.E. (1957) Progress in the biological control of undesirable plants in Hawaii. *Proceedings of the 9th Pacific Science Congress* **9**, 124-126.

505.   Pemberton, R.W. (1985) Native plant considerations in the biological control of leafy spurge. *Proceedings of the 6th International Symposium on Biological Control of Weeds*, 365-390.

506.   Pemberton, R.W. (1986) The distribution of halogeton in North America. *Journal of Range Management* **39**, 281-282.

507.   Pemberton, R.W. (1986) The impact of a stem-boring insect on the tissues, physiology, and reproduction of Russian thistle. *Entomologia Experimentalis et Applicata* **42**, 169-177.

508.   Pemberton, R.W. (personal communication 1991) United States Department of Agriculture, Agriculture Research Service, Biological Control of Weeds Laboratory, Albany 94710, United States of America.

509.   Pemberton, R.W. (1992) Leafy Spurge, *Euphorbia esula* L. (Euphorbiaceae). In; Nechols, J.R.; Andres, L.A.; Beardsley, J.W.; Goeden, R.D.; Jackson, C.G. *(Eds) Biological Control in the U.S. Western Region: Accomplishments and Benefits of Regional Research Project W-84 (1964-1989).* Berkeley; University of California, Division of Agriculture and Natural Resources, in press.

510.   Pemberton, R.W.; Rees, N.E. (1990) Host specificity and establishment of *Aphthona flava* Guill. (Chrysomelidae), a biological control agent of leafy spurge (*Euphorbia esula* L.) in the United States. *Proceedings of the Entomological Society of Washington* **92**, 351-357.

511.   Pemberton, R.W.; Turner, C.E. (1990) Biological control of *Senecio jacobaea* in northern California, an enduring success. *Entomophaga* **35**, 71-77.

512.   Perkins, R.C.L.; Swezey, O.H. (1924) The introduction into Hawaii of insects that attack lantana. *Bulletin of the Hawaiian Sugar Plantation Association Experimental Station* **16**, 83 pp.

513.   Peschken, D.P. (1977) Biological control of creeping thistle *(Cirsium arvense):* analysis of releases of *Altica carduorum* (Col.: Chrysomelidae) in Canada. *Entomophaga* **22**, 425-428.

514.   Peschken, D.P. (1979) Biological control of weeds in Canada with the aid of insects and nematodes. *Zeitschrift fur Angewandte Entomologie* **88**, 1-16.

515.   Peschken, D.P. (1979) Host specificity and suitability of *Tephritis dilacerata* [Dip.: Tephritidae]: a candidate for the biological control of perennial sow-thistle (*Sonchus arvensis*) [Compositae] in Canada. *Entomophaga* **24**, 455-461.

516.   Peschken, D.P. (1984) *Cirsium arvense* (L.) Scop., Canada thistle (Compositae). In; Kelleher, J.S.; Hulme, M.A. *(Eds) Biological Control Programmes Against Insects And Weeds In Canada 1969-1980.* London; Commonwealth Agricultural Bureaux, pp. 139-146.

517.   Peschken, D.P. (1984) *Sonchus arvensis* L., perennial sow-thistle, *S. oleraceus* L. annual sow-thistle and *S. asper* (L.) Hill, spiny annual sow-thistle (Compositae). In; Kelleher, J.S.; Hulme, M.A. *(Eds) Biological Control Programmes Against Insect And Weeds In Canada 1969-1980.* London; Commonwealth Agricultural Bureaux, pp. 205-209.

518.   Peschken, D.P. (personal communication 1991) Regina Research Station, Box 440, Regina, Saskatchewan, S4P 3A2, Canada.

519.   Peschken, D.P.; Beecher, R.W. (1973) *Ceutorhynchus litura* (Coleoptera: Curculionidae): biology and first releases for the biological control of the weed Canada thistle *(Cirsium arvense)* in Ontario, Canada. *Canadian Entomologist* **105**, 1489-1494.

520.   Peschken, D.P.; Wilkinson, A.T.S. (1981) Biocontrol of Canada thistle *(Cirsium arvense):* Releases and effectiveness of *Ceutorhynchus litura* (Coleoptera: Curculionidae) in Canada. *Canadian Entomologist* **113**, 777-785.

521.   Peschken, D.P.; Finnamore, D.B.; Watson, A.K. (1982) Biocontrol of the weed Canada thistle *(Cirsium arvense)* : releases and development of the gall fly *Urophora carduii* (Diptera : Tephritidae) in Canada. *Canadian Entomologist* **114**, 349-357.

522.   Peschken, D.P.; Derby, J.L. (1988) Host specificity of *Liriomyza sonchi* Hendel (Diptera: Agromyzidae), a potential biological agent for the control of weedy sow-thistles *Sonchus* spp., in Canada. *Canadian Entomologist* **120**, 593-600.

523.   Peschken, D.P.; McClay, A.S.; Derby, J.L.; DeClerk, R. (1989) *Cystiphora sonchi* (Bremi) (Diptera: Cecidomyiidae), a new biological control agent established on the weed perennial sow-thistle (*Sonchus arvensis* L.) (Compositate) in Canada. *Canadian Entomologist* **121**, 781-791.

524.   Pettey, F.W. (1948) The biological control of prickly pears in South Africa. *Science Bulletin, South African Department of Agriculture* **271**, 163 pp.

525.   Philip, B.A.; Winks, C.J.; Joynt, P.W.; Sutherland, O.R.W. (1988) Current status of biological control of alligator weed in New Zealand. *Proceedings of the 41st New Zealand Weed and Pest Control Conference*, 61-65.

526.   Philipose, M.T. (1976) Fifty years of aquatic weed control in India. In; Varshney, C.K.; Rzoska, J *(Eds) Aquatic Weeds in South East Asia.* The Hague; W. Junk, pp. 215-223.

527.   Philippart, J.C.; Ruwet, J.C. (1982) Ecology and distribution of Tilapias. In; Pullin, R.S.V.; Lowe-McConnell, R.H. *(Eds) The Biology and Culture of Tilapias.* Manila; ICLARM, 432 pp.

528.   Piper, G.L. (1985) Biological control of weeds in Washington: status report. *Proceedings of the 6th International Symposium on Biological Control of Weeds*, 817-826.

529.   Piper, G.L. (personal communication 1991) Department of Entomology, Washington State University, Pullman, Washington 99164-6432, United States of America.

530.   Piper, G.L.; Andres, L.A. (1992) Canada thistle, *Cirsium arvense* (L.) Scop. (Asteraceae). In; Nechols, J.R.; Andres, L.A.; Beardsley, J.W.; Goeden, R.D.; Jackson, C.G. *(Eds) Biological Control in the U.S. Western Region: Accomplishments and Benefits of Regional Research Project W-84 (1964-1989).* Berkeley; University of California, Division of Agriculture and Natural Resources, in press.

531.   Piper, G.L.; Andres, L.A. (1992) Rush skeletonweed, *Chondrilla juncea* L. (Asteraceae). In; Nechols, J.R.; Andres, L.A.; Beardsley, J.W.; Goeden, R.D.; Jackson, C.G. *(Eds) Biological Control in the U.S. Western Region: Accomplishments and Benefits of Regional Research Project W-84 (1964-1989).* Berkeley; University of California, Division of Agriculture and Natural Resources, in press.

532.   Piper, G.L.; Rosenthal, S.S. (1992) Diffuse knapweed, *Centaurea diffusa* Lamarck (Asteraceae). In; Nechols, J.R.; Andres, L.A.; Beardsley, J.W.; Goeden, R.D.; Jackson, C.G. *(Eds) Biological Control in the U.S. Western Region: Accomplishments and Benefits of Regional Research Project W-84 (1964-1989).* Berkeley; University of California, Division of Agriculture and Natural Resources, in press.

533.   Pitty, A. (personal communication 1991) Sección de Malezas, Departamento de Protección Vegetal, Apartado Postal 93, Tegucigalpa, D.C., Honduras, C.A.

534.   Poinar, G.O. jr. (1964) Observations on nutgrass insects in Hawaii with notes on the host range of *Bactra truclenta* Meyrich and *Athesapeuta cyperi* Marshall. *Proceedings of the Hawaiian Entomological Society* **18**, 417-423.

535.   Popay, A.I.; Lyttle, L.A.; Edmonds, D.K.; Phung, H.T. (1984) Incidence of the nodding thistle receptacle weevil on nodding and slender winged thistles. *Proceedings of the 37th New Zealand Weed and Pest Control Conference*, 28-32.

536.   Porter, D.M. (1972) The genera of Zygophyllaceae in southeastern United States. *Journal Arnold Arboretum* **53**, 531-552.

537.   Powell, R.D.; Myers, J.H. (1988) The effect of *Sphenoptera jugoslavica* Obenb. (Col., Bupresidae) on its host plant *Centaurea diffusa* Lam. (Compositae). *Journal of Applied Entomology* **106**, 25-45.

538.   Procter, D.L.C. (1984) Biological control of the aquatic weed *Salvinia molesta* D.S. Mitchell in Botswana using the weevils *Cyrtobagous singularis* and *Cyrtobagous* sp. nov. *Botswana Notes and Records* **15**, 99-101.

539.   Purea, M. (personal communication 1981) Ministry of Agriculture and Fisheries, P.O. Box 96, Rarotonga, Cook Islands.

540.   Puttler, B. (personal communication 1990) University of Missouri, Integrated Pest Management, Columbia, Missouri 65211, United States of America.

541.   Puttler, B.; Long, S.H.; Peters, E.J. (1978) Establishment in Missouri of *Rhinocyllus conicus* for the biological control of musk thistle. *Weed Science* **26**, 188-190.

542.   Randall, J.E. (1960) New fishes for Hawaii. *Sea Frontiers* **6**, 33-43.

543.   Rao, V.P. (1971) Biological control of pests in Fiji. *Miscellaneous Publication, Commonwealth Institute of Biological Control* **2**, 38 pp.

544.   Rao, V.P.; Ghani, M.A.; Sankaran, T.; Mathur, K.C. (1971) Review of biological control of insects and other pests in Southeast Asia and the Pacific region. *Technical Communication, Commonwealth Institute of Biological Control* **6**, 59-95.

545.   Rees, N.E. (1977) Impact of *Rhinocyllus conicus* on thistles in southwestern Montana. *Environmental Entomology* **6**, 839-842.

546.   Rees, N.E. (1990) Establishment, dispersal and influence of *Ceutorhynchus litura* on Canada thistle (*Cirisium arvense*) in the Gallatin valley of Montana. *Weed Science* **38**, 198-200.

547.   Rees, N.E. (personal communication 1991) United States Department of Agriculture, Rangeland Weeds Laboratory, Bozeman, Montana 59717, United States of America.

548.   Rees, N.E.; Pemberton, R.W.; Rizza, A.; Pecora, P. (1986) First recovery of *Oberea erythrocephala* on the leafy spurge complex in the United States. *Weed Science* **34**, 395-397.

549.   Reimer, N.J.; Beardsley, J.W., jr. (1989) Effectiveness of *Liothrips urichi* (Thysanoptera: Phlaeothripidae) introduced for biological control of *Clidemia hirta* in Hawaii. *Environmental Entomology* **18**, 1141-1146.

550.   Reschke, M. (1978) Untersuchungen zur Entwicklung von Unkrautbekampfungssystemen in Entwasserungsgraben im Weser-Ems- Gebiet. *Proceedings of the 5th International Symposium on Aquatic Weeds*, 231-238.

551.   Reznik, S.Y. (1989) Ovipositional selectivity, population density and efficiency of the ambrosia leaf beetle. *Proceedings of the Zoological Institute* **189**, 45-55. (In Russuian with English abstract)(Abstract service summary cited).

552.   Reznik, S.Y.; Kovalev, O.V.; Maryushkina, V.Y.; Kalinin, O.M.; Ilyina, E.G.; Bart, A.G. (1986) Distribution pattern of the ragweed leaf-beetle *Zygogramma saturalis* F. (Coleoptera, Chrysomelidae) in the zone of high population density. *Entomologicheskoe Obozreniye* **65**, 244-250. (In Russian with English abstract)

553.   Richards, K. (personal communication 1986) Department of Agriculture, South Perth, Western Australia 6151, Australia.

554.   Ridings, W.H.; Mitchell, D.J.; Schoulties, C.L.; El-Gholl, N.E. (1978) Biological control of milkweed vine in Florida citrus groves with a pathotype of *Phytophthora citrophthora. Proceedings of the 4th International Symposium on Biological Control of Weeds*, 224-240.

555.   Riotte, J.C.E.; Uchida, G. (1979) Butterflies of the Hawaiian Islands. *Journal of Research on the Lepidoptera* **17**, 33-39.

556.   Roberts, L.I.N.; Winks, C.J.; Sutherland, O.R.W.; Galbreath, R.A. (1984) Progress of biological control of alligator weed in New Zealand. *Proceedings of the 37th New Zealand Weed and Pest Control Conference*, 50-54.

557.   Roberts, L.I.N.; Sutherland, O.R.W. (1989) *Alternanthera philoxeroides* (C. Martius) Grisebach, alligator weed (Amaranthaceae). In; Cameron, P.J.; Hill, R.L.; Bain, J.; Thomas, W.P. *(Eds)* A review of biological control of invertebrate pests and weeds in New Zealand 1874 to 1987. *Technical communication, CAB International Institute of Biological Control* **10**, pp. 325-330.

558.   Robinson, A.F.; Orr, C.C.; Abernathy, J.R. (1978) Distribution of *Nothanguina phyllobia* and its potential as a biological control agent of silverleaf nightshade. *Journal of Nematology* **10**, 362-366.

559.   Robinson, G.W. (1986) Weed control in land drainage channels in England and Wales with reference to conservation. *Proceedings of the 7th International Symposium on Aquatic Weeds*, 257-261.

560.   Roché, C.T.; Roché, B.F. jr. (1989) Introductory notes on squarrose knapweed (*Centaurea virgata* Lam. ssp. *squarrosa* Gugl.). *Northwest Science* **63**, 246-252.

561.   Room, P.M. (personal communication 1991) Commonwealth Scientific and Industrial Research Organisation, Division of Entomology, Long Pocket Laboratories, Private Bag No. 3, Indooroopilly, Queensland 4068, Australia.

562.   Room, P.M.; Harley, K.L.S.; Forno, I.W.; Sands, D.P.A. (1981) Successful control of the floating weed salvinia. *Nature (London)* **294**, 78-80.

563.   Room, P.M.; Forno, I.W.; Taylor, M.F.J. (1984) Establishment in Australia of two insects for the biological control of the floating weed *Salvinia molesta. Bulletin of Entomological Research* **74**, 505-516.

564.   Room, P.M.; Thomas, P.A. (1985) Nitrogen and establishment of a beetle for biological control of the floating weed *Salvinia molesta* in Papua New Guinea. *Journal of Applied Ecology* **22**, 139-156.

565.   Room, P.M.; Gunatilaka, G.A.; Shivanathan, P.; Fernando, I.V.S. (1989) Control of *Salvinia molesta* in Sri Lanka by *Cyrtobagous salviniae. Proceedings of 7th International Symposium on Biological Control of weeds*, 285-290.

566.   Room, P.M.; Fernando, I.V.S. (1991) Weed invasions countered by biological conrol: *Salvinia molesta* and *Eichhornia crassipes* in Sri Lanka. *Aquatic Botany*, in press.

567.   Rose, D.J.W. (personal communication 1979) Centre for Overseas Pest Research, College House, Wrights Lane, London, W8 5SJ, United Kingdom.

568.   Rosenthal, S.S. (1983) Current status and potential for biological control of field bindweed, *Convolvulus arvensis*, with *Aceria convolvuli*. In; Hoy, M.S.; Knutson, L.; Cunningham, G.L. *(Eds.) Biological Control of Pests by Mites, Prodeedings of a Conference, April 1982, Berkeley, California.* Agricultural Experiment Station, University of California, Special Publication 3304, pp. 57-60.

569.   Rosenthal, S.S. (personal communication 1991) United States Department of Agriculture, Agricultural Research Service, Rangeland Weeds Laboratory, Bozeman, Montana 59717, United States of America.

570.   Rosenthal, S.S. (1992) Field Bindweed, *Convolvulus arvensis* L. (Convolvulaceae). In; Nechols, J.R.; Andres, L.A.; Beardsley, J.W.; Goeden, R.D.; Jackson, C.G. *(Eds) Biological Control in the U.S. Western Region: Accomplishments and Benefits of Regional Research Project W-84 (1964-1989).* Berkeley; University of California, Division of Agriculture and Natural Resources, in press.

571.   Rosenthal, S.S.; Clement, S.L.; Hostettler, N.; Mimmocchi, T. (1988) Biology of *Tyta luctuosa* [Lepidoptera: Noctuidae] and its potential value as a biological control agent for the weed *Convolvulus arvensis*. *Entomophaga* **33**, 185-192.

572.   Rosenthal, S.S.; Platts, B.E. (1990) Host specificity of *Aceria (Eriophyes)* Malherbe, [Acari: Eriophyidae], a biological control agent for the weed *Convolvulus arvensis* [Convolvulaceae]. *Entomophaga* **35**, 459-463.

573.   Rosenthal, S.S.; Piper, G.L. (1992) Bull thistle, *Cirsium vulgare* (Savi) Ten. (Asteraceae). In; Nechols, J.R.; Andres, L.A.; Beardsley, J.W.; Goeden, R.D.; Jackson, C.G. *(Eds) Biological Control in the U.S. Western Region: Accomplishments and Benefits of Regional Research Project W-84 (1964-1989)*. Berkeley; University of California, Division of Agriculture and Natural Resources, in press.

574.   Rosenthal, S.S.; Piper, G.L., (1992) Russian knapweed, *Centaurea (Acroptilon) repens* L. In; Nechols, J.R.; Andres, L.A.; Beardsley, J.W.; Goeden, R.D.; Jackson, C.G. *(Eds) Biological Control in the U.S. Western Region: Accomplishments and Benefits of Regional Research Project W-84 (1964-1989)*. Berkeley; University of California, Division of Agriculture and Natural Resources, in press.

575.   Ross, J.H. (Ed) (1976) Flora of Southern Africa. *Department of Agricultural Technical Services South Africa* **22**, 152-153.

576.   Rowe, D.K. (1989) Algal blooms. In; Cameron, P.J.; Hill, R.L.; Bain, J.; Thomas, W.P. *(Eds)* A review of biological control of invertebrate pests and weeds in New Zealand 1874 to 1987. *Technical communication, CAB International Institute of Biological Control* **10**, pp. 321-324.

577.   Rowe, D.J.; Kok, L.T. (1984) Potential of *Rhinocyllus conicus* to adapt to the plumeless thistle, *Carduus acanthoides*, in Virginia. *Virginia Journal of Science* **35**, 192-196.

578.   Rowe, D.K.; Hill, R.L. (1989) Aquatic macrophytes, waterweeds. In; Cameron, P.J.; Hill, R.L.; Bain, J.; Thomas, W.P. *(Eds)* A review of biological control of invertebrate pests and weeds in New Zealand 1874 to 1987. *Technical communication, CAB International Institute of Biological Control* **10**, pp. 331-337.

579.   Sands, D.P.A. (personal communication 1991) Commonwealth Scientific and Industrial Research Organisation, Division of Entomology, Long Pocket Laboratories, Private Bag No. 3, Indooroopilly, Queensland 4068, Australia.

580.   Sankaran, T. (1973) Biological control of weeds in India. A review of introductions and current investigations of natural enemies. *Proceedings of the 2nd International Symposium on Biological Control of Weeds*, 82-88.

581.   Sankaran, T. (personal communication 1979) Commonwealth Institute of Biological Control, Bellary Road, P.O. Box 603, Bangalore, 560 006, India.

582.   Satheesan, N.V.; Lyla, K.R.; Joy, P.J.; Joesph, D. (1987) Establishment of *Pareuchaetes pseudoinsulata* Rego Barros (= *Ammalo insulata* Walk.), an arctiid caterpillar, for the biological control of *Chromolaena odorata*. *Agricultural Research Journal, Kerala* **25**, 142-143.

583.   Scheele, S.M.; Syrett, P. (1987) The broom twigminer, *Leucoptera spartifoliella* (Lepidoptera: Lyonetiidae) in New Zealand. *New Zealand Entomologist* **10**, 133-137.

584.   Scheibelreiter, G.K. (1980) Biological control of *Lantana camara* L. (Verbenaceae) in Ghana. *Zeitschrift fur Angewandte Entomologie* **90**, 99-103.

585.   Schlettwein, C.H.G. (1985) Distribution and densities of *Cyrtobagous singularis* Hustache (Coleoptera: Curculionidae) on *Salvinia molesta* Mitchell in the Eastern Caprivi Zipfel. *Madoqua* **14**, 291-293.

586.   Schlettwein, C.H.G.; Hamman, P.F. (1984) The control of *Salvinia molesta* in the Eastern Caprivi zipfel. *South West Africa Annual*, 49-51.

587.   Schmidl, L. (1972) Studies on the control of ragwort, *Senecio jacobaea* L., with the Cinnabar Moth, *Callimorpha jacobaeae* (L.) (Arctiidae: Lepidoptera), in Victoria. *Weed Research* **12**, 46-57.

588.   Schmidl, L. (1981) Ragwort, *Senecio jacobaea* L. in Victoria and renewed attempts to establish the cinnabar moth, *Tyria jacobaeae* L. for its control. *Proceedings of the 5th International Symposium on Biological Control of Weeds*, 603-607.

589.   Schoonbee, H.J. (1991) Biological control of fennel-leaved pondweed, *Potamogeton pectinatus* (Potamogetonaceae), in South Africa. *Agriculture, Ecosystems and Environment* **37**, 231-238.

590.   Schoonbee, H.J.; Vermaak, J.; Swanepoel, J.H. (1985) Use of the Chinese grass carp, *Ctenopharyngodon idella*, in the control of the submerged water weed *Potamogeton pectinatus* in an inland lake in the Transvaal, South Africa. *Proceedings of the 6th International Symposium on Biological Control of Weeds*, 557-565.

591.   Schreiner, I. (1989) Biological control introductions in the Caroline and Marshall Islands. *Proceedings, Hawaiian Entomological Society* **29**, 57-69.

592.   Schröder, D. (1980) The biological control of thistles. *Biocontrol News and Information* **1**, 9-26.

593.   Schröder, D. (personal communication 1991) CAB International Institute of Biological Control, European Station, 1 Chemin des Grillons, CH-2800 Delémont, Switzerland.

594.   Scott, J.K. (personal communication 1991) Commonwealth Scientific and Industrial Research Organisation, Division of Entomology, Private Bag P.O., Wembley, Western Australia 6014, Australia.

595.   Scott, J.K.; Sagliocco, J.L. (1991) *Chamaesphecia doryliformis* (Ochsenheimer) (Lep.: Sesiidae), a second root borer for the control of *Rumex* spp. (Polygonaceae) in Australia. *Entomophaga* **35**, in press.

596.   Seibert, F. (1989) Biological control of the weed, *Chromolaena odorata* [Asteraceae] by *Pareuchaetes pseudoinsulata* [Lep.: Arctiidae] on Guam and the Northern Mariana Islands. *Entomophaga* **34**, 531-539.

597.   Sen-Sarma, P.K. (personal communication 1979) Forest Research Institute, Dehra Dun, India.

598.   Shireman, J.V.; Smith, C.R. (1983) Synopsis of biological data on the grass carp. *FAOUN, FAO Fisheries Synopsis* **135**, pp. 9-12 and 39-40.

599.   Sim, T. (personal communication 1991) Kansas State Board of Agriculture, Topeka, Kansas, United States of America.

600.   Simmonds, H.W. (1932) A list of insects introduced into Fiji for the biological control of pests and weeds. *Agricultural Journal of Fiji* **5**, 5-9.

601.   Simmonds, F.J. (1933) The biological control of the weed *Clidemia hirta* D. Don, in Fiji. *Bulletin of Entomological Research* **24**, 345-348.

602.   Simmonds, H.W. (1934) Biological control of noxious weeds with special reference to the plants *Clidemia hirta* (the curse) and *Stachytarpheta jamaicensis* (blue rat tail). *Agricultural Journal of Fiji* **7**, 3-10.

603.   Simmonds, F.J. (1949) Initial success of attempts at the biological control of the weed *Cordia macrostachya* (Jacq.) R. and S. in Mauritius. *Tropical Agriculture* **26**, 135-136.

604.   Simmonds, F.J. (1967) Biological control of pests of veterinary importance. *Veterinary Bulletin (London)* **37**, 71-85.

605.   Simmonds, F.J. (1980) Biological control of *Cordia curassavica* (Boraginaceae) in Malaysia. *Entomophaga* **25**, 363-364.

606.   Simmonds, F.J. (1981) Control of *Cordia curassavica* in Sri Lanka. *Biocontrol News and Information* **2**, 2.

607.   Simmonds, F.J.; Bennett, F.D. (1966) Biological control of *Opuntia* spp. by *Cactoblastis cactorum* in the Leeward Isands (West Indies). *Entomophaga* **11**, 183-189.

608.   Simmonds, H.W. (1928) Lantana bug, "*Teleonemia lantanae* Distant". *Agricultural Journal of Fiji* **1**, 16-21.

609.   Simmonds, H.W. (1931) Noxious weeds and their control in Fiji. II. Biological Control. *Agricultural Journal of Fiji* **4**, 29-31.

610.   Simmonds, H.W. (1937) The biological control of the weed, *Clidemia hirta* commonly known in Fiji as "the curse". *Agricultural Journal of Fiji* **8**, 37-39.

611.   Singh, R.S.; Prasad, R.S.; Solly, R.K. (1982) The status of *Neochetina eichhorniae* (Coleoptera Curculionidae) as biological control agent for water hyacinth *Eichhornia crassipes* (Mart) Solms (Fam.: Pontideriaceae) in Fiji. *Regional Workshop on Biological Control of Water Hyacinth, Bangalore*, 35-38.

612.   Smith, M.J. (1959) Notes on insects especially *Gymnaetron* spp. (Coleoptera: Curculionidae), associated with toadflax, *Linnaria vulgaris* Miller (Scrophulariaceae), in North America. *Canadian Entomologist* **41**, 116-121.

613.   Smith, R.J. jr. (1986) Biological control of northern jointvetch *(Aeschynomene virginica)* in rice *(Oryza sativa)* and soybean *(Glycine max)* - a researcher's view. *Weed Science* **34** (Supplement 1), 17-23.

614.   Sommer, G. (personal communication 1991) CAB International Institute of Biological Control, European Station, 1 Chemin des Grillons, CH-2800 Delémont, Switzerland.

615.   Spencer, K.A. (1973) *Agromyzidae (Diptera) of Economic Importance.* The Hague; Dr. W. Junk, B.V., 418 pp.

617.   Stegmaier, C.E. jr. (1973) Colonization of the puncturevine stem weevil, *Microlarinus lypriformis* (Coleoptera: Curculionidae) with notes on parasitism in south Florida. *The Florida Entomologist* **56**, 235-241.

618.   Stinnson, C.S.A. (personal communication 1991) CAB International Institute of Biological Control, European Station, 1 Chemin des Grillons, CH-2800 Delémont, Switzerland.

619.   Story, J.M. (1979) Biological weed control in Montana. *Bulletin, Montana Agricultural Experimental Station* **717**, 15 pp.

620.   Story, J.M. (1985) First report of the dispersal into Montana of *Urophora quadrifasciata* (Diptera : Tephritidae), a fly released in Canada for biological control of spotted and diffuse knapweed. *Canadian Entomologist* **117**, 1061-1062.

621.   Story, J.M. (1985) Status of biological weed control in Montana. *Proceedings of the 6th International Symposium on Biological Control of Weeds*, 837-842.

622.   Story, J.M. (personal communication 1990) Western Agricultural Research Center, Montana State University, Corvallis, Montana 59828, United States of America.

623.   Story, J.M. (1992) Spotted knapweed, *Centaurea maculosa* Lamarck (Asteraceae). In; Nechols, J.R.; Andres, L.A.; Beardsley, J.W.; Goeden, R.D.; Jackson, C.G. *(Eds) Biological Control in the U.S. Western Region: Accomplishments and Benefits of Regional Research Project W-84 (1964-1989).* Berkeley; University of California, Division of Agriculture and Natural Resources, in press.

624.   Story, J.M.; Nowierski, R.M. (1984) Increase and dispersal of *Urophora affinis* (Diptera: Tephritidae) on spotted knapweed in western Montana. *Environmental Entomology* **13**, 1151-1156.

625.   Story, J.M.; Nowierski, R.M.; Boggs, K.W. (1987) Distribution of *Urophora affinis* and *U. quadrifasciata*, two flies introduced for biological control of spotted knapweed (*Centaurea maculosa*) in Montana. *Weed Science.* **35**, 145-148.

626.   Story, J.M.; Boggs, K.W.; Nowierski, R.M. (1989) Effect of two introduced seed head flies on spotted knapweed. *Montana AgResearch* **5**, 14-17.

627.   Story, J.M.; Boggs, K.W.; Good, W.R. (1991) First report of the establishment of *Agapeta zoegana* L. (Lepidoptera: Cochylidae) on spotted knapweed, *Centaurea maculosa* Lamarck, in the United States. *Canadian Entomologist* **123**, 411-412.

628.   Story, J.M.; Boggs, K.W.; Good, W.R.; Harris, P.; Nowierski, R.M. (1991) *Metzneria paucipunctella* Zeller (Lepidoptera: Gellechiidae), a moth introduced against spotted knapweed: its feeding strategy and impact on two introduced *Urophora* spp. (Diptera: Tephritidae). *Canadian Entomologist* **123**, in press.

629.   Stott, B. (1977) On the question of the introduction of the grass-carp *(Ctenopharyngodon idella* Val.) into the United Kingdom. *Fisheries Management* **8**, 63-71.

630.   Stott, B.; Cross, D.G.; Iszard, R.E.; Robson, T.O. (1971) Recent work on grass carp in the United Kingdom from the standpoint of its economics in controlling submerged aquatic plants. *Proceedings of the 3rd International Symposium on Aquatic Weeds*, 105-116. [*Weed Abstracts* (1972) **21**, 37-38].

631.   Stott, B.; Buckley, B.R. (1978) Costs for controlling aquatic weeds with grass carp as compared with conventional methods. *Proceedings of the 5th International Symposium on Aquatic Weeds*, 253-260.

✱ Reference 616 has been deleted

632. Suasa-ard, W.; Napompeth, B. (1982) Investigations on *Episammia pectinicornis* (Hampson) (Lepidoptera: Noctuidae) for biological control of the waterlettuce in Thailand. *Technical Bulletin, National Biological Control Research Centre, Kasetsart University/National Research Council* **3**, 10 pp.

633. Subramanian, T.V. (1934) The lantana seedfly in India, *Agromyza (Ophiomyia) lantanae* Froggatt. *Indian Journal of Agricultural Science* **4**, 468-471.

634. Summerville, W.A.T. (1933) Two insect enemies of nut grass. *Queensland Agricultural Journal* **40**, 284-287.

635. Supkoff, D.M.; Joley, D.B.; Marois, J.J. (1988) Effect of introduced biological control organisms on the density of *Chondrilla juncea* in California. *Journal of Applied Ecology* **25**, 1089-1095.

636. Surles, W.W.; Kok, L.T. (1978) *Carduus thistle* seed destruction by *Rhinocyllus conicus*. *Weed Science* **26**, 264-269.

637. Sutton, D.L. (1977) Grass carp *(Ctenopharyngodon idella* Val.) in North America. *Aquatic Botany* **3**, 157-164.

638. Sweetman, H.L. (1935) Successful examples of biological control of pest insects and plants. *Bulletin of Entomological Research* **26**, 373-377.

639. Sweezey, O.H. (1923) Records of Introduction of Beneficial Insects into the Hawaiian Islands. *Proceedings of the Hawaiian Entomological Society* **5**, 299-304.

640. Sweezey, O.H. (1964) Recent introductions of beneficial insects in Hawaii. *Journal of Economic Entomology* **19**, 714-720.

641. Syed, R.A. (1977) An attempt on biological control of *Eupatorium odoratum* L. f. in Sabah, Malaysia. *Proceedings of the 6th Asian-Pacific Weed Science Society Conference*, 459-466. [*Weed Abstracts* (1980) **29**, 2955].

642. Syrett, P. (1983) Biological control of ragwort in New Zealand: a review. *Australian Weeds* **2**, 96-101.

643. Syrett, P. (1989) *Senecio jacobaea* L., ragwort (Aseraceae). In; Cameron, P.J.; Hill, R.L.; Bain, J.; Thomas, W.P. *(Eds)* A review of biological control of invertebrate pests and weeds in New Zealand 1874 to 1987. *Technical communication, CAB International Institute of Biological Control* **10**, pp. 361-366.

644. Syrett, P. (personal communication 1991) Department of Scientific and Industrial Research Plant Protection, Private Bag, Christchurch, New Zealand.

645. Syrett, P.; Scheele, S.M.; Philip, B.A. (1984) Renewed activity in biological control of ragwort. *Proceedings of the 37th New Zealand Weed and Pest Control Conference*, 37-41.

646. Syrett, P.; Hancox, N.A. (1985) Effect of an introduced beetle on St John's wort. *Proceedings of the 38th New Zealand Weed and Pest Control Conference*, 154-157.

647. Syrett, P.; O'Donnell, D.J. (1987) A seed-feeding beetle for biological control of broom. *Proceedings of the 40th New Zealand Weed and Pest control Conference*, 19-22.

648. Tanner, C.C.; Wells, R.D.S.; Mitchell, C.P. (1990) Re-establishment of native macrophytes in Lake Parkinson following weed control by grass carp. *New Zealand Journal of Marine and Freshwater Research* **24**, 181-186.

649. TeBeest, D.O. (1984) Biological control of weeds with microbial herbicides. *Fitopatologia Brasileira* **9**, 443-453.

650. Templeton, G.E.; TeBeest, D.O.; Smith, R.J. jr (1978) Development of an endemic fungal pathogen as a mycoherbicide for biocontrol of northern jointvetch in rice. *Proceedings of the 4th International Symposium on Biological Control of Weeds*, 214-216.

651. Templeton, G.E.; Greaves, M.P. (1984) Biological control of weeds with fungal pathogens. *Tropical Pest Management* **30**, 333-338.

652. Thistleton, B. (personal communication 1989) South Pacific Commission, Plant Protection Service, Private Mail Bag, Suva, Fiji.

653. Thomas, P.A.; Room, P.M. (1986) Taxonomy and control of *Salvinia molesta*. *Nature (London)* **320**, 581-584.

654. Tillyard, R.J. (1934) The entomological control of noxious weeds in the Pacific Region. *Proceedings of the 5th Pacific Science Congress*, **5**, 3547-3557.

655.   Tomley, A.J. (personal communication 1991) Department of Lands, Alan Fletcher Research Station, Sherwood, Queensland 4075, Australia.

656.   Tomley, A.J.; McFadyen, R.E. (1985) Biological control of Harrisia cactus, *Eriocereus martinii*, in central Queensland by the mealybug, *Hypogeococcus festerianus*, nine years after release. *Proceedings of the 6th International Symposium on Biological Control of Weeds*, 843-847.

657.   Trujillo, E.E. (1985) Biological control of Hamakua pa-makani with *Cercosporella* sp. in Hawaii. *Proceedings of the 6th International Symposium on Biological Control of Weeds*, 661-671.

658.   Trujillo, P.W. (personal communication 1991) Department of Plant Pathology, University of Hawaii, Honolulu 96822, United States of America.

659.   Trujillo, E.E.; Latterell, F.M.; Rossi, A.E. (1986) *Colletotrichum gloeosporioides*, a possible biological control agent for *Clidemia hirta* in Hawaiian forests. *Plant Disease* **70**, 974-976.

660.   Trujillo, E.E.; Aragaki, M.; Shoemaker, R.A. (1988) Infection, disease development, and axenic culture of *Entyloma compositarum*, the cause of Hamakua pamakani blight in Hawaii. *Plant Disease* **72**, 355-357.

661.   Trumble, J.T.; Kok, L.T. (1982) Integrated pest management techniques in thistle suppression in pastures of North America. *Weed Research* **22**, 345-359.

662.   Tryon, H. (1910) The wild cochineal insect, with reference to its injurious action on prickly pear (*Opuntia* spp.) in India, etc., and to its availability for the subjugation of this plant in Queensland and elsewhere. *Queensland Agricultural Journal* **25**, 188-197.

663.   Tryon, H. (1912) Insects for checking growth or dissemination of lantana. *Queensland Agricultural Journal* **29**, 493-498.

664.   Tryon, H. (1915) Nut grass-destroying coccid and its mitigation. *Queensland Agricultural Journal* **3**, 72.

665.   Tsuchiya, M. (1979) Control of Aquatic weeds by grass carp (*Ctenopharyngodon idella* Val.) *Japan Agricultural Research Quarterly* **13**, 200-203. [*Biocontrol News and Information* (1981) **2**, abstract 351].

666.   Tuduri, J.C.G.; Martorell, L.F.; Gaud, S.M. (1979) Geographical distribution and host plants of the cactus moth, *Cactoblastis cactorum* Berg) in Puerto Rico and the United States Virgin Islands. *Journal of Agriculture of the University of Puerto Rico* **55**, 130-137.

667.   Turner, C.E.; Pemberton, R.W.; Rosenthal, S.S. (1987) Host utilization of native *Cirsium* thistles (Asteraceae) by the introduced weevil *Rhinocyllus conicus* (Coleoptera: Curculionidae) in California. *Environmental Entomology* **16**, 111-115.

668.   Turner, C.E.; Johnson, J.B.; McCaffrey, J.P. (1992) Yellow starthistle, *Centaurea solstitialis* L. (Asteraceae). In; Nechols, J.R.; Andres, L.A.; Beardsley, J.W.; Goeden, R.D.; Jackson, C.G. *(Eds) Biological Control in the U.S. Western Region: Accomplishments and Benefits of Regional Research Project W-84 (1964-1989)*. Berkeley; University of California, Division of Agriculture and Natural Resources, in press.

669.   Ung, S.H.; Yunis, A. (1981) The present status of the biological control of *Cordia curassavica* in Malaysia. *Proceedings of the 5th International Symposium on Biological Control of Weeds*, 489-498.

670.   United States of America Department of Agriculture, Soil Conservation Service. (1982) *National List of Scientific Plant Names 1, List of plant names*, SCS-TP-159, 416 pp.

671.   United States of America Department of Agriculture, Soil Conservation Service. (1982) *National List of Scientific Plant Names 2, Synonymy, SCS-TP-159*, 438 pp.

672.   Valladares, G.R. (1986) The genus *Ophiomyia Braschnikov* (Dipt., Agromyzidae) in Argentina. *Entomologist's Monthly Magazine* **122**, 111-115. [*Biocontrol News and Information* (1986) **7**, abstract 1798].

673.   van der Zweerde, W. (1990) Chapter 9. Biological Control of Aquatic Weeds. (d) Biological control of aquatic weeds by means of phytophagous fish. In; Pieterse, A.H.; Murphy, K.J. *(Eds) Aquatic Weeds. The Ecology and Management of Nuisance Aquatic Vegetation*. Oxford University Press, Oxford, pp. 201-221.

674.   Verigin, B.V. (1979) The role of herbivorous fishes at reconstruction of Ichthyo-fauna under the conditions of anthropogenic evolution of waterbodies. *Proceedings of the Grass Carp Conference, Gainesville*, 139-145.

675.   Villaneuva, H.L.; Faure, G.O. (1959) Biological control of St. John's-wort in Chile. *FAO Plant Protection Bulletin* **7**, 144-146.

676.   Vogel, E.; Oliver, A.D. jr. (1969) Evaluation of *Arzama densa* as an aid in the control of water hyacinth in Louisiana. *Journal of Economic Entomology* **62**, 142-145.

677.   Vogel, E; Oliver, A.D. jr. (1969) Life history and some factors affecting the population of *Arzama densa* in Louisiana. *Annals of the Entomological Society of America* **62**, 749-752.

678.   Vyalkh, A.K.; Zheryagin, V.G. (1977) Factors contributing to the infection of common ragweed (*Ambrosia artemisiifolia*) by the white rust causal agent, *Albugo tragopogonis* Schroet. *Mikologiya i Fitopatologiya* **11**, 135-139. [*Weed Abstracts* (1978) **27**, 2673].

679.   Walker, H.L. (1982) Seedling blight of sicklepod caused by *Alternaria cassiae*. *Plant Disease* **66**, 426-428.

680.   Walker, H.L.; Riley, J.A. (1982) Evaluation of *Alternaria cassiae* for the biocontrol of sicklepod (*Cassia obtusifolia*). *Weed Science* **30**, 651-654.

681.   Waloff, N. (1966) Scotch broom (*Sarothamnus scoparius* (L.) Wimmer) and its insect fauna introduced into the Pacific Northwest of America. *Journal of Applied Ecology* **3**, 293-311.

682.   Wan, F.H.; Wang, R. (1990) A cage study on the control effects of *Ambrosia artemisiifolia* by the introduced biological control agent, *Zygogramma suturalis* (Col.: Chrysomelidae). *Chinese Journal of Biological Control* **6**, 8-12. (In Chinese with English abstract).

683.   Wang, R. (1989) Progress towards biological control of weeds in China. *Proceedings of the 7th International Symposium on Biological Control of Weeds*, 689-693.

684.   Wapshere, A.J. (1974) An ecological study of an attempt at biological control of Noogoora burr (*Xanthium strumarium*). *Australian Journal of Agricultural Research* **25**, 275-292.

685.   Ward, R.H.; Pienkowski, R.L. (1978) Biology of *Cassida rubiginosa*, a thistle-feeding shield beetle. *Annals of the Entomological Society of America* **71**, 585-591.

686.   Waterhouse, D.F.; Norris, K.R. (1987) *Biological Control: Pacific Prospects*. Melbourne; Inkata Press, pp. 332-341.

687.   Watson, A.K.; Harris, P. (1984) *Acroptilon repens* (L.) DC., Russian knapweed (Compositae). In; Kelleher, J.S.; Hulme, M.A. *(Eds) Biological Control Programmes Against Insects And Weeds In Canada 1969-1980*. London; Commomwealth Agricultural Bureaux, pp. 105-110.

688.   Weber, P.W. (1951) Recent liberations of beneficial insects in Hawaii. *Proceedings of the Hawaiian Entomological Society* **14**, 327-330.

689.   Weber, P.W. (1954) Recent liberations of beneficial insects - III. *Proceedings of the Hawaiian Entomological Society* **15**, 369-371.

690.   Weber, P.W. (1955) Recent liberations of beneficial insects in Hawaii - IV. *Proceedings of the Hawaiian Entomological Society* **15**, 635-638.

691.   Weber, P.W. (1956) Recent introductions for biological control in Hawaii - XVI. *Proceedings of the Hawaiian Entomological Society* **16**, 162-164.

692.   Weber, E. (1974) Bekampfung unerwunschter Wasserpflanzen durch den weissen Amur. *Proceedings of the 4th International Symposium on Aquatic Weeds*, 134-138.

693.   Wehling, W.F.; Piper, G.L. (1988) Efficacy diminution of the rush skeletonweed gall midge, *Cystiphora schmidtti* (Diptera: Cecidomyiidae), by an indigenous parasitoid. *Pan-Pacific Entomologist* **64**, 83-85.

694.   Weller, B. (personal communications 1985) Department of Agriculture, Livestock and Forestry, Port Villa, Vanuatu.

695.   Wester, L.L.; Wood, H.B. (1977) Koster's curse *(Clidema hirta)*, a weed pest in Hawaiian forests. *Environmental Conservation* **4**, 35-41.

696.   White, I.M.; Clement, S.L.; (1987) Systematic notes on *Urophora* (Diptera, Tephritidae) species associated with *Centaurea solstitialis* (Asteraceae, Cardueae) and other Palaearctic weeds adventive in North America. *Proceedings of the Entomological Society of Washington* **89**, 571-580.

697.   Williams, J.R. (1951) The control of the black sage in Mauritius by *Schematiza cordiae* Barb. (Col. Galerucid.) *Bulletin of Entomological Research* **42**, 455-463.

698. Willson, B.W. (1979) The current status of biological control of rangeland weed projects in Australia. *Invited Reviews and Situation Papers, Australian Applied Entomological Research Conference, Lawes*, 214-222.

699. Willson, B.W. (1985) The biological control of *Acacia nilotica* indica in Australia. *Proceedings of the 6th International Symposium on Biological Control of Weeds*, 849-853.

700. Willson, B.W. (personal communication 1991) Department of Lands, Alan Fletcher Research Station, Sherwood, Queensland 4075, Australia.

701. Wilson, C.G. (personal communication 1990) Department of Primary Industries and Fisheries, Berrimah Research Centre, Berrimah, Northern Territory 0828, Australia.

702. Wilson, C.G.: Flanagan, G.T. (1990) Establishment and spread of *Neurostrota gunniella* on *Mimosa pigra* in the Northern Territory. *Proceedings of the 9th Australian Weeds Conference*, 505-507.

703. Wilson, C.G.; Flanagan, G.J. (1991) Establishment of *Acanthoscelides quadridentatus* (Schaeffer) and *A. puniceus* Johnson (Coleoptera: Bruchidae) on *Mimosa pigra* L. in northern Australia. *Journal of the Australian Entomological Society* **30**, 279-280.

704. Wilson, C.L. (1969) Use of plant pathogens in weed control. *Annual Review of Phytopathology* **7**, 411-434.

705. Wilson, F. (1943) The entomological control of St. John's wort *(Hypericum perforatum)* (L.). With particular reference to the insect enemies of the weed in Southern France. *Bulletin, Australian Commonwealth Council of Science and Industrial Research* **169**, 87 pp.

706. Wilson, F. (1960) A review of the biological control of insects and weeds in Australia and Australian New Guinea. *Technical Communication, Commonwealth Institute of Biological Control* **1**, 51-68.

707. Winder, J.A.; Harley, K.L.S. (1984) The phytophagous insects on Lantana in Brazil and their potential for biological control in Australia. *Tropical Pest Management* **29**, 346-362.

708. Winder, J.A.; Harley, K.L.S.; Kassulke, R.C. (1984) *Uroplata lantanae* Buzzi and Winder (Coleoptera: Chrysomelidae: Hispinae), a potential biological control agent of *Lantana camara* in Australia. *Bulletin of Entomological Research* **74**, 327-340.

709. Winder, J.A.; Sands, D.P.A.; Kassulke, R.C. (1988) The life history, host specificity and potential of *Alagoasa parana* Samuelson (Coleoptera: Chrysomelidae) for biological control of *Lantana camara* in Australia. *Bulletin of Entomological Research* **78**, 511-518.

710. Winks, C.J. (personal communication 1991) Department of Scientific and Industrial Research Plant Protection, Private Bag, Auckland, New Zealand.

711. Woodburn, T.L. (personal communication 1990) Commonwealth Scientific and Industrial Research Organisation, Division of Entomology, G.P.O. Box 1700, Canberra, Australian Capital Territory 2601, Australia.

712. Wright, A.D. (1981) Biological control of water hyacinth in Australia. *Proceedings of the 5th International Symposium on Biological Control of Weeds*, 529-535.

713. Wright, A.D. (1982) Progress towards biological control of water hyacinth in Australia. *Regional Workshop on Biological Control of Water Hyacinth, Bangalore*, 31-33.

714. Wright, A.D. (personal communication 1991) Commonwealth Scientific and Industrial Research Organisation, Division of Entomology, P.M.B. 3, Indooroopilly, Queensland 4068, Australia.

715. Wymore, L.A.; Watson, A.K.; Gotlieb, A.R. (1987) Interaction between *Colletotrichum coccodes* and Thidiazuron for control of velvetleaf (*Abutilon theophrasti*). *Weed Science* **35**, 377-383.

716. Wymore, L.A.; Watson, A.K. (1989) Interaction between a velvetleaf isolate of *Colletotrichum coccodes* and Thidiazuron for velvetleaf (*Abutilon theophrasti*) control in the field. *Weed Science* **37**, 478-483.

717. Yano, K.; Heppner, J.B. (1983) Description of Hamakua pamakani plume moth from Hawaii (Lepidoptera: Pterophoridae). *Proceedings of the Hawaiian Entomological Society* **24**, 335-341.

718. Yoshioka, E.R.; Isherwood, M.O.; Markin, G.P. (1991) Progress of biological control of gorse in Hawaii. *Western Society of Weed Science* **44**, 75-78.

719.   Young, R.G. (1982) Recent work on biological control in Papua New Guinea and some suggestions for the future. *Tropical Pest Management* **28**, 107-114.

720.   Zhang, Z.; Wei, Y.; He, D. (1988) Biology of a gall fly, *Procecidochares utilis* [Dip.: Tephritidae] and its impact on croftonweed, *Eupatorium adenophorum*. *Chinese Journal of Biological Control* **4**, 10-13. (In Chinese with English abstract).

721.   Zimmermann, E.C. (1958) *Insects of Hawaii. Volume 7, Macrolepidoptera.* Honolulu; University Press of Hawaii. pp. 478-487.

722.   Zimmerman, E.C (1978) *Insects of Hawaii. Volume 9, Microlepidoptera.* Honolulu; University Press of Hawaii. pp. 611-643.

723.   Zimmermann, H.G. (1991) Biological control of mesquite, *Prosopis* spp. (Fabaceae), in South Africa. *Agriculture, Ecosystems and Environment* **37**, 175-186.

724.   Zimmermann, H.G. (1991) Biological control of spear thistle, *Cirsium vulgare* (Asteraceae), in South Africa. *Agriculture, Ecosystems and Environment* **37**, 199-205.

725.   Zimmermann, H.G. (personal communication 1991) Department of Agriculture and Water Supply, Plant Protection Research Institute, P.O. Box 330, Uitenhage 6230, Republic of South Africa.

726.   Zimmermann, H.G.; Moran, V.C. (1991) Biological control of prickly pear, *Opuntia ficus-indica* (Cactaceae), in South Africa. *Agriculture, Ecosystems and Environment* **37**, 29-35.

727.   Zon, J.C.J. van (1977) Grass carp *(Ctenopharyngodon idella* Val.) in Europe. *Aquatic Botany* **3**, 143-155.

728.   Zon, J.C.J. van (1979) The grass carp for weed control. *Proceedings of the 1st British Freshwater Fisheries Conference*, 61-66 and 115-117.

729.   Zon, J.C.J. van (personal communication 1980) Centre for Agrobiological Research, Bornsesteeg 65, P.O. Box 14, 6700 AA Wageningen, The Netherlands.

730.   Zweerde, W. van der. (1985) Grass carp for the biological control of waterweeds. *Gewasbescherming* **16**, 153-161. [*Biocontrol News and Information* (1986) **7**, abstract 216].

731.   Zwölfer, H.; Harris, P. (1984) Biology and host specificity of *Rhinocyllus conicus* (Froel.) (Col., Curculionidae), a successful agent for biocontrol of the thistle *Carduus nutans* L. *Zeitschrift fuer Angewandte Entomologie* **97**, 36-62.

ABBREVIATIONS

a. Research Organisations

AP   ASEAN Plant Quarantine Centre and Training Institute, Serdang, Selangor, Malaysia

AUPPI   All-Union Plant Protection Institute, Leningrad, 190000, U.S.S.R.

BAF   Board of Agriculture and Forestry, Hawaii, United States of America

BIOTROP   SEAMEO Regional Centre for Tropical Biology, Indonesia

BWA   Bundesanstalt Wasserbiologie u. Abwasserforschung, Austria

BWRA   Bavarian Water Research Agency, West Germany

CAAS   Chinese Academy of Agricultural Sciences, Beijing, People's Republic of China.

CAR   Center Agrobiological Research, Netherlands

CBG   Calcutta Botanical Gardens, India

CDA   Agriculture Canada, Canada

CI   Cawthron Institute, New Zealand

CIFRI   Central Inland Fisheries Research Institute, India

CPPB*   Commonwealth Prickly Pear Board, Australia

CPPTI   Central Plant Protection Training Institute, Hyderabad, India

CSIR*   Council for Scientific and Industrial Research, Australia - see CSIRO

CSIRO   Commonwealth Scientific and Industrial Research Organization, Australia

DAA   Department of Agriculture, Antigua

DAC   Department of Agriculture, Cook Islands

DAF   Department of Agriculture, Fiji

DAFF   Department of Agriculture, Forests and Fisheries, Western Samoa

DAI   Department of Agriculture, Indonesia

DAIN   Department of Agriculture, Mysore, India

DAK   Department of Agriculture, Kenya

DAM   Department of Agriculture, Montserrat

DAMA   Department of Agriculture, Malaysia

DANSW   Department of Agriculture, New South Wales, Australia

DASL   Department of Agriculture, Sri Lanka

DAT   Department of Agriculture, Tanzania

DAV   Department of Agriculture, Victoria, Australia

DAW   Department of Agriculture, Western Australia, Australia

DCE   Keith Turnbull Research Station, Department of Conservation and Environment, Victoria, Australia

DNC   Division of Nature Conservation, Transvaal Provisional Administration, Transvaal, South Africa

DPIF   Department of Primary Industries and Fisheries, Northern Territory, Australia

DPIT   Department of Primary Industries, Tasmania

DSIR   Department of Scientific and Industrial Research, New Zealand

DWAB   Department of Water Affairs, Botswana

DWAN   Department of Water Affairs, Windhoek, Namibia/South West Africa

EAP   Escuela Agricola Panamericana, Honduras

FAO   Food and Agricultural Organisation, United Nations

FCN   Forestry Commission, New South Wales, Australia

FDA   Florida Department of Agriculture and Consumer Service, Florida, U.S.A.

FRI   Forest Research Institute, India

FRIC   Fisheries Research Institute, Czechoslavakia

GM   Government of Madras, India

HDOA   Hawaiian Department of Agriculture, United States of America

IBF   Institute Binnenfischerei, Berlin, Federal Republic of Germany

IC   Imperial College, University of Wales, Cardiff, Great Britain

ICARDA   International Center for Agricultural Research in the Dry Areas, Syria

IFI   Inland Fisheries Institute, Poland

IIBC   International Institute of Biological Control, United Kingdom

IIHR   Indian Institute of Horticultural Research

INIA   Estacion Experimental Carillanca, Temuco, Chile

INTA   Department of Plant Pathology, INTA, Castelar, Argentina

IPP   Institute for Plant Protection, Zagreb, Yugoslavia

KAU   Kerala Agricultural University, India

---

* Organisation no longer exists or has been renamed

KIEC	Kunming Institute of Ecology, People's Republic of China		**QDL**	Queensland Department of Lands, Australia
KRS	Koronivia Research Station, Ministry of Agriculture and Fisheries, Fiji Islands		**RAU**	Rand Afrikaans University, Johannesburg, South Africa
KU	Kelaniya University, Kelaniya, Sri Lanka		**RSTO**	De La Recherche Scientifique Et Technique Outre-Mer, New Caledonia
MAF	Ministry of Agriculture, Forestry and Fisheries, Japan		**RU**	Department of Zoology and Entomology, Rhodes University, Grahamstown, Republic of South Africa
MAFF	Ministry of Agriculture, Fisheries and Food, Great Britain			

State **(State Institutions of the United States of America)**

MAL	Ministry of Agriculture and Lands, Solomon Islands		**(1)**	Virginia Polytechnic. Institute and State University
MAM	Ministry of Agriculture, Mauritius		**(2)**	University of Arkansas
MAMA	Ministry of Agriculture, Madagascar		**(3)**	University of Florida, Gainesville
MANZ	Ministry of Agriculture and Fisheries, New Zealand		**(4)**	University of California, Berkeley
MAR	Ministry of Agriculture, Zimbabwe		**(5)**	University of California, Riverside
MARDI	Malaysian Agricultural Research and Development Institute, Serdang, Selangor, Malaysia		**(6)**	University of Idaho
			(7)	Montana State University
MAZ	Ministry of Agriculture, Zambia		**(8)**	Oregon State University
MEF	Ministry Eaux et Forets, Belgium		**(9)**	Washington State University
MIE	Ministry of Irrigation, Egypt		**(10)**	Kansas State University, Manhattan
MOA	Ministry of Agriculture, Chile		**(11)**	University of North Dakota, Fargo
MSU	Moscow State University, U.S.S.R.		**(12)**	University of South Dakota, Brookings
MU	McGill University, Quebec, Canada		**(13)**	University of Wyoming, Laramie
NBCRC	National Biological Control Research Centre, Kasetsart University, Bangkok, Thailand		**(14)**	California Department of Food and Agriculture, Sacremento
			(15)	Oregon State Department of Agriculture, Salem
NCC	Noumea Chamber of Commerce, Noumea, New Caledonia		**(16)**	Aquatic Research Group, Coachella, California
PCA	Philippine Coconut Authority, Davao Research Center, Davao, Philippines		**(17)**	University of Central Florida, Orlando, Florida
PCC	Panama Canal Commission. (Formerly Panama Canal Company)		**(18)**	Florida Department of Natural Resources, Tallahassee
PIJ	Prefecture Ishikawa, Japan		**(19)**	South Florida Water Management District, West Palm Beach
PNGDAL	Department of Agriculture and Livestock, Papua New Guinea		**(20)**	Maryland Department of Agriculture, Annapolis
PO	Pflanzenschutcamt Oldenburg, Western Germany		**(21)**	Utah State University, Logan
PPIB	Plant Protection Institute, Belgrade, Yugoslavia		**(22)**	University of California, Davis
			(23)	Louisiana State University, Baton Rouge
PPRI	Department of Agriculture and Fisheries, Plant Protection Research Institute, Pretoria, Republic of South Africa		**(24)**	Texas A & M University, College Station
			(25)	University of Missouri, Columbia
PPRIZ	Plant Protection Research institute, Zimbabwe		**(26)**	Oklahoma State University, Stillwater
			(27)	North Dakota State University, Grand Forks
PPTC*	Prickly Pear Travelling Commission, Australia		**TDA**	Tasmanian Department of Agriculture, Australia
QDAS*	Queensland Department of Agriculture and Stock, Australia - now Department of Primary Industries, Queensland, Australia		**UBC**	University of British Columbia, Canada
			UAC	Universidad Austral de Chile, Valdivia, Chile

* Organisation no longer exists or has been renamed

UG	University of Guelph, Canada
UH	University of Hawaii, Hawaii, United States of America
UKS	University of Khartoum, Sudan
UOG	University of Guam, Mangilao, Guam
USAE	United State Army Corps of Engineers
USDA	**(United States Department of Agriculture, United States of America)**
(1)	Beltsville, Maryland
(2)	Frederick, Maryland
(3)	Gainesville, Florida
(4)	Fort Lauderdale, Florida
(5)	Stoneville, Mississippi
(6)	Lubbock, Texas
(7)	Albany, California

(8)	Lincoln, Nebraska
(9)	Temple, Texas
(10)	Bozeman, Montana
(11)	Columbia, Missouri
(12)	Rome, Italy
(13)	Hurlingham, Argentina
USDAA	United States Department of Agriculture at Hurlingham, Argentina
WPRC	Water Pollution Research Centre, Sweden
WRO	Weed Research Organization, Great Britain
ZIAS	Zoological Institute and Academy of Science, Leningrad, U.S.S.R.

b. States of the United States of America

AL	Alabama		**NC**	North Carolina
AR	Arkansas		**ND**	North Dakota
AZ	Arizona		**NE**	Nebraska
CA	California		**NJ**	New Jersey
CO	Colorado		**NM**	New Mexico
DE	Delaware		**NV**	Nevada
FL	Florida		**NY**	New York
GA	Georgia		**OH**	Ohio
HI	Hawaii		**OK**	Oklahoma
IA	Iowa		**OR**	Oregon
ID	Idaho		**PA**	Pennsylvania
IL	Illinois		**SC**	South Carolina
IN	Indiana		**SD**	South Dakota
KS	Kansas		**TN**	Tennessee
KY	Kentucky		**TX**	Texas
LA	Louisiana		**UT**	Utah
MA	Massachusetts		**VA**	Virginia
MD	Maryland		**WA**	Washington
MN	Minnesota		**WI**	Wisconsin
MO	Missouri		**WV**	West Virginia
MS	Mississippi		**WY**	Wyoming
MT	Montana			

SCIENTIFIC NAMES OF WEEDS INDEX

(Scientific Names of Weeds Index)

COMMON NAMES OF WEEDS INDEX

(Common Names of Weeds Index)

SCIENTIFIC NAMES OF CONTROL AGENTS INDEX

(Scientific Names of Control Agents Index)

Chrysomela quadrigemina - see
  Chrysolina quadrigemina
Chrysomela varians - see
  Chrysolina varians
Cochylis atricapitana 30
Coleophora klimeschiella 52
Coleophora parthenica 52, 53
Colletotrichum coccodes 125
Colletotrichum gloeosporioides
  71, 122-125
Comostolopsis germana 24
Crasimorpha infuscata 3
Cremastobombycia lantanella 90
Crocidosema lantana - see
  Epinotia lantana
Croesia zimmermani 83
Ctenopharyngodon idella 110
Cuphodes profluens 73
Cyanotricha necyria 75
Cydmaea binotata 82
Cyphocleonus achates 15, 18
Cyrtobagous salviniae 84, 136
Cyrtobagous singularis 85, 136
Cystiphora schmidti 20
Cystiphora sonchi 33

D

Dactylopius austrinus 37, 43, 47,
  49
Dactylopius ceylonicus 37, 49,
  132
Dactylopius coccus 48
Dactylopius confusus 39, 46, 50,
  120, 121
Dactylopius opuntiae 38, 39,
  42-49, 51, 120, 121, 132
Dactylopius tomentosus 41, 120,
  121
Dactylopius sp 40, 132
Dasineura capitigena - see
  Spurgia capitigena
Dialectica scalariella 34
Diastema tigris 90
Disonycha argentinensis 2
Disonycha glabrata 118

E

Entyloma ageratinae 6
Entyloma compositarum 6
Epiblema strenuana 7, 29, 34
Epinotia lantana 91, 138
Epipagis albiguttalis - see
  Sameodes albiguttalis
Epipsammea pectinicornis 3, 118
Episammea pectinicornis - see
  Epipsammea pectinicornis
Episimus utilis 3
Eriocereophaga humeridens 35
Eriococcus orariensis 135
Eriophyes chondrillae 21
Erytenna consputa 82

Euaresta aequalis 34
Euaresta bella 7
Euaresta bullans 130
Euclasta whalleyi 4
Eulocastra argentisparsa 88
Eurytoma attiva 61
Eustenopus villosus 19
Eutreta xanthochaeta 91
Eutreta sparsa - see *Eutreta*
  xanthochaeta
Evander xanthomelas - see
  Parevander xanthomelas

F

Frumenta nephelomicta 88
Fusarium oxysporum 119, 125

G

Gastrophysa atrocyanea 126
Gymnaetron antirrhini 87, 137

H

Heilipodus intricatus 9
Heilipodus ventralis 28
Hepialus sp 91
Heteropsylla sp 73
Hydrellia balciunasi 69
Hydrellia pakistanae 70
Hyles euphorbiae 63, 65
Hylemia jacobaeae - see
  Botanophila jacobaeae
Hylemia seneciella - see
  Botanophila seneciella
Hypena strigata 92, 138
Hypogeococcus festerianus 35, 36
Hypolixus truncatulus 118
Hypophthalmichthys molitrix 114

L

Lantanophaga pusillidactyla 93,
  138
Lema cyanella 26
Leptobyrsa decora 93, 139
Leptogalumna sp - see
  Orthogalumna terebrantis
Leucoptera spartifoliella 67, 133
Lioplacis elliptica 9
Liothrips mikaniae 28
Liothrips urichi 71, 134
Liriomyza sonchi 33
Listronotus setosipennis 29
Lithraeus atronotatus 3
Litodactylus leucogaster - see
  Phytobius leucogaster
Lius poseidon 71
Lixus cribricollis 76
Lobesia euphorbiana 66
Longitarsus albineus 35
Longitarsus flavicornis 31

Longitarsus jacobaeae 31
Longitarsus sp 31
Lorita baccharivora 9

M

Mecas saturnina 34
Megacyllene mellyi 9
Melanagromyza cuscutae 59, 60,
  123
Melanagromyza eupatoriella 23
Melanterius acaciae 72
Melanterius servulus 75
Melanterius ventralis 72
Melitara dentata 40
Melitara doddalis 42
Melitara prodenialis 37, 40, 42,
  46, 120, 121
Melitara sp 42
Mescinia nr. *parvula* 23
Metallactus nigrofasciatus 9
Metallactus patagonicus 10
Metamasius spinolae 40
Metriona bicolor 122
Metriona purpurata 122
Metrogaleruca obscura 62
Metzneria paucipunctella 15, 18
Microlarinus lareynii 108, 109
Microlarinus lypriformis 108,
  109, 141
Mimorista flavidissimalis 42, 46
Mimorista pulchellalis 37
Moneilema armatum 40
Moneilema crassum 40
Moneilema ulkei 42, 45, 46, 48
Moneilema variolare 42

N

Namangana pectinicornis - see
  Epipsammea pectinicornis
Nanaia sp 37
Neochetina bruchi 78, 126
Neochetina eichhorniae 78, 135
Neodiplogrammus quadrivittatus
  67
Neogalea esula 94
Neohydronomus affinis 4
Neohydronomus pulcellus - see
  Neohydronomus affinis
Neurostrota gunniella 74
Nothanguina phyllobia 126
Nupserha antennata - see
  Nupserha vexator
Nupserha vexator 34

(Scientific Names of Control Agents Index)